Maha Samadhi: Antardhyana

With kind regards, ॐ and prem

Maha Samadhi: Antardhyana

Realizing the Absolute

From the teachings of Swami Sivananda Saraswati
and Swami Satyananda Saraswati

Yoga Publications Trust, Munger, Bihar, India

© Sivananda Math 2010

All rights reserved. No part of this publication may be reproduced, transmitted or stored in a retrieval system, in any form or by any means, without permission in writing from Yoga Publications Trust.

The terms Satyananda Yoga® and Bihar Yoga® are registered trademarks owned by International Yoga Fellowship Movement (IYFM). The use of the same in this book is with permission and should not in any way be taken as affecting the validity of the marks.

Published by Yoga Publications Trust
First edition 2010

ISBN: 978-81-86336-89-2

Publisher and distributor: Yoga Publications Trust, Ganga Darshan, Munger, Bihar, India.

Website: www.biharyoga.net
www.rikhiapeeth.net

Printed at Thomson Press (India) Limited, New Delhi, 110001

Dedication

*In humility we offer this dedication to
Swami Sivananda Saraswati, who initiated
Swami Satyananda Saraswati into the secrets of yoga.*

Contents

Introduction   1

Samadhi
From the teachings of Swami Sivananda Saraswati
  1. What is Samadhi?   7
  2. Samadhi – An Overview   13
  3. The State of Moksha   19
  4. Samadhi According to the Upanishads   23
  5. Nirvikalpa Samadhi   26
  6. Sahaja Samadhi   33
  7. Raja Yoga Samadhi   37
  8. Vedantic Samadhi   42
  9. Bhakti, Hatha, Jnana and Kundalini Yoga Samadhis   46
  10. States of Consciousness   54
  11. Samadhi and Sleep   62
  12. Overcoming Obstacles to Samadhi   67
  13. Advice for Samadhi Aspirants   73
  14. Guru, Disciple and Sadhana   79
  15. Jivanmukti and Videhamukti   85
  16. A Sage's Experience   99

Samadhi
From the teachings of Swami Satyananda Saraswati

17. Samadhi	105
18. Realms of Superconsciousness	113
19. Samadhi in a Nutshell	120
20. Stages of Samadhi	128
21. Dharmamegha Samadhi	140
22. The Attainment of Kaivalya	146
23. Planes of Consciousness	149
24. Transformations in Consciousness	157
25. The Supreme Being is Changeless	165
26. The Absolute Experience	170
27. Transcending the Realm of Duality	179
28. Yogic Preparation for Samadhi	190
29. Realization to Overcome Suffering	198
30. Karma Yoga and Samadhi	205
31. Bhakti Yoga and Samadhi	212
32. Samadhi – Culmination of Yogic Effort	218
33. The Spiritual Quest	223
34. The Necessity of Sadhana	229
35. Awakening Inner Awareness	236
36. Samadhi – An Inner Journey Through Life	246
37. Enlightenment is a Process	253
38. The Guru	260
39. Awaken God From Within	267

Glossary 279

Introduction

We present an extraordinary thesis on the ultimate of yogic life, the state of samadhi. This unique collection of spiritual discourses illuminates the subject of samadhi from the rare perspective of the direct personal experiences and profound insights of two enlightened masters, our gurus Swami Sivananda Saraswati and Swami Satyananda Saraswati.

Samadhi is the culminating point in the spiritual quest. This quest is an ancient one. It is not a quest for morality, or for goodness, purity or obedience. It is a quest given to humankind to realize the transcendental consciousness, to reach that point of evolution where all our earthly karmas are finished with. The external experiences that we have in the relative world through the eyes, the ears and the other senses is not the highest knowledge; there are deeper forms of experience than this. The senses, mind and intellect are finite instruments; they cannot penetrate into the heart of the ultimate truth and attain transcendental knowledge.

In order to experience the ultimate reality one has to transcend these boundaries, because God is beyond the limited, finite mind. If we know how to turn our mind from the outer world to the inner world, this inner realm will lead us to the expansion of consciousness. When consciousness expands and becomes one with totality or God, it is called samadhi. And, it is only within the experiences of samadhi that we will come to know the infinite facets of existence within us. It is only through samadhi that we can realize the knowledge of the eternal by which everything is known.

Every great guru has had the highest experience of samadhi, and in India, for thousands of years these gurus have revealed the mystical truths about this state. They have spoken of samadhi as the fulfilment of man's vision and destiny, and explained how for one who has had this experience nothing of worldly life is needed anymore because samadhi is the wealth of all wealth. They have described samadhi variously as an extraordinary moment that may come in the life of an individual when the ego is completely fused and lost; as the direct and everlasting experience of absolute consciousness; as the end of all relative existence; as union with God where the individual soul merges with the mighty supreme soul and becomes highest consciousness, supreme peace and infinite; and as indescribable bliss, boundless joy and love for all.

These teachings unfold the experience of samadhi as one of fullness and completion of the human personality. They describe samadhi as an evolutionary process, where consciousness undergoes a graduated sequence of experiences which change and move progressively in continuity, each stage of evolution fusing into the next. Our exceptional authors categorize and classify, in finest detail, the various experiences that consciousness undergoes as it moves from where the awakening begins to the point where the state of samadhi becomes stable. They include accounts of samadhi experiences and give full descriptions of the states of the *jivanmuktas*, the liberated sages, who are established in the highest transcendental, divine knowledge and live in the world with an abiding realization of the secret oneness of existence.

Both Swami Sivananda and Swami Satyananda say that although the seed of samadhi is already in everyone, it is only through gradual accomplishments in the practice of sadhana that the aspirant will be able to enter the domain of samadhi and develop that seed into a fully grown tree. In this respect they emphasize the necessity of practising a regular sadhana of traditional yogic techniques so as to break through the barrier of illusion that separates the aspirant from union with the Divine. They stress that the aspirant must not only receive the appropriate direction and encouragement for sadhana from an accomplished teacher, but must also learn how to give proper expression to the spiritual power generated through their practices so as to utilize that energy in a positive and uplifting way.

Aspirants are particularly advised never to shun the active life and to always integrate their sadhana with the essentials of karma yoga, bhakti yoga, raja yoga and jnana yoga. It is also explained that although many aspirants have fantastic experiences during their practices which they mistake for samadhi, none of them are absolute because 'someone' is experiencing them. As long as there is experience and experiencer, there is ego, and where there is ego, there cannot be the experience of samadhi. The reader is certain to gain an understanding that the practices for samadhi are dealing with the evolution of consciousness, and thus appreciate that the attainment of samadhi should definitely take more than a lifetime.

The teachings on samadhi in this book are conveyed in various ways. Many judicious technical descriptions and definitions of samadhi are given, all clearly explained and often illustrated by references to various scriptures, yet there are also sections where the insight on samadhi is expressed as if it were pure poetry. These teachings describe, discuss and compare the experiences of samadhi in the various branches of the yogic science, as well as in the systems of tantra, vedanta and samkhya. But the reader is called upon to remember that it is the same consciousness which is undergoing the samadhi experience, although the approach and expression may differ.

We hope that the explanations, perspectives and revelations on samadhi presented in these pages will help to remove much of the erroneous intellectual speculation and scholarly misunderstanding that surrounds the subject.

This book is an inspiration to all who seek to understand the experience of the Absolute. It is offered in veneration to Swami Satyananda Saraswati, who attained maha samadhi at midnight on 5th December, 2009.

In the words of Swami Satyananda, "It is only in samadhi that all the highest purities of peace, light, bliss and ecstasy appear. No amount of enjoyment in life can equal this rare experience. Whether you call it emancipation, salvation, darshan, enlightenment, nirvikalpa samadhi, *adwaita anubhuti*, the non-dual experience, moksha, nirvana, shoonya or kaivalya, kundalini awakening or God-realization or union with God or absolute experience, it's all the same. There are many, many other names for the experience of samadhi. It has no name and it has every name. It is beautiful, it is splendid. It is the last door which opens into the temple of unimaginable bliss. It is the final goal and ultimate purpose of human existence."

Samadhi

From the teachings of Swami Sivananda Saraswati

8th November, 1943

Beloved aspirants.

Samadhi is blissful union with the Supreme Self. It leads to the direct intuitive realization of the infinite.

It is an inner divine experience which is beyond the reach of speech and mind.

You will have to realize this yourself through deep meditation. The senses, the mind and the intellect cease functioning. There is neither time nor causation here.

May you rest in samadhi.

Swami Sivananda

1
What is Samadhi?

Samadhi is union with God, union with the Absolute. It is a state of everlasting joy and perennial peace, a state of supreme and eternal bliss. Samadhi is the experience of the light of the Absolute and the end of all relative existence. It is the direct and everlasting experience of superconsciousness, *adhyatmic anubhava.*

    Samadhi is the state of absolute consciousness where the mind does not seek anything, where the mind is at perfect rest, where the knower and the known have become one. In samadhi the mind is still, the mind is silenced, the thoughts are controlled and all the surging, bubbling emotions are subdued. The yogi passes into the transcendental calm or the stupendous ocean of silence and attains transcendental knowledge of Brahman or the eternal. Samadhi is a state of full wisdom. The mind merges with *Brahman*, the absolute reality. Individuality melts. Everlasting bliss is attained.

    Samadhi is the experience of fullness and completion of the personality. It is not abolition or annihilation of the personality, rather it is deliverance from the delusion of personality. This divine experience arises when the ego and the mind are dissolved, when the senses, mind and intellect cease functioning. Just as a river joins the ocean, the individual soul mixes with the mighty *Atman*, the supreme soul, and becomes the highest consciousness, transcendental bliss and attains the highest realization. All limitations and differences disappear. The sage is free from pain, sorrow, fear and delusion.

When the mind is completely absorbed in one object of meditation, it is termed *samadhi*. In samadhi there is neither *dhyana* nor *dhyata*, meditation or meditator. The meditator and the meditated, the thinker and the thought, the worshipper and the worshipped, become identical. The triad vanishes. The mind loses its own consciousness and becomes identical with the object of meditation. The mind does not function at all in samadhi; it becomes absorbed in Brahman.

In samadhi there is neither thinking nor hearing nor smelling nor seeing. It is an experience wholly beyond the orbit of the senses. There is neither physical nor mental consciousness, only spiritual consciousness. The seer and the sight become one. There is only existence, *sat,* and that is one's real essence. When the water dries up in a pool, the reflection of the sun in the water also vanishes. When the mind melts in Brahman, when the mind-lake dries up, the reflected consciousness also vanishes. The *jivatman,* the individual personality, goes away. Only existence remains.

Samadhi is freedom from birth and death, freedom from all sorts of pains; there is no perception of duality. *Avidya,* ignorance, is absent in samadhi. Samadhi transcends the three states of consciousness: *jagrat,* the waking state, *swapna,* the dream state, and *sushupti,* the deep sleep state. Samadhi is the fourth state, known as *turiya,* where there is no play of the mind, where the mind is dissolved in Brahman. It is the fourth dimension where there is infinite bliss. It is the state of absolute consciousness which baffles all attempts at description. Turiya is the last door which opens into the temple of the unspeakable bliss of Brahman. Samadhi is the final goal of all, it is *mukti,* freedom, *moksha,* liberation. These terms are synonymous.

Perfect awareness, unity and oneness
Samadhi is not an stone-like, inert state, as many people imagine, not a state of lethargy, idleness or inertia. It is intense awareness of the highest reality, the highest intuition which

reveals to the meditator things as they are, in which eternal peace is experienced. It is a condition of perfect awareness, a magnificent experience of unity and oneness, where the higher Self alone exists. It is life in the pure spirit, in the Atman, in the Divine. When the limitations of empirical existence are transcended, universal life is intensified and one has a rich inner life, an expanded cosmic life and supra-cosmic life, too.

As long as one is established in samadhi, *samadhi nishtha,* there is only Brahman or the Absolute. *Niranta samadhi,* continuous samadhi, does not mean sitting blindfolded; it refers to the renunciation of attachment to the body, regarding the individual soul and the supreme soul as one, and knowing that the practitioner himself is Paramatman, and is acting upon this knowledge. Samadhi means absorption of the mind. Wherever one goes, one beholds the one Self everywhere. The coexistence of both abnegation and knowledge of the Self constitutes niranta samadhi. Self-knowledge is *Brahmanishtha,* being established in the realization of Brahman. One who has acquired this has no body.

In samadhi there is revelation or insight or intuition. *Jnana chakshu,* the third eye of wisdom, opens by itself when the *Brahmakara vritti,* the vortex leading to Brahman, is raised. The sage born of samadhi experience becomes established in his own Self. He is endowed with cosmic vision and transcendental, divine knowledge.

In samadhi the yogi abandons the sense of his own being and enters into the being of God. He loses his personality in the Divine and becomes an embodiment of bliss, peace, joy and knowledge. The yogi has dissolved his personality in the sea of God. He is drowned and forgotten there until he becomes simply the instrument of God. When his mouth opens, it speaks God's words without effort or forethought through direct intuition and, when he raises his hand, God flows again through that to work a miracle.

Samadhi is not mere emotional enthusiasm or exhilaration. It is the direct, unique, intuitive experience of the highest truth or absolute consciousness or the ultimate reality.

There is perfect awareness in samadhi which is beyond expression. The aspirant rests in his centre now – the goal of his search – and realizes absolute freedom, independence and perfection. The mind becomes Brahman when it is purified and brought into the samadhi state.

The state of samadhi is beyond description, beyond the reach of the mind and speech. Even in worldly experience, the taste of an apple cannot be expressed to someone who has not tasted it, or the nature of a colour to a blind person. Only this much can be said. You have to experience it yourself through constant meditation practice.

The aspirant rests in Atman

In the state of samadhi there is perfect stillness, perfect mental poise; there is no mental tension, no mental inhibition, no *vikalpa*, or imagination, of any sort. This is the goal of life. All mental activities, the functions of the intellect and the ten senses cease entirely. The aspirant now rests in the Atman. There is no distinction between subject and object. The world and the pairs of opposites vanish absolutely. The aspirant attains knowledge of the Self, supreme peace and infinite bliss and joy. This state is indescribable; it has to be felt and experienced by the aspirant.

In samadhi the purified mind withdraws from external objects, from its natural or habitual occupation and looks within. It concentrates on the innermost Self and becomes fixed upon the Atman, which is not touched by the mind. It resolves itself in the Atman, its source, and becomes Atman itself. It takes the form of Atman, just as camphor becomes the fire itself. The knowledge of Brahman or Atman is real experience, not mere knowing. 'To know Brahman is to become Brahman – *Brahmavid Brahmaiva bhavati*' is the emphatic declaration of the Upanishads.

The scriptures tell us that the knower of Brahman knows everything, that one who has truly entered into samadhi has detailed knowledge of all subjects. '*Kasminnu Bhagavo vijnate sarvamidam, vijnatam bhavati* – What is that, O Lord, which by being known, all this becomes known?' One knows all languages and can speak and understand them. One knows all the sciences. One knows the past, present and the future.

The sadhaka who attains samadhi will feel the presence of the Lord at all times. He will feel divine ecstasy and possess all the divine qualities. He will have a pure mind and a pure heart, and shed tears of divine love, *prem*. He will have holy communion with the Lord.

It is extremely difficult to enter the state of samadhi. It requires long preparation. Samadhi cannot be experienced by chance. All visible objects merge in the invisible or the unseen. The individual soul becomes that which it contemplates.

Samadhi is sleepless sleep

Samadhi is a sleepless sleep in which the senses and the veil of ignorance are destroyed by the fire of knowledge. The aspirant enjoys the perfect joy of freedom and infinite, supracosmic, vast experiences and the supreme silence of the imperishable. If one can consciously induce a state like deep sleep, it is no longer deep sleep but samadhi.

Generally, in what is called dreamless sleep either one does not remember what one dreamt or one fell into absolute unconsciousness, which is a taste of death. But there is the possibility of a sleep in which one enters into absolute silence, immortality and peace in all parts of one's being and consciousness merges into *satchidananda*, truth-consciousness-bliss, the supreme reality. It can hardly be called sleep, for there is perfect awareness. It is called samadhi, and one can remain in that condition for a few minutes or hours or days. Even a few minutes will give more rest and refreshment than hours of ordinary sleep.

Try to attain that sleepless sleep wherein the senses and the mind remain in a state of quietude and the intellect ceases to function. This sleepless sleep is *maha nidra*, or the state of superconsciousness. It is perfect awareness wherein the individual soul has merged into the supreme soul. There is no waking from this sleep. The show of names and forms eventually vanishes. The individual soul becomes the supreme soul. This is samadhi. Just as salt mingled with water becomes one with the water, so the mind mingled with Brahman ultimately becomes Brahman. This world, which is the creation of the mind, also melts away in Brahman and becomes Brahman itself.

We may think that a person is dead, whereas he may be in a state of trance, catalepsy, ecstasy or samadhi. These states resemble death; the outward signs are similar. A yogi can stop the heartbeat at will and remain in a state of samadhi, the superconscious state, for hours or days. There is neither heartbeat nor breathing during the state of samadhi. This is sleepless sleep or perfect awareness. When one comes back down to physical consciousness, the heartbeat and respiration revive. Science cannot explain this and doctors are dumbfounded when they witness these phenomena.

Samadhi is a cosmic experience
Samadhi transcends duality of all kinds and is undisturbed by the ego. It is the experience of fullness and one who has realized samadhi becomes silent, wise and illumined, free from worry. There is complete satisfaction, a feeling of having attained all that was to be known. Samadhi leaves a permanent mark on the aspirant who experiences it. For one who sees the all-pervading, tranquil, blissful Atman, nothing remains to be attained. Know this perfect Atman and attain eternal satisfaction and perennial joy.

Samadhi gives a new orientation to life, a new perspective of reality. Even if one obtains a momentary glimpse of the supreme, a new element enters the heart and the whole heart is revolutionized. The vision in samadhi is not seeing or sensing in any form; it is of the nature of *aparoksha anubhuti*, personal, direct experience of the Absolute.

Samadhi or nirvana or divine vision is the birthright of every human being, not the monopoly of sannyasins or ascetics alone. It is the goal of human life. All our miseries, birth, old age and death can end only by the realization of God. Realization can be had by meditation on God. There is no other way. O Mokshapriya! Struggle hard. Obtain the grace of the guru and Ishwara. You will enjoy the supreme bliss of samadhi.

2

Samadhi – An Overview

The ground floor represents the life of passion in the sense universe. The first storey corresponds to savikalpa samadhi. The second storey is equivalent to nirvikalpa samadhi. The third storey represents the sahaja state or attainment of a *jivanmukta*, one liberated in life.

Savikalpa samadhi can be compared to a moving bullock cart. When the cart stops, that is nirvikalpa samadhi. When the bulls are detached from the cart, that is the sahaja samadhi state. When the yogi has reached the last perfect stage of samadhi, and all the impressions are totally annihilated, he at once attains liberation and becomes a jivanmukti in this very life.

The intellect and the mind have their own limitations. They can operate only in the earthly plane. It is only through intuitive insight that one can attain this transcendental knowledge of the Absolute in samadhi and become free from the cycle of births and deaths. There is no other way. It is emphatically declared in the *Shvetashvatara Upanishad* 3:8: "I know that great Purusha who is resplendent like the sun and who is beyond the darkness of ignorance. Only by knowing Him can immortality be attained, as there is no other road to eternal bliss." It is only through samadhi that one can know the 'unknowable', see the 'unseeable', and gain entrance into that which is 'inaccessible'.

The steps in samadhi differ in aspirants according to the nature of their sadhana and the yoga they are practising. A raja yogi obtains savichara, nirvichara, savitarka, nirvitarka, asmita, ananda and the asamprajnata samadhis, and attains nirodha samadhi by restraining the mental modifications, *vrittis*. It is only the raja yogi who attempts annihilation of the vrittis, *chitta vritti nirodha*, the nirodha samadhi of Maharishi Patanjali (*Yoga Sutras* 1:2).

A bhakta or devotee obtains bhava samadhi and maha bhava samadhi through a purified mind and supreme devotion to the Lord. Faith, devotion, admiration, a taste for singing the Lord's name, firm devoutness, intense attachment to the Lord, steady absorption in God, and transcendental love, *maha bhava*, the highest dedication, are the stages through which a devotee passes. A bhakta sees Narayana or Krishna in all objects. He also does not check the vrittis. Like the vedantin who studies the Vedas, he changes his mental attitude. It is the mind that creates all the differences and separateness. The world is all *ananda*, bliss. If only you change your angle of vision, your mental attitude, you will find heaven on earth.

A jnani or vedantin experiences ecstasy, insight, intuition, revelation, illumination and supreme bliss. He passes through the stages of *moha*, darkness and void, the stage in which there is neither perception nor non-perception, the stage of infinite consciousness and bliss. The samadhi of the jnani is effortless and spontaneous. Wherever the mind goes, it experiences samadhi. For a jnana yogi there is neither 'in samadhi' nor 'out of samadhi'; he is forever in contact with the divine or supreme wisdom. He enjoys freedom, bliss and peace every moment of his life. Hence it is called sahaja samadhi. One drinks the nectar of immortality in this very life.

The fruit of samadhi
The fruit of savikalpa samadhi is nirvikalpa samadhi. In the lower samadhis of savikalpa, the vrittis are dissolved into the pure sattwa guna, the state of luminosity, whereas in nirvikalpa samadhi the vritti is dissolved into Brahman itself, just as water is absorbed into a hot iron.

Used in the highest sense, samadhi is neither self-forgetfulness nor sleep. It is a powerful state of transcendental self-awareness. One who comes down from it may live and move about in the same ordinary way as before, and there may not be any strikingly perceptible change in his life and behaviour to the casual beholder. But all the same, the change in consciousness is undeniably there; the personality is transformed.

The stupid bee, knowing that flowers are blossoming in a certain tree and setting out with terrific speed, passes it, and, in turning back, reaches it when the juice is finished. Another stupid bee, setting out at a low speed, reaches it when the juice is finished. A clever bee, on the other hand, setting out with just the necessary speed, easily reaches the bunch of flowers, takes the juice to its heart's content and, turning it into honey, enjoys its taste.

In the same way, when the sign appears, an aspirant makes strong efforts, saying, "I will quickly attain samadhi," but his mind, through excessive strain, becomes distracted and he is not able to attain ecstasy or samadhi. Another person, seeing fault in excessive effort, gives up, saying, "What is the use of samadhi to me now?" His mind becomes idle and he, too, is not able to attain samadhi. But one who releases with an intelligent, calm, uniform force the slack mind from slackness and the distracted mind from distraction drives it towards the goal of oneness with Brahman, and attains nirvikalpa samadhi. Become like such a one.

Contemplate on the Atman, fill the mind with Atman, then the mind becomes identified with Brahman. As you think, so you become. Think you are Brahman, Brahman you will become. When the mind is withdrawn from objects and deep reflection sets in, the objective consciousness is shut down, and savitarka samadhi commences. Analysis and synthesis, investigation and abstract reasoning take place. This is samadhi with reasoning. Evil thoughts cannot enter now, as the mind is sattwic.

One should look upon all beings with an equal eye and remain unattached like air. One who thus keeps a healthy mind, works for others, and lives a regular disciplined life for an extended period can realize Brahman and attain nirvikalpa samadhi, the highest state of samadhi.

A sudden stroke of mystic illumination puts an end to all empirical existence and the very idea of remembrance of such a thing as this world, or the narrow individuality of the spirit in this world, absolutely leaves. Now all the seeds or impressions are totally burnt by the fire of knowledge, and liberation, jivanmukti, is attained at once in this very life.

Jada and chaitanya samadhi

Samadhi is of two kinds, *jada* or inert samadhi and *chaitanya* or conscious samadhi. In chaitanya samadhi there is perfect awareness. In jada samadhi the sadhaka is unconscious. There is a popular belief that samadhi means sitting in a state of absolute consciousness in the lotus pose, with perfect suspension of the breath. Most people think that a person established in samadhi should have no consciousness of his surroundings, and should be absolutely insensible even if a knife is thrust into his body. The samadhi of the yogi who has himself buried underground for hours, days, weeks or months is jada samadhi. Such samadhis certainly exist, but they are all jada samadhis induced by hatha yoga kriyas like khechari mudra and pranayama.

Once a well-dressed man showed me a newspaper article about a swami who had had himself buried underground in a box for forty-two days. The event had been witnessed by government officials, university professors, medical doctors and other distinguished persons, and no doubt the matter was so interesting that it would impress any intelligent thinker or scientist. However, I had to tell my co-traveller that this swami was demonstrating jada samadhi, simulated or pseudo samadhi.

Such feats or exploits may amaze spectators and deceive worldly people, but have nothing to do with real yoga, and are not signs that a person has reached the highest peak of yogic perfection or realization. Generally, these shows are only performed by pseudo-yogis, who run after name, fame and money and thus face a hopeless downfall in spirituality. Only those who have purified their heart, who are extremely devoted to God, can enter into the highest state of yoga, and such people do not demonstrate it in public.

Jada samadhi is a state more or less like deep sleep. It does not give realization or knowledge of the Self, there is no transcendental experience or divine wisdom involved. The samskaras and vasanas are not destroyed. It does not grant *moksha* or final liberation.

In chaitanya samadhi the yogi comes down with divine knowledge. He gives inspired talks and messages and those who hear him are very elevated. The *vasanas*, subtle desires, are destroyed by this samadhi and the yogi attains perfect liberation. One who is established in chaitanya samadhi keeps the mind and body in perfect balance and utilizes them in the service of humanity with *atmabhava*, seeing everything as the Self.

Aspire for samadhi

Mankind has a constant inner yearning to know more and more, to live eternally and to enjoy perpetual happiness. The knowledge gained through the senses in the relative world is not the highest knowledge, and cannot give permanent satisfaction and everlasting peace. It is limited knowledge, and there is always a sense of void in spite of one's intellectual attainments, an urge in the mind to attain transcendental knowledge, the knowledge of the eternal by which everything is known.

You know that you are always hankering after absolute peace, bliss and immortality. You know that these things cannot be had in the finite, perishable objects of this world, but only in God or the Absolute, only by realizing the Self, realizing God. That is man's foremost duty. Therefore, it is most important to do something to know God, to know the Self. Man is born for something more than taking birth, earning wealth, enjoying and suffering, and then dying.

Samadhi is a means of liberation from birth and death. It leads to direct intuitive perception of the truth or the infinite. It puts an end to all the troubles of life and the cause of rebirth. It destroys the samskaras which give rise to fresh births. It helps one to tide over even unalterable or *prarabdha karma*, even though the fruition of one's past karmas has not ended. Whatever one does or thinks is all indelibly impressed in the layers of the subconscious mind. These impressions can be burnt or obliterated only by the dawn of knowledge of Atman, the supreme Self.

Aspire for samadhi. Perfect inward renunciation, total purification, earnest sadhana, faith, concentration of mind, contemplation and discernment of the direct perceptions brought about by meditation become the means to attain samadhi. When that eternal truth is realized, this creation will appear as the sport of the Lord.

The ultimate light upon this highly subtle matter has to come through personal realization alone. Your heart must expand; your faith must become deep rooted. Share what you have with others, awaken your spirit of renunciation. Cultivate all the good qualities like compassion, selflessness and egolessness. The seeker has to be resolutely bold and active in the quest through patience and perseverance upon this spiritual path until the ultimate goal of samadhi is attained.

3

The State of Moksha

Moksha or emancipation is the highest exaltation of the Self in its pristine nature of supreme perfection. It is consciousness of the supreme reality; not becoming something which previously did not exist, not travelling to another world of greater joy. It is the knowledge of eternal existence, the awareness of the essential nature of pure being. It is the freedom attained by knowing that we are always free. Knowledge is not merely the cause of freedom, but is itself freedom. Moksha is to realize one's Self, to be Oneself, to be the All.

Absolute consciousness does not know, for it is knowledge. It does not enjoy, for it is enjoyment. It is not 'existent' but 'existence'. It is the simple knowing, the great knowing, so mysterious and complicated, the ever unsolved problem, the only problem of the whole universe. And yet, it is the only truth to the knower. The curious riddle, somehow, makes one feel that, truly, nothing happens in infinity, though worlds may seem to roll in it.

That which is so simply said as 'existence-consciousness' and which is so easy to understand is, after all, the hardest nut to crack, never understood, never known, never realized by any individual, except the most rare being. Whatever is spoken or thought is not the truth as it is. Truth is the union of the cosmic thinker and cosmic thinking.

Moksha is neither a mass of consciousness nor self-consciousness. It is the very life and order of the universe, ever-present, unchanging. It transcends even the sense of immortality which also is conceptual. The light of the Absolute puts a sudden end to all relative existence and the world does not exist even as a remembrance.

Absolute reality

There is no such thing as inert, inanimate, dead matter or blind force. It is all supreme force, knowledge and bliss without motion or mind. There are no planes of existence, no states of consciousness, and no degrees of reality. This is the most blessed and supreme state of absolute freedom and conscious eternal life, not a conviction but actual being. It is the awful grandeur of utter negation of limitation and experience of the infinite, not mere continued personal life. It is the complete dissolution of thought in simple existence which is the mightiest nothing!

It is an immediate here and now of spacelessness and timelessness, the inexpressible, beyond joy and sorrow, beyond knowledge and ignorance, beyond life and death, beyond all that is beyond! It is the fullest Reality, the most complete consciousness, the most immense power, and the most intense bliss. Truth, knowledge, power, happiness and immortality are its shadows. Unseen, transcendental, unthinkable, imperishable, the loftiest, the deepest, the Truth – That, is the Absolute. The light of limitless suns is darkness in its presence. It oversteps the boundaries of being and nullifies all ideas of existence. It swallows the mind and the ego and annihilates the individual consciousness to the very extreme. It is the thunder that breaks the heart of the universe, the lightning that fuses all sense of empirical reality. The bubble bursts into the ocean; the soul merges into the Supreme Reality.

Nothing is beyond That. It is neither form nor content nor existence. The soul sinks into it by an experience of all fullness. It has no name. It is that which is. It is not love nor grace, neither world nor soul, neither God nor freedom nor light. For all these are relative conceptions. Satchidananda is the highest logical description, but merely an intellectual prop.

It is the essence of essence, where eternity and infinity embrace one another to form its centre of experience. It is the life of life. Birthlessness and deathlessness float in it like ripples. It is the supreme death of all, and yet it is the highest peak of real life. It puts an end to the vicious circle of transmigratory life.

Only those who experience the highest samadhi, and no others, have eternal peace. For one whose desires are completely satisfied, who is totally perfected, all desires dissolve themselves here itself. The liberated one becomes unlimited. Time, age and death, sorrow, merit and demerit do not go there. Fearless is the state of the bliss of Brahman.

Samadhi is the supreme treasure. The freed souls enter into Brahman; they are liberated beyond mortal nature. The constitution of individuality becomes unified in the imperishable supreme; they are liberated from name and form. They reach the transcendental divine being. This is immortality.

Liberated souls

Liberated souls think and work through the higher spiritual nature, not through the mind and sense organs of the lower nature. They have the unceasing immediacy of the consciousness of everything, an awareness of the innermost objective essence of the complete universe. They can have entire knowledge of the universe through self-identification with anything in the universe.

The experience of self-dissolution in the state of samadhi is, in some respects, similar to the deep sleep of the worldly individual who also, at the end of the day, dissolves his body consciousness into the unconscious power which is superimposed on the atma. But the difference between the two dissolutions is in the fact that in the highest samadhi there is no further forced coming back to universe consciousness, no subsequent dreaming and waking state, and there is absolute experience. Whereas in the case of the worldly individual, there is a forced returning to body consciousness and subsequent dreaming and waking states, and there is no experience of the Self.

There is karma in the worldly individual because of ignorance, but in samadhi there is vidya, universal consciousness of absolute self-consciousness alone. Hence, there is no karma. Desire and action in an individual are the outcome of the darkness of ignorance, but they do not exist in *vidya*, which is the light of knowledge.

Moksha does not mean physical separation from all worldly affairs, but a state of mind which is free from all impure vasanas, passions, and clinging to worldly things, yet works as usual amidst them. God must be realized in and through the world. This is the central teaching of the *Bhagavad Gita* and of *Yoga Vasishtha* also.

4
Samadhi According to the Upanishads

1. Samadhi is that state of pure consciousness, the supreme blissful state, free from the triads: the meditator, meditated and meditation. It is the state where the *jivatma* (individual soul) becomes one with the *paramatma* (supreme soul).

2. The state of mind that is steady like the flame of a lamp in a windless place, which has given up the idea of meditator and meditation, and which constantly dwells in Brahman, is samadhi.

3. The mind, when it is free from thoughts, desires and motion, merges in the supreme Brahman. This state is samadhi.

4. When through knowledge of the Self, which is seated within one's heart, one attains *vijnana*, direct realization, and when the body idea is completely eradicated and absolute peace is attained, in that state the vrittis, mind and intellect are destroyed. This state of obliteration of mind is samadhi.

5. Having controlled the prana and apana during *kumbhaka* (breath retention) with the gaze steadily fixed at the tip of the nose, performing shanmukha mudra with the fingers of both hands, the mind merges itself in the sound of *pranava*, Aum.

6. After the dribbling of nectar, like the milk from the cow's udder, the senses become calm by withdrawal, and then results *manonasha*, destruction of the mind.

7. When the five organs of knowledge are at rest together with the mind and when the intellect ceases functioning or becomes calm, that the seers call the highest state, samadhi.

8. When all *sankalpas*, desires of the mind, become calm, when the mind is neither waking nor sleeping, when it is motionless and calm like a stone, the highest Brahmic state of samadhi is attained.

9. When the prana moves in the middle of sushumna, leaving both ida and pingala, the mind becomes steady. The perfect state of tranquillity of mind is the Brahmic state of samadhi, called *manonmani*.

10. When the *chitta* or mind is free from all flickering desires, when the mind is destroyed, the peaceful state which ensues is similar to sushupti or deep sleep, yet the yogi is awake.

11. That state is neither waking nor dreaming on account of the absence of sankalpa or desires. It is also not *sushupti*, sleep, because of the absence of inertness there.

12. Knowledge of sattwa or Brahman, which is like the fire burning up the grass of *vasanas*, subtle desires, is indicated by the word samadhi, and not the state of inertia or mere silence.

13. The complete eradication of vrittis caused by the destruction of thoughts by generating the *Brahmakara vritti*, or meditation on Brahman, is called samadhi.

14. 'I am the Supreme Brahman; I am Brahman alone': when this one thought remains to the exclusion of all other thoughts, it is called samadhi.

15. The rising of the knowledge of the identity of jivatman and paramatman and complete forgetfulness of meditation is called samadhi.
16. The state of steadiness of the mind, free from all craving for sensual enjoyment, free from ideas of sensual enjoyment, free from ideas of acquiring and giving up, that state of fullness of mind is called samadhi.
17. The merging of the mind into the atman, like salt put into water, is called samadhi.
18. The samadhi wherein there is destruction of the vasanas or vrittis of the mind and which brings us face to face with the enjoyment of the supreme blissful state is termed asamprajnata samadhi – dear to the yogins!
19. Samadhi is that real state of direct realization of the supreme Self which is all auspiciousness, which is all full, all-pervading and fills the above, below and the intervening spaces.

5
Nirvikalpa Samadhi

Nirvikalpa samadhi is that state in which one's identity with the universal reality is realized. When the mind ceases functioning, when all the thoughts subside, when all consciousness of the body and the outer world is effaced from the mind, the individual soul completely merges into the supreme soul, into universal consciousness.

Nirvikalpa samadhi is that blessed state in which the mystery of life is revealed. It is that serene state in which the meditator enters into sleepless sleep. It is the highest realization known as the superconscious state, and as *turiya* or the fourth state.

The lower samadhis, *jada* (inert) or *savikalpa* (with imagination), cannot give liberation as there are still subtle *samskaras* or impressions in the mind. However, in nirvikalpa samadhi the mind has no support or *alambana*; there are no samskaras or vasanas, all have been burnt or fried in toto. Nirvikalpa is the experience of oneness with the Absolute where the highest reality is intuited in all its wholeness. It is the state of one's own spiritual experience. There are no words to fully describe nirvikalpa samadhi. It is an experience of supreme peace and bliss.

Nirvikalpa samadhi is oneness with the Supreme Being. One who has attained this oneness can never be separated from it. It is the state of perfect awareness of one's real essence. All names and forms vanish, all mental modifications cease; there is consciousness of infinite space. This also disappears and then there is a state of nothingness. The little 'I' has melted. There is no consciousness of anything internal or external; there is neither 'I' nor 'you', neither 'he' nor 'she', neither 'here' nor 'there', neither 'this' nor 'that', neither 'above' nor 'below'. The differentiating mind has vanished. The ideas of class, creed and colour have now gone. All barriers, all sense of duality, differences and separateness have disappeared. There is no idea of time and space, there is only eternity. The jiva has realized its identity with Brahman.

Death of the mind

The world is a mental creation, a mere impression only. There is no world during sleep. It may be argued that the world exists for the waking person. It is true, if there is mind, there is world. What then is the mind? It is a bundle of impressions, ideas, and habits. The two currents of *raga* and *dwesha*, likes and dislikes, keep up the life of the mind. If these two currents are destroyed, there is death of the mind, or *manonasha*.

The yogi who has achieved manonasha cannot perceive the world. If you can consciously destroy the mind through samadhi, this world disappears. Just as you see a rope as a rope and not as a snake only when the illusory impression, *bhranti,* of a snake has vanished, so also you see Brahman only when the bhranti of the world and body has disappeared through realization of the Self.

Nirvikalpa samadhi is pure absolute consciousness. It is Christ consciousness. Here there are no names and forms, no sound or colour, neither matter nor energy. Jesus said, "The kingdom of God is within you." The kingdom of God is not a place but a state of consciousness. It is non-dual consciousness wherein the mind, senses and intellect cease functioning. It is the realm of intuition.

The immortal state

Suddenly illumination dawns, and the culmination of man's evolution is attained. In this state there is no movement of *prana*, the life force, there is neither inhalation nor exhalation.

It is the immortal state without birth or death, without decay or disease, without pain or sorrow.

The Supreme Being is realized by the yogi at the highest stage of this spiritual experience. One who rests in nirvikalpa samadhi will be beyond all the effects of *prakriti* or matter. *Purusha,* or pure consciousness, alone is the seer, the *drashta.* The *gunas*, qualities, and their modifications are the *drishyam* or the seen. When the purusha attains *kaivalya,* or absolute independence, in the state of nirvikalpa samadhi, the gunas and their modifications have no further purpose and return to their origin, prakriti. *Buddhi,* intellect, *ahamkara*, egoism, and *manas,* mind, are only modifications of the threefold gunas and also merge into their original sources, one after another.

Although one can enter into lower samadhi without any moral perfection, nirvikalpa samadhi can never be had without ethical perfection. Note this point very carefully. However, God's grace alone can take one into the realms of this transcendental experience.

Can a person in nirvikalpa samadhi break it at will?
Yes.

Can one in samadhi be misunderstood by outsiders as dead and lost?
Yes.

The scriptures say that a person who has attained nirvikalpa samadhi does not say so publicly. So how are we to know that a person has attained the highest wisdom or not?
By observing his actions, behaviour and speech. He performs all actions with equal vision and perfect serenity, and maintains a balanced mind, cosmic love, peace and bliss under all conditions.

How can a person know he has attained nirvikalpa samadhi?
If his experiences tally with the experience of the seers of the Upanishads, if he enjoys absolute bliss and peace, if he

maintains unperturbed serenity of mind in the worst situations, and if his doubts have been rent asunder; if he beholds unity in diversity, and if he feels that he is the self in all beings and the whole world is his body; if he is perfectly free from desires for sensual objects, likes, dislikes, egoism, anger, lust, mineness, pride and attachment, then he can be sure that he has attained samadhi, Self-realization.

How can we know that the divine experience of nirvikalpa samadhi described by mystics and saints is true?
There is a power in their words. Contact with them is elevating and inspiring. They are ever peaceful, joyful, and blissful, free from greed, anger, likes and dislikes. Their experiences are in accord with the experiences sages describe in the *Bhagavad Gita* and the Upanishads.

AN EXPERIENCE OF THE DIVINE

"The floodgate of joy broke into his soul; he was inundated with waves of indescribable ecstasy. Worlds that had been merely words before – bliss, immortality, eternity, truth, divine love – became, in the twinkling of an eye, the core of his being, the essence of his life, the only possible reality. Realization that these deep, everlasting founts of joy exist in every heart, that this immortal life underlies all the mortality of humanity, that this eternal, all-inclusive love envelops, supports and guides every particle and atom of creation burst upon him with a divine certainty that caused his whole being to pour forth a flood of praise and gratitude.

He knew, not with his mind alone, but with his heart and soul, with every cell and molecule. The sublime splendour and joy of this discovery was so vast that he felt that centuries, millenniums, countless aeons of suffering were less than nothing, if by such means that bliss could be obtained. Sin, sorrow, death are now but words, without meaning.

He was aware during this first period of illumination and during the months that followed of a number of physiological changes within himself. The most striking was what seemed like a re-arrangement of the molecular structure in his brain, or the opening up of new cell territory. Ceaselessly, day and night, he was conscious of this work going on. It seemed as though a kind of electric drill was boring out new cellular thought channels.

Another important change was felt in his spinal column. The whole spine seemed turned into iron for several months, so that when he sat to meditate on God, he felt anchored forever, able to sit in one place eternally without motion or consciousness of any bodily functions. At times an influx of superhuman strength invaded him and he felt that he was carrying the whole universe on his shoulders. He felt the elixir of life, the nectar of immortality, flowing in his veins as an actual, tangible force. It seemed like quicksilver or a sort of electrical fluid light flowed throughout his body.

During the months of illumination, he felt no need for food or sleep. But he conformed his outward life to the pattern of his household and ate and slept when his family did. All food seemed pure spirit to him, and in sleep he was pillowed on the 'everlasting arms', awakening to a joy beyond description.

He had previously suffered from heavy colds and had been a constant smoker; now his body was purged of all sickness, and the desire for cigarettes was completely wiped from his consciousness. His family and friends were aware of a great change in his appearance and manner; his face shone with radiant light, his eyes were pools of joy. Strangers spoke to him, irresistibly drawn by a strange sympathy. On the street-car, children would come over to sit on his lap, asking him to visit them.

For him the whole universe was bathed in a sea of love. He would often say, "Now at last I know what love is!" This is God's love, unconquerable, all-satisfying love. He knew beyond all doubt that love creates and sustains the universe, and that all creatures, human or subhuman, were destined to discover this immortal bliss that is the very essence of life. He felt his mind expand, his understanding reach out endlessly widening, growing, touching everything in the universe, binding all things, all thought to himself. He was the centre of everywhere, but his circumference was nowhere.

The air that he breathed was friendly, intimate, and conscious of life. He felt all the world was 'home' to him, that he could never feel strange or alien in any place again; that the mountains, the seas, the distant lands which he had never seen would be as much his own as the home of his boyhood. Everywhere he looked he saw the dance of nature; the air was filled with myriad moving pinpricks of light.

During these months he went about his daily duties as usual, but with a hitherto unknown efficiency and speed. He was a student at college during this period, and passed all his examinations without looking at a textbook. His mind was bathed in a sea of knowledge. Typed papers flew off his machine, complete, without errors, in a fourth of his customary time. Fatigue was unknown to him; his work seemed like child's play, happy and carefree. When he conversed in person or on the phone, to him the other person's voice was God manifesting in another of His fascinating disguises.

In the midst of his work, he would suddenly be freshly overwhelmed by the goodness of God who had given him this incredible, unspeakable happiness. His breath would stop completely at such times; the awe which he felt would be accompanied by an absolute stillness within and without. Time and space were swallowed up, gone without a trace like all unreality. Underlying his consciousness was a sense of immeasurable and unutterable gratitude, a longing for others to know the joy which lay within them. But most of all, a divine knowledge, beyond all human comprehension, that all was well with the world, that everything was leading to the goal of cosmic consciousness and immortal bliss."

The state of samadhi or cosmic consciousness can be attained by the practices of yoga. Yogic techniques provide a definite way to contact God, and the techniques are available to all people in all circumstances. This is proof in itself that divine knowledge is indeed an inherent faculty of everyone, not only the experience of a chosen few.

Purify your heart. Meditate. You will attain samadhi. May you attain this everlasting abode of peace and immortality, which was attained by Tukaram, Tulsidas, Ram Das, Mira, Kabir, Prahlada, Ramanuja, Gouranga, Madhava, Lord Buddha, Lord Jesus, and Dhruva of yore.

6
Sahaja Samadhi

When a sage becomes established in samadhi, his outer consciousness also automatically follows this attainment. The inward perfection cannot but express itself as a distinct transformation in outer consciousness. Later, a stage is reached when the inner and the outer consciousness partake of the very same quality with hardly any difference between the two. This is the state of *sahaja samadhi*, where the superconscious state has become spontaneous and natural.

Sahaja samadhi is an extension of samadhi so that it covers all the twenty-four hours of the day, not only when one sits in meditation. The reality of God and the unreality of names and forms, and the inner realization that the individual self is none other than the supreme Self that pervades everything, comes to stay in sahaja samadhi. The samadhi that the sadhaka strives to experience through *bahiranga*, external, and then *antaranga*, internal, sadhana becomes one's *sahaja* or natural state.

In that state the ego, the world and one's own body appear like a pane of glass on which a thin coating of moisture has settled. You are able to see through it, yet you see the glass pane because of the moisture; the glass pane is transparent except for a slight opacity. The yogi in sahaja samadhi perceives the world in exactly the same manner as a person who knows that a mirage is a mirage; he sees the water-like spectacle without being deluded into believing that it is actually water.

What part does the mantra of the breath, Soham, play in sahaja samadhi? Does the world exist in sahaja samadhi?

There is a slight sattwic trace of ego in the yogi who enjoys sahaja samadhi. This enables him to live, experience and work, but as he is rooted in the consciousness of *Soham*, 'That am I', he is not affected by living, experiencing and working. Lord Krishna has given the exact description of this state in the second chapter of the *Bhagavad Gita* when he describes the state of *sthita prajna*, steady wisdom. In sahaja samadhi, the Soham disposition or *bhavana* becomes automatic, continuous and natural. In nirvikalpa samadhi, there is not even the Soham bhavana, as there is no one to feel Soham.

Why struggle for sahaja samadhi when one is contented in the nirvikalpa state?

No one need struggle to pass from one stage of samadhi to another; it is an automatic process. Even the 'struggle' that the yogi puts forth is intended only to maintain the sahaja state. The slender thread of sattwic ego should be prevented from assuming rajasic proportions. Though such a downfall is very rare, there are instances in the scriptures where a slight heedlessness spoils the game. If, as Lord Krishna puts it at the end of the *Bhagavad Gita*, the sahaja state is maintained until the very end of life, until the *prarabdha* or irrevocable karma is exhausted, one attains Brahma nirvana.

Sahaja being a God-conscious state, the yogi vigorously engages in *lokasangraham*, the upliftment of humanity, selfless service, and cosmic love. Karma is rapidly worn out, and the supreme culmination is hastened. At the same time all chances of even the slightest descent from the high sahaja state are prevented.

Jesus: a sage in sahaja samadhi

Two thousand years ago, divinity incarnated upon this planet to show humanity the glorious path to everlasting life by actually living the divine life upon this earth. The great Jesus embodied the qualities of *satya*, truth, *ahimsa*, non-violence, and *brahmacharya*, chastity. These three strands were woven into the very fabric of the divine life he lived. During his entire life, Christ lived as the visible expression of the highest truth. He was a living witness to the supreme reality essentially indwelling in man. In his dealings with the outside world, he was ahimsa incarnate.

With words brimming with the true spirit of ahimsa, Jesus preached the doctrine of non-retaliation. Present your left cheek to the assailant who hits you on the right. If a man takes away your coat forcibly, offer him your cloak too. No test, struggle, torment or persecution whatsoever could ruffle him to anger or retaliation. In his personal life he was indeed purity itself. He said, "Unless you become like little children you cannot enter the kingdom of heaven." You have to be absolutely pure like the innocent little ones.

An almost supernal spotless purity rested like a divine mantle upon his sublime personality. His life was a wonderful combination of jnana, bhakti and karma, based upon *para vairagya*, supreme non-attachment. An ideal integral development of head, heart and hand rendered his life a model for mankind to emulate for all eternity. Christ was ever conscious of his inseparable identity with the supreme Self. Yet deep devotion and love for the personal God constantly found expression in him in the form of prayers, praises and glorification.

In his day-to-day life he was the very personification of the spirit of karma yoga. His entire life was a continuous ministry to the afflicted. His feet moved only to reach where aid was needed. If his hands moved, it was only to help the troubled and oppressed. His tongue spoke only to utter soft, honeyed words of compassion, consolation, inspiration and enlightenment. With a glance of his luminous yogic eyes Jesus awakened, elevated and transformed those upon whom he gazed. He felt, thought, talked and acted for the good of others. Amidst all this he dwelt in unbroken awareness of the assertion 'I and my Father are one'. His life was that of a sage in sahaja samadhi.

In Jesus the man, the aspirant or sadhaka finds two traits to be faithfully emulated. One is an admirable moral courage in being a witness to truth. His life displays a silent yet supreme heroism in the face of the most determined opposition, persecution and misunderstanding. He has also set an example of how a true seeker repulses temptations on the spiritual path. Long before the outward drama of crucifixion, Jesus voluntarily crucified himself by annihilating the lower self and living a purely divine life.

Great rishi that he was, the man from Galilee exemplified the *sthitadhih muni*, the sage of steady wisdom, described by Lord Krishna in the *Bhagavad Gita*. Jesus was a sage forever absorbed in the Self, perfectly balanced in the midst of opposites. He never lost his calm even for a single moment of his intensely lived life. He neither rejoiced in pleasure nor grieved in pain. Looking with perfect equal vision upon friend and foe, intent only upon universal welfare, he exemplifies the perfected siddha.

The compassionate voice of this God-man called aloud to all mankind, "Come to me, all you that are weary and burdened", and promised to "relieve their load" and grant them rest. "Come! Come! Come!" was His divine call. And how? "Cast your cares upon God for He cares for you. Your work is to intently think of Him and Him alone. Never care for anything else for does He not look after the lilies in the field and the birds in the air? Depend on Him and He will care for you." For, as is the promise of Lord Krishna: "To those who worship Me alone, thinking of no other, of those ever united, I secure what is not already possessed and preserve what they already possess." (*Bhagavad Gita* 9:22)

7

Raja Yoga Samadhi

According to raja yoga, samadhi is mainly of two kinds: samprajnata and asamprajnata. In the former, the seeds of samskaras are not destroyed. In the latter, the samskaras are fried or annihilated entirely. That is the reason why samprajnata samadhi is also called *sabija samadhi*, samadhi with seed. Asamprajnata samadhi is also known as *nirbija samadhi*, without seed or samskara. Samprajnata samadhi leads to asamprajnata samadhi.

Samprajnata or savikalpa samadhi
Samprajnata samadhi is also known as savikalpa samadhi. This samadhi brings perfect knowledge of the object of meditation. The mind continuously, and to the exclusion of all other objects, assumes the nature of and becomes one with the object of contemplation. The yogi attains the power of controlling nature in this samadhi.

In savikalpa samadhi there is the consciousness, "I am meditating, Brahman is the object of meditation." There is consciousness of the triad of knower, knowledge and the known. In savikalpa samadhi the karmas and the impressions or *samskaras* are not burnt whereas in nirvikalpa samadhi all of these are totally annihilated. Savikalpa samadhi is a state of preparation. Nirvikalpa samadhi is the ultimate goal.

Samprajnata or savikalpa samadhi is of four kinds: savitarka, savichara, ananda and asmita. All these samadhis have something to grasp; there is argumentation or questioning. They give intense joy but they are not the finest and ultimate forms of samadhi. They cover the gross or the subtle elements of nature and the sense organs. They give direct knowledge of the elements, objects and instruments of knowledge and some freedom.

These stages are in the form of steps of an ascending staircase. To begin with meditation must be done on a gross form. When one advances in this meditation, one can take to abstract meditation or meditation on subtle concepts or ideas. The mind should be gradually trained in meditation. It cannot all at once enter into asamprajnata samadhi or that state which constitutes the highest and subtlest essence. This is the reason why Maharishi Patanjali has prescribed the practice of various kinds of lower samadhis.

Savitarka and nirvitarka samadhi

Savitarka samadhi is samadhi with reasoning. In savitarka samadhi concentration is practised on gross objects and their nature in relation to time and space. This is a gross form of samadhi. When the yogi meditates on the elements as they are, by taking them out of time and space, then it is called *nirvitarka samadhi*, or samadhi without questioning, reasoning or argumentation. This is a subtle form of samadhi.

In savitarka samadhi there is a fanciful notion of word, object and idea. There are three factors in the comprehension of a word, for example, 'cow': (i) cow, the word (ii) cow, the object, and (iii) cow, the idea in the mind. When the meditator imagines these three to be one and the same, it is an instance of *vikalpa* or fanciful notion of the word, object and idea. There is no such notion in nirvitarka samadhi, where there is no intellectual argumentation or logic.

Savichara and nirvichara samadhi

Savichara samadhi is samadhi with reflection and reasoning. *Nirvichara samadhi* is samadhi without logic and enquiry. If one meditates on the subtle elements, *tanmatras*, and their nature in relation to time and space, it is savichara samadhi, i.e. samadhi with deliberation or discrimination. This is more subtle than savitarka and nirvitarka samadhis. The five gross elements are derived from the tanmatras, the root elements, through the process of quintuplication or mixing. Meditation goes a step higher in this samadhi than in the previous one. The yogi will attain knowledge of the subtle elements and obtain control over them. He will gain direct perception of the various subtle forms of the object, culminating in primordial matter, *moola prakriti*.

Meditation on the subtle elements by taking them out of time and space, by thinking of them as they are, constitutes nirvichara samadhi, i.e. samadhi without deliberation or discrimination. As there is only pure sattwa in the mind, owing to the eradication of rajas and tamas, the yogi enjoys internal peace and subjective luminosity. The mind is very steady now. The Purusha, who is all bliss, all knowledge and all purity, can only be realized when the mind is perfectly steady and is filled with purity. The yogi obtains simultaneous knowledge of everything.

Ananda samadhi

Ananda samadhi is a joyous samadhi. In this samadhi the gross and the subtle elements are given up. The yogi meditates on the sattwic mind itself. He thinks of the mind which is devoid of rajas and tamas. Through this type of samadhi there arises in the yogi a peculiar perception in the form of intense joy.

Asmita samadhi

In this samadhi the mind is the object of meditation. It bestows the knowledge of the subject of all experiences. The self knows the Self. Only the sattwic state of the ego remains. The yogi can think of himself now as without his gross body. He feels that he has a fine body. This samadhi takes the yogi to the root of experiences and shows the way to freedom.

The yogi feels, "I am, *asmi*, other than this body." He experiences that the gross, subtle and joyous samadhis are not the highest samadhis. He finds defects in them also and becomes disgusted with them (even though they are infinitely more blissful than the miserable mundane life), because even lower kinds of samadhi act as an obstacle on the path of the aspirant and prevent him from striving to reach the highest nirvikalpa samadhi. He proceeds further and practises asmita samadhi. He experiences consciousness of the self, *asmita*. He experiences a feeling of 'enough' and develops dispassion in its highest form, *para vairagya*. This finally leads to the development of asamprajnata samadhi.

Asamprajnata samadhi

This is the highest form of samadhi, attained by removing the hold of prakriti through yogic practices and disciplines. This comes after the final discrimination between prakriti and purusha, and in raja yoga samadhi, according to Patanjali, greater stress is laid upon this discrimination between prakriti and purusha. This highest samadhi of raja yoga is also known as nirbija samadhi and nirvikalpa samadhi. In asamprajnata samadhi there is no ego consciousness. The ego and mind melt and fuse in Brahman.

All the seeds or impressions are burnt by the fire of knowledge attained in nirvikalpa samadhi. This samadhi brings *kaivalya*, absolute independence. It the culmination or climax of yoga and bestows supreme, undying peace or knowledge. The yogi enjoys the transcendental glories of the Self and has perfect freedom from mental life. The sense of time is replaced by a sense of eternity.

When the yogi attains perfection in raja yoga by entering into asamprajnata samadhi, the nirvikalpa state, all the samskaras and vasanas which bring on rebirths are totally fried or burnt up. This can only be attained when there is perfect *nirodha*, perfect control or restraint of the mind. *Nirvikalpa* means that in which there is no *vikalpa*, no thought, no imagination, no functioning of the mind or senses. All the five *kleshas* or afflictions: ignorance, egoism, likes and dislikes, and clinging to mundane life, are destroyed and the bonds of karma are annihilated. Egoism is burnt to ashes. All the *vrittis*, the modifications of the mind, totally cease, and the mind is freed from distractions, attachments and all other defects. It rests unmoved like the flame of a lamp sheltered from the wind. The yogi becomes an *apta kama*, one whose desires are all gratified. There is only pure consciousness or awareness. There is full illumination.

However, a mere glimpse of the Truth cannot free one from birth and death. Only when the yogi is perfectly established in nirvikalpa samadhi will the seed of rebirth be burnt entirely. The only sadhana for attaining nirvikalpa samadhi is *para vairagya,* supreme dispassion. Here the yogi completely disconnects from prakriti and its effects. Hence it is also called asamprajnata samadhi.

The Purusha must eventually realize his own native state of divine glory, kaivalya or final liberation. He feels absolute freedom upon attaining kaivalya, the highest goal of raja yoga. The five kleshas are destroyed. The gunas, having fulfilled their objects of enjoyment and attachment, entirely cease to act. The past and the future are blended into the present. The yogi has transcended time and space. Everything is 'now!' Everything is 'here!' All sorrows have ceased, all miseries have disappeared, all doubts are dispelled. It is a state like the ocean without waves, without even a ripple. There is eternal freedom. The sum total of all knowledge of the three worlds, of all secular sciences, becomes nothing but mere husk when compared to the infinite knowledge of a yogi who has attained kaivalya. Glory, glory to such exalted yogis!

In this samadhi the yogi sees without eyes, tastes without a tongue, hears without ears, smells without a nose and touches without skin. In this samadhi the yogi's sankalpas can work miracles; he simply wills and everything comes into being. This state is described in *Taittiriya Aranyaka* (1:2:5): "The blind man pierced the pearl, the fingerless put a thread into it, the neckless wore it and the tongueless praised it."

When the yogi has reached the highest state of nirvikalpa samadhi, he at once attains liberation in this very life. He has attained the state of perennial joy, of fullness and perfection, the state of supreme peace. He attains immortality, the highest, or transcendental wisdom. His bliss is unending.

8

Vedantic Samadhi

There is a difference between the nirvikalpa state of a raja yogi and the nirvikalpa state of a vedantin. The former concerns the mind; the latter concerns the pure Atman or Brahman only. In raja yoga samadhi, the object of meditation remains. In vedantic samadhi, existence alone remains.

According to Vedanta, annihilation of *avidya*, ignorance, leads to samadhi. A vedantin says, "Nothing is mine or everything is mine." As the world is mere appearance, he is quite right in saying, "Nothing is mine". As he has realized the Self, as the world has no permanent existence apart from Brahman or the Self, he says, "Everything is mine." He has controlled the organ of smell and *prithvi tattwa*, the earth element, and so all objects of smell and sense belong to him. He has controlled the palate or tongue and *apas tattwa*, the water element, and so all objects of taste, fruits and other delicacies belong to him. He has controlled the organ of sight or eye and *agni tattwa*, the fire element, and so all objects of sight and beauties and gardens belong to him. He has controlled the organ of touch and *vayu tattwa*, the air element, and so all the objects of touch belong to him. He has controlled the organ of hearing and *akasha tattwa*, the space element, and so all sounds and music belong to him.

The vedantin enjoys the eternal bliss and natural easiness of sahaja samadhi. He remains as a *sakshi* or silent witness. He does not make any serious attempt to control the psychic or thought currents. He raises the *Brahmakara vritti*, where the mind flows towards Brahman, by meditating on the significance of the *mahavakya* or great saying, *Tat Twam Asi*, 'I am That'. The chitta is modified into the form of Brahmakara vritti. All other modifications are withdrawn. This vritti annihilates ignorance, avidya dies by itself, and Brahman shines out as the aspirant realizes his identity. When this vritti is intermittent, the sage attains savikalpa samadhi. When it is continuous, the highest form of samadhi, nirvikalpa samadhi, is attained.

Destroy the ego

There are four ways of destroying the ego, *ahamkara*: two adwaitic methods, positive and negative; one bhakti method of ungrudging, unreserved, and absolute self-surrender, *atma nivedana*; and the fourth, the complete self-sacrifice of *nishkama* karma yogis.

Purify the mind by japa, pranayama, satsang, swadhyaya, daan, yajna, tapas and selfless service. Then fix it on God. Destroy the *sankalpa-vikalpa*, thought and counter-thought, of the mind. Unite the currents of the mind with the spiritual current. Abandon the idea or notion of duality, of 'I', 'he', 'you', etc. Instead have *Brahma bhavana*, feeling that all is Brahman, then samadhi or the superconscious state will supervene automatically.

The negative vedantic method is denial: "I am not the body, I am not the mind." Brahman alone is real. The world is unreal. Jiva is identical with Brahman.' The world includes the body. Meditate on this idea and the ego will vanish. The positive method is that everything is Brahman, there is nothing but Brahman.

In Vedanta there are two kinds of samadhis: adwaita bhavanaroopa samadhi and adwaita avastharoopa samadhi. The aspirant meditates on the formula *Aham Brahmasmi*, 'I am Brahman', or *Tat Twam Asi*, 'I am That', the great sayings of the Upanishads. In the beginning stage it is called *adwaita bhavanaroopa*, where the aspirant tries to identify himself with the non-dual consciousness. But later on, through constant *nididhyasana*, deep meditation, when he is established in his own Self, it is called *adwaita avastharoopa samadhi*, where one is fully established in non-dual consciousness. The thing-in-itself, the transcendent, alone remains. Sri Shankaracharya, Dattatreya, Vyasa, Vasishtha, Sukadeva, Sanaka, Sanandana, Sanatkumara, Padmapada and many other Indian sages had this experience.

There are four fundamental, vital verses in the *Avadhoota Gita* of Dattatreya. He gives it in his own experience. It is very useful for students of Vedanta to meditate on those formulas. These verses are:

> Why do you weep, my child? There are no names and forms in you. There is neither bondage nor liberation, neither good nor evil. Stand up. Gird your loins. Fight with the mind and the senses and rest in your own satchidananda swaroopa. The world is not in you. It is only sankalpa. (1:17)

> I am imperishable, infinite, a mass of pure consciousness. The physical mountain appears solid but this knowledge of atma is more solid and massive than the Himalayas. I do not know what pleasure is or what pain is. (1:7)

> The mental actions are not in you. The actions of the body are not in you. The actions of speech are not in you. Purity, nectar, beyond the reach of the senses – this is your divine, essential, Brahmic nature. (1:8) Meditation on this third verse will free you from the bondage of karmas.

> Then he denies the whole world. For one who is established in his own essence, the names and forms and the world vanish. Mahat is the first manifestation of the Absolute, and then sprang up the mind, the senses, the tanmatras and the five elements, giving rise to the world. Where is *varna*, caste, where are the *ashramas*, the four stages of life? Everything is Brahman. There is no world! (1:45) This is the highest experience of a sage or a jnani.

Therefore, let us try to enter into this non-dual consciousness by reflection and meditation on these formulas and attain the state of jivanmukti and highest illumination and rest in our essential nature. Let us radiate joy and peace and bliss to all those who come in contact with us. Let us radiate joy and peace and bliss to the different corners of the whole world.

The whole world is your body

Pull up all walls that separate you from others. The whole world is your body. Feel this. Feel your oneness with all life. If you see difference, there is absence of love. Feel your presence in the tree, stone, sun, moon, stars, animals, etc. All is the Self. All is One.

Remember there is no world. You are not the body; you are all-pervading Atman or pure spirit. You are *akarta*, the non-doer. You are the silent *sakshi* or witness. There is Atman everywhere. Feel the indwelling intelligence. When you see a fruit say, "This is an Atma." See the essence in all forms. Reject the outer sheaths and illusory appearances. This will lead to *bahir* or external nirvikalpa samadhi. There is no need to close the eyes. For this kind of sadhana, no asana or room is needed.

This sadhana is suitable for intelligent people of the world. This is work combined with jnana. The light of the supreme Brahman is appearing as mind and universe. The world is nothing but mind. The world is a long dream. This is the essence of Vedanta or jnana yoga in a nutshell. Digest it, absorb it, assimilate it. Proclaim it everywhere. Become fearless. Shine as Brahman. Rejoice always in the *satchidananda*, truth-existence-bliss, within.

9
Bhakti, Hatha, Jnana and Kundalini Yoga Samadhis

Bhakti yoga

In bhakti yoga there is absence of the least tinge of pride and self-assertion. The *bhakta* or devotee becomes one with the cosmic will through unreserved self-surrender. He resigns completely to the Lord and obtains His grace. Grace is a mighty spiritual force, which transforms the entire being of the devotee, infusing him with inspiration and a new divine life. Grace makes surrender complete; it removes all the obstacles, snares and pitfalls on the spiritual path. Only through grace is the devotee's whole being galvanized and rejuvenated. Through divine grace there is an inflow of divine energy into the entire being, which is properly moulded for divine realization and divine instrumentality. The individual becomes one with the cosmic will. Without grace, perfect union in *bhava samadhi*, the superconscious state attained by bhaktas through intense divine emotion, is not possible.

There are nine modes or methods of bhakti: *shravana*, hearing about God; *kirtan*, singing the names of God; *smarana*, remembrance; *padaseva*, service at the feet of God; *archana*, offering of flowers, etc.; *vandana*, prostrations and prayers; *dasya*, the attitude of a servant; *sakhya*, friendship with the Lord; and *atma nivedana*, self-surrender. Self-surrender draws down grace, it makes the devotee feel the reality of the Divine and the Lord's readiness to bestow help at all times.

When established in samadhi, the bhakta who meditates on the form of Lord Krishna will see Krishna and only Krishna everywhere. All other forms will disappear. This is one kind of spiritual experience. He will also see himself as Krishna. The gopis of Vrindavan, Gauranga and Ekanath had this experience. Those who meditate on the all-pervading Krishna will have another kind of cosmic experience, like Arjuna, who had consciousness of the whole universe in cosmic consciousness.

In bhava samadhi the mind of the devotee is highly elevated through pure emotion and devotion. He forgets the body and the world; his mind is wholly absorbed in the Lord. Tukaram, a great bhakta who attained bhava samadhi, was an agricultural peasant, unable even to sign his name. He was always singing kirtan of Lord Krishna's name, 'Vitala Vitala', with cymbals in his hands. He had darshan of Lord Krishna in the physical form. His inner sight, *divya drishti*, was opened by *sankirtan*, continuous kirtan. His inspiring *abhangas*, devotional songs, are texts for MA students at Bombay University. From where did the unlettered, illiterate Tuka derive his knowledge? He tapped the fountain of knowledge through sankirtan and penetrated into the divine source through bhava samadhi.

Ramakrishna Paramahamsa also could not sign his name, but he was able to remove the doubts of erudite scholars. From where did he get this super-intuitional knowledge? He also tapped the divine source.

Just as fire has the natural property of burning inflammable things, so also the name of God has the power of burning sins, samskaras and vasanas and bestowing eternal bliss and everlasting peace on those who repeat the Lord's name. Just as burning is a natural quality inherent in fire, so too the power of destroying sins at their very root and branch and bringing the aspirant into blissful union with the Lord through bhava samadhi is natural and inherent in God's name.

Take refuge in the name. Sing the Lord's name incessantly. Remember the name of the Lord with every incoming and outgoing breath. In this age, *nama smarana,* remembrance of the Lord's name, or japa is the easiest, quickest, safest and surest way to reach God and to attain the immortality and perennial joy of bhava samadhi.

Glory to the Lord. Glory to His Name. Sing 'Hari Om,' 'Sri Rama,' 'Radheshyam,' 'Hare Rama Hare Rama Rama Rama Hare Hare, Hare Krishna Hare Krishna Krishna Krishna Hare Hare.'

Hatha yoga

A hatha yogi draws all the prana from the different parts of the body and takes it to sahasrara chakra, the thousand-petalled lotus at the top of the head. Then he enters into samadhi, the superconscious state. Therefore, it is very difficult to bring him down to objective consciousness by merely shaking his body.

Prana and apana, which move in the chest and abdomen respectively, are united by the yogic processes of jalandhara, mooladhara and uddiyana bandhas, and the united prana-apana is driven into the sushumna nadi of the spinal canal. The pranas, when thus driven, also draw up the mind along the sushumna nadi, also known as brahma nadi. During the ascent in sushumna nadi, the three *granthis* or knots, brahma granthi at mooladhara chakra, vishnu granthi at manipura chakra and rudra granthi at ajna chakra, should be cut asunder by yogic efforts. These knots prevent the ascent of kundalini.

Bhastrika pranayama breaks down these knots. Kula kundalini shakti lies dormant in mooladhara chakra in the form of a coiled serpent with three and a half coils, face downwards. When it is awakened by spiritual sadhana, it ascends upwards towards sahasrara chakra at the crown of the head and takes the mind and prana with it.

When the mind is in sushumna nadi, the yogi is shut out from the objective, physical consciousness of the world. One is practically dead to the world; one sees various visions and moves in the mental, ethereal space of chidakasha. The experience of samadhi begins to unfold from this point.

Jnana yoga

Jnana yoga samadhi is of two kinds: savikalpa and nirvikalpa. Again savikalpa is of two kinds: *drishyanuvid*, when it is connected with an object, and s*habdanuvid*, when it is connected with a sound.

When one meditates on consciousness as the witness for the modifications of the mind, such as desires, etc., which are regarded as perceivable objects, this is inner or *antar drishyanuvid savikalpa samadhi*. When one meditates and actually feels 'I am unattached, satchidananda, self-luminous, *adwaita swaroopa* (non-dual self)', it is *antar shabdanuvid savikalpa samadhi*.

That steady state of mind like the unflickering flame of a lamp in a place free from wind, wherein one becomes indifferent to both objects and sounds, owing to total merging in the realization of one's own real Self, Brahman, is termed *antar nirvikalpa samadhi*.

When samadhi is associated with the sound, 'I am Brahman', *Aham Brahmasmi*, it is *shabdanuvid samadhi*. When it is not associated with this sound, it is *ashabdanuvid samadhi*.

There is neither darkness nor void in this experience; it is all light. There is neither sound nor touch nor form here. It is a magnanimous experience of unity or oneness. There is neither time nor causation here. One becomes omniscient and omnipotent, a *sarvavid* or knower of everything. One knows the whole story of creation. One attains immortality, higher knowledge and eternal bliss.

When one is established in the highest nirvikalpa samadhi, there is nothing to see, nothing to hear, nothing to smell, nothing to feel. There is no body consciousness. There is full consciousness of Brahman. There is nothing but the Self. It is a grand experience. You will be struck with awe and wonder.

This experience arises when the ego and the mind are dissolved. It is a state to be attained through one's own effort. It is limitless, divisionless and infinite, an experience of being and of pure consciousness. When this experience is realized, the mind, desires, actions and feelings of joy and sorrow vanish into a void.

The individuality has gone now, the little 'I' has melted. The mind that differentiates has vanished. All barriers, all sense of duality, difference and separateness have disappeared. There is no idea of time and space, there is only eternity.

Sing Om. Om is your real name. Om is Atman. Om is Brahman. Om is existence-knowledge-bliss absolute. Om is silence. Om is your centre. Om is your refuge. Om is the heart, *hridaya*. Do japa of Om. Chant Om. Feel Om. Live in Om. Om is everything. Hum Om. Live in truth. Feel His presence always everywhere, in flowers and in trees, in stones and in chairs, in birds and in dogs, in the sun and in the stars. Enter the silence. Rejoice in the Atman. Rejoice in the light of truth, knowledge, and bliss. There is a vast ocean of bliss and knowledge at the back of the mind. Drive the mind back to its source.

Remember Om. Remember Soham, Om Shivoham, Shivoham, Aham Brahmasmi, Analhaq. Truth is One. These mantras remind us of our identity with the supreme soul. These *mahavakyas*, great sentences of the Upanishads, blow out this little false ego, this illusory 'I', into an airy nothing.

Silence is Atman. Atman is *maha mouna*, great silence. Rest in the centre in Atman, draw peace and strength, and do not forget this centre whatever your circumstances may be. This knowledge of Atman has to be kept steady like the steady flow of oil from one vessel to another. One must become established in the centre. Be up and doing, my friends.

When you think of the Atman, when thoughts of objects subside, this Brahma vritti arises from the pure mind. When the flow of the Brahmic idea is quite steady, you will be inundated with ideas of the Self alone.

A little earnest practice is an indispensable requisite. Jnana yoga can be practised at all times. Sometimes when you are free and when you have leisure, you can retire into a room for deep meditation. For jnana yoga, no asana or room is necessary. Keep up the feeling of the idea of infinity while walking, talking, eating, etc.

It is very difficult for a worldly person with practical intelligence to mentally visualize how a jnani sees the physical universe while he is working. When you put a drop of blood under a microscope and examine it carefully, you see millions of red blood corpuscles, white cells, leucocytes, lymphocytes, nuclei, pigments, etc. and are struck with wonder. Similarly, a jnani with the eye of Atman, divya chakshu, sees in the whole world all the details of creation. He sees a person's astral body, the casual body with its samskaras, the pranic aura, psychic aura, magnetic aura, etc. He sees the whole world within himself, as part and parcel of his own Self, through the cosmic eye. He does not see names and forms. He is a paramahamsa. The world has entirely vanished for him, and he is quite unable to work.

A samadhi jnani will not experience pain even if his limbs are amputated. Take the case of Shams Tabriez. When he was skinned alive, he laughed and uttered, "Analhaq, analhaq." *Analhaq* means 'I am He'. It is similar to *Soham*, meaning 'I am That'.

Kundalini yoga
Mother kundalini shakti unites with Lord Shiva in sahasrara during nirvikalpa samadhi. This is real *maithuna* or blissful union. It is due to *divya bhava* or divine disposition. One must rise from *pashu bhava*, the animal nature, to divya bhava through satsang, service of guru, renunciation and dispassion, discrimination, japa and meditation practice.

Worship of the Divine Mother with intense faith and perfect devotion and self-surrender will help one to attain her grace. Through her grace alone, one can attain knowledge of the imperishable in nirvikalpa samadhi.

How the yogi comes down from samadhi
A raja yogi or bhakti yogi or jnana yogi can be brought down to normal objective consciousness by merely shaking the body or blowing a conch. Chudala brought down her husband, Sikhidhvaja, from samadhi by chanting vedic songs to him.

Lord Hari brought Prahlada down from his samadhi by blowing his conch.

Sikhidhvaja entered into nirvikalpa samadhi, and he was as immovable as a pillar. His wife, Queen Chudala, roared like a lion but this did not wake him up from his samadhi. So she tossed him up and down and even when the body fell to the ground, he did not regain consciousness. She then concentrated her mind and in her yogic vision she found that there was some residue of sattwa remaining in his heart, which indicated to her that there was intelligence animating his body.

Like flowers and fruits latent in a seed, a residue of sattwa, the cause of intelligence, rests always in the heart of one who is in samadhi. The queen entered into the subtle body of her king and caused his heart to vibrate. Then she returned to her own body and chanted the *Sama Veda* songs. With this, Sikhidhvaja came back to external consciousness. It is only through the residue of sattwa that jivanmuktas are awakened to an external perception of objects.

Prahlada seated himself in nirvikalpa samadhi for five thousand years. Lord Hari blew his conch, Panchahajanya, intimating his arrival to Prahlada. Prahlada slowly recovered consciousness on the physical plane, and slowly opened his eyes. Prana and apana began to percolate throughout the nadis. In the twinkling of an eye, his mind become gross and life began to glow again in his eyes, mind and prana.

In the case of jivanmuktas, the pure vasanas exist like burnt seeds, and will never reproduce. These pure vasanas are associated with sattwa guna and atmic dhyana. They exist in jivanmuktas like vasanas in deep sleep. Even after a lapse of a thousand years, the pure vasanas will be latent in the heart of jivanmuktas and will melt away gradually. It is only through these pure vasanas that jivanmuktas are awakened to perception of the external world.

You are surrounded by the wild fire of samsara and the three fires. You are travelling in the forest fire of infatuation. The tiger-mind is threatening to devour you. You are captured by the six thieves of lust, anger, greed, attachment, etc., and stung by the snake of desire. Find out the means of escape at once. Approach a spiritual preceptor and serve him with faith and devotion. Obtain spiritual instructions from him and follow them to the very letter. Free yourself from the thraldom of mind and matter by entering into nirvikalpa samadhi.

Highest fruit of yoga

Samadhi is the highest fruit of yoga. Through self-purification, through the eradication of all bad habits and samskaras and the cultivation of good and virtuous qualities, through the practices of yama and niyama, asana, pranayama, pratyahara, dharana and dhyana, resembling the steady flame of a candle, a pious sadhaka tries to have a glimpse of samadhi. Through repeated attempts it becomes a daily occurrence. Gradually he then begins to feel an inner joy, to devote the early morning hours to drink its ambrosial sweetness. Then he comes down to the common plane to perform his normal duties. When he thus advances, he prolongs his life too. And when he feels that he has lived long enough on this plane, he desires to enter into samadhi, never to return to the living abode of mortals. His breath becomes fixed in the nerves of the brain at the crown of the head, *brahmarandhra*, and the body becomes completely lifeless. Left to itself, the body gradually decays.

In some parts of India it is the custom to strike the head of a sannyasin with a coconut to break the skull before the body is consigned to its burial place. For it is commonly believed that sannyasins practise samadhi and their final passing away is termed as entering into *maha samadhi*, or highest samadhi.

Bear in mind that samadhi is the culminating point in the spiritual quest. The spiritual wealth of this supreme state cannot be assessed by anyone. The fortunate sadhaka tries to enter into it more deeply every day. It is the *akshaya* state, the state of deathlessness. I wish you all divine access into this treasure house of celestial knowledge.

10

States of Consciousness

There are various states or dimensions of consciousness, ranging from the conscious state, related to the senses and the material universe, right through to the transcendental or absolute state of consciousness experienced in the final stage of samadhi.

The conscious state

Consciousness means *prajna*, awareness. There is physical consciousness, where one is conscious of the body and one's surroundings, and the visible objects of this universe. In mental consciousness, one feels the operations of the mind, the sentiments, thoughts and feelings. Very few people have mental consciousness; most people only have consciousness of their body. Only those who have a subtle intellect, who have knowledge of psychology, who practise a little concentration, meditation and introspection, will be able to know about mental consciousness.

The subconscious state

Then comes the subconscious wherein all the *samskaras* or latent impressions are stored. From the subconscious, through memory, ideas come to the surface of the mind, to the conscious state. In Sanskrit the subconscious is known as *chitta*. An action is performed. An object is desired and experienced. The experience goes to the subconscious mind, and remains there until a stimulus is received from the external world or from within through memory. The ideas and samskaras then come to the surface of the mind. A *vasana* or subtle desire becomes a samskara and a samskara becomes a vasana. Action produces an impression and the impression goads one to repeat an action again. There is no end to this vicious circle.

The samskaras imprinted on the subconscious mind force one to take rebirth again and again. These samskaras can only be destroyed by the realization of Brahman, the absolute reality, the experience of samadhi. Only then is one free from births and deaths and does one become a *jivanmukta*, liberated in this life.

The aspirant will have to be careful about producing impressions in the subconscious mind. Doing good deeds, having sublime thoughts, and doing japa and kirtan will produce good samskaras and destroy the negative impressions. By being good and doing good and practising meditation, good samskaras can be generated in the subconscious mind.

The superconscious state

Then we have the superconscious state, para Brahman, where there are neither names nor forms, darkness nor light, east nor west, nor visible objects. It is the state of pure absolute consciousness. The goal of life is to attain this superconscious state, also known as nirvikalpa samadhi or asamprajnata samadhi. One has to transcend the body and mind to attain the superconscious state.

According to raja yoga there are various kinds of savikalpa samadhis below the superconscious state. These are known as the states of savitarka, nirvitarka, savichara, nirvichara, ananda and asmita. Vedanta also recognizes various states of savikalpa samadhi below the superconscious state, which are known as antar drishyanuvid, antar shabdanuvid, bahya drishyanuvid and bahya shabdanuvid. They are the lower states of samadhi where the triad of the knower, knowledge and the known, or the seer, sight and the seen, still exist. Above the state of savikalpa samadhi there is asamprajnata samadhi or nirvikalpa samadhi, also known as nirbija samadhi. There are no vrittis, no vasanas, no imagination, and no sankalpas in that state; the senses and the mind are completely subdued. In fact, the mind, emotions and imagination have no further use. There is only pure consciousness. That is our goal. That is para Brahman.

In samadhi or the superconscious state the yogi abandons the sense of his own being and enters only into the being of God. This rare experience gives the yogi great bliss. He feels that the Lord is sporting in all things as pure consciousness. He actually loses the sense of the material nature of things around him. Pure emotions rise in the heart and he begins to love every creature. He experiences the whole world as nothing but pure consciousness, and even tables, chairs, men, women and other things all appear to be made of this consciousness.

Cosmic consciousness

There are several different degrees of samadhi, from the gross or savitarka samadhi to the highest or nirvikalpa samadhi. In the lower form of samadhi the yogi attains cosmic consciousness, which progresses to absolute consciousness in nirvikalpa samadhi. In the state of absolute consciousness the seer, the sight and the things seen become one. In cosmic consciousness there is yet the seer and the seen. It is doubtless a very subtle experience, a divine experience. In the Upanishads one who has experience in cosmic consciousness is called *sarvavid*, one who knows everything in detail.

In cosmic consciousness the lower mind is withdrawn from the external objective world, the senses are abstracted in the mind, and the individual mind becomes one with the cosmic mind or *Hiranyagarbha*, the soul of the universe. The functions of the intellect, the objective mind and the senses are suspended. The yogi becomes a living soul and sees into the life of things through his new divine eye of intuition or wisdom. The yogi who has experience of cosmic consciousness acquires all the divine powers. He attains many kinds of psychic powers which are described in the *Srimad Bhagavatam* and the *Raja Yoga Sutras* of Maharishi Patanjali.

Cosmic consciousness is a 'state' of consciousness that comes to very few human beings. Reports of it come from all times, races and countries. It is described as perfect awareness of the oneness of life, a consciousness that the universe is filled with one life, an actual perception and awareness that the universe is full of life, motion and mind, and that there is no such thing as blind force or dead matter, but that all is alive, vibrating and intelligent. In fact, the descriptions of those who have had glimpses of this state would indicate that they see the universe as all-mind, that all is mind at last.

In the moment of 'illumination' there came to those experiencing it a sense of 'in-touch-ness' with universal knowledge and life, impossible to describe, accompanied by a joy beyond understanding. The period of 'illumination' lasts for a very short time, only a few moments, then fades away and leaves but a memory. Cosmic consciousness means more than an intellectual conviction, belief or realization of the facts as stated, for an actual vision and consciousness of these things comes in the moment of illumination.

There are others who found themselves in the spiritual presence of something of awful grandeur and spiritual rank and were completely dazed and bewildered at the sight. They did not understand the nature of the Absolute and when they had sufficiently recovered, they reported that they had been 'in the presence of God', meaning their particular conception of the divine in their own particular religious creed or school. They saw nothing to cause them to identify with their particular conception of deity, except that they thought that 'it must be God', and knowing no other God except their own particular conception they naturally identified that something with 'God' as they conceived Him to be.

Reports from all religions are filled with accounts of so-called miraculous occurrences. The Christian saints report that they "saw the light of God's countenance". The Mohammedan reports that he caught a glimpse of the face of Allah, and the Buddhist tells us that he saw Buddha under the tree. The Brahmin has seen the face of Brahman and the various Hindu sects have people who give similar reports regarding their own particular deities. The Persians and even the ancient Egyptians have left records of similar occurrences.

These conflicting reports have led to the belief, on the part of those who did not understand the nature of the phenomenon, that these things were all imagination and fancy, if indeed not falsehood and imposture. But the yogis know better. They know that underneath these varying reports there is a common ground of truth, which will be apparent to anyone investigating the matter. They know that these people were temporarily lifted above the ordinary plane of consciousness and were made aware of the existence of a being higher than mortal. The yogi accepts these reports of the various mystics, saints and inspired ones, and accounts for them all by laws perfectly natural in yoga philosophy, but which may appear as supernatural to those who have not studied along these lines.

Cosmic consciousness is an inherent, natural faculty of all men and women, but it is inactive or non-functioning in the majority of human beings. Yogic training and discipline are necessary to awaken the exalted blissful state of cosmic consciousness. The bhava samadhi of bhakti yoga, the lower samadhis of raja yoga: savitarka, savichara, nirvichara asmita, ritambhara prajna, etc., and the lower samadhis of Vedanta, all lead to the experience of cosmic consciousness. The approaches may be different but the fruit is the same. As we have seen, the experiences are common: intuition, revelation, inspiration and ecstasy are synonymous terms.

Turiya or absolute consciousness

Turiya is the substratum or the absolute being underlying all states of consciousness. Known also as the fourth state, turiya pervades yet, at the same time, transcends the three lower states of consciousness, subconsciousness and unconsciousness; waking, dreaming and sleeping. Turiya totally absorbs and resolves all these states into the light of pure consciousness. Therefore, turiya is not consciousness in the ordinary sense but consciousness in its transcendental essence.

The *jivatma* or individual spirit is not the common link beneath all states of consciousness, that link is turiya. The individual consciousness, the jivatma, mostly experiences one state of consciousness at a time. This compartmental experience is due to the fact that the three lower states of consciousness overlap one another, so that when one state functions the others are covered over, although still latent with potential. But with the dawn of turiya, this delimitation disappears and the jivatma consciousness is replaced by absolute consciousness.

The individual jiva's consciousness is dependent upon its physical basis in so far as it is called upon to be manifest and function at the physical and mental levels in the waking and dream states of consciousness. Even when consciousness becomes independent of its physical moorings in the state of deep sleep – when it withdraws into the astral or psychic level – upon waking it once again has to function upon the physical and mental planes through the mind and senses. As such, worldly experience is in essence nothing but the individual consciousness, whereas turiya, pure consciousness, is absolutely independent of any physical basis whatsoever. In the state of turiya, individuality no longer exists; it merges into the all-pervading consciousness.

When one completely negates the manifold distinctions of the world and realizes the undivided, one essence, *satchidananda*, existence-knowledge-bliss, one is said to be in *turiya,* pure consciousness. This state of turiya is latent in every human being, and when one becomes established in this state the transcendental experience of truth, which had previously been just an intellectual abstraction, now becomes a definite living reality. When the experience of turiya or superconsciousness is attained in highest samadhi, the consciousness never again experiences the same worldly vision that it had before this experience. Henceforth, the yogi is an enlightened being, and real spiritual life begins.

In the state of turiya, the silent witness, the *sakshi bhava*, vanishes and the jnani is enthroned in pure nirvikalpa, drowned in atmic bliss. This unified consciousness becomes the basis of the jnani's perception. There is now at-one-ment; the individual and universal no longer exist as two factors. The jnani's vision is now at all times, and under all circumstances, identical with the invisible existence, knowledge and bliss. It pervades all persons and all objects. It is beyond all limitations. It perceives unity in diversity. The entire world of diversity is perceived in a different light altogether. All ideas of heterogeneity are completely annihilated. Being thus established in the Self the jnani arrives at the final state of peace, the goal of life, and attains freedom from all forms of bondage.

The state of turiya is often referred to as the state of *jivanmukti*, liberated while living. It is also called the state of videhamukti. Some say that videhamukti can be had only when the jnani throws off his physical body; however, this view is incorrect. In videhamukti the jnani is unconscious of his body, and this happens while he is still alive. However, when the jnani enters the highest stage of turiya, even the most subtle body consciousness disappears and the world completely vanishes for him. He now needs to be fed by a caretaker. This jnani cannot live for more than fourteen days. His state is described in the shrutis: There is no such thing as diversity.'

The dual consciousness of a jivanmukta

In dual consciousness the sage is resting in his own essence, enjoying supreme bliss, and at the same time he works in this world, like the famous King Janaka. He has dual consciousness; he has not forgotten his own pure, Brahmic state, and at the same time he has consciousness of the world. This is the state of a *jivanmukta,* who is liberated in life, who rests in his own essence and also utilizes his mind for serving humanity. If the mind is completely destroyed as in a *videhamukta*, he cannot work in this world.

In a jivanmukta the whole mind is not destroyed. Rajas and tamas have been destroyed but the sattwic ego remains. It is through this state of sattwa that he beholds the world within himself. In a videhamukta the whole mind is destroyed; he is completely absorbed in para Brahman.

Through sadhana the aspirant raises his awareness into higher states of consciousness. He becomes aware of *Brahmakara vritti*, thinking of Brahman to the exclusion of all other thoughts. He begins to think, "I am *satchidananda swaroopa,* an embodiment of existence-knowledge-bliss."

11
Samadhi and Sleep

Samadhi is deep sleep with full knowledge of the Self. This sleepless sleep is attained when the five *jnanendriyas* or sensory organs have been burnt in the fire of wisdom, when one has extricated oneself from the clutches of ignorance and controlled all the desires. This is not a state of nothingness. One enters into a condition of absolute awareness in which time and place disappear; every place is here, every period of time is now, and everything is 'I'. In this state one has attained bliss and eternal life.

During cosmic consciousness one is in touch with universal knowledge and life. The divine principle flows through one. The little individual personality is lost; the individual will has become merged with the cosmic will. One has *tattwa jnana*, knowledge of truth, and sees the real universe, which is the essence or background of the universe of matter, energy and mind. One is in a state of bliss and ecstasy beyond understanding and description. This is a cognitive trance where the knowledge, the knowable and the knower exist.

In *sushupti*, the state of deep sleep, there is neither the play of the mind nor the play of the senses. There are no objects; there is neither attraction nor repulsion. From where is the bliss in sleep derived? Everyone says, "I slept soundly. I knew nothing. I was very happy asleep." During sleep one rests in satchidananda and enjoys the atmic bliss which is independent of objects. The difference between sleep and samadhi is that in sleep there is the veil of ignorance and in samadhi this veil is removed.

Four conclusions can be drawn from sleep: you exist, there is a feeling of continuity of consciousness; there is *adwaita*, one alone exists without another; you are *ananda swaroopa*, the essence of bliss; and the world is *anitya*, finite. The world is a mere play of the mind. It is phenomenal appearance only; names and forms are illusory.

If there is mind, there is also the world. If destruction of the mind, *manonasha*, can be produced consciously through sadhana, the world will disappear. You will cognize the Atman everywhere. Even in the daytime, you become one with Atman whenever a desire is gratified. When you enjoy an object, you become mindless for a short time. You rest in your own Self and enjoy atmic bliss, spiritual ananda. Ignorant people attribute their happiness to external objects, while they actually derive their happiness from their own Self within. They are deluded owing to the force of *maya* and *avidya*, illusion and ignorance.

If a worldly person is asked, "Who is it that is awake? Who is it that dreams? Who is it that sleeps?" he will answer, "It is I who am awake. It is I who dream. It is I who sleep." If you ask him, "What is this I?" he will say, "This body is the 'I'." He will tell you that it is the body that sleeps when the brain is tired or exhausted. It is the body that dreams when the brain is disturbed, and it is the body that wakes up when the brain is refreshed after sound sleep. A psychologist who has made a special study of the mind will say that the mind which has its seat in the brain is the 'I'. He says that the mind is inseparable from the brain, and it perishes along with the physical body.

Some ignorant aspirants mistake deep sleep and *tamas*, inertia, for the state of samadhi. They pose by closing their eyes. But samadhi is perfect awareness of the Self. It is extremely difficult to enter the state of samadhi. Struggle hard. Obtain the grace of guru and Ishwara. Live in seclusion, meditate ceaselessly and you will enjoy the supreme bliss of samadhi.

Life after death

The metaphysician and the spiritualist hold that the mind continues to exist somewhere after the death of the body. According to psychologists, metaphysicians and spiritualists, it is the mind that wakes up, dreams and sleeps, and this mind is the 'I'.

A theologist says that there is a soul which is quite independent of the body and the mind, and it is this soul that wakes up, dreams and sleeps, and the soul is the 'I'. This soul enters another body, in accordance with the law of karma.

A vedantin says that this body, or the mind, or the soul is not the 'I'. There is one pure consciousness or Atman in all beings, which is infinite, eternal, all-pervading, self-existent, self-luminous and self-contained; it is partless, timeless, spaceless, birthless and deathless. This is the real 'I'. This 'I' never wakes, dreams or sleeps. It is always the seer or the silent witness, the *sakshi*, of the three states of waking, dreaming and sleeping. It is *turiya* or the fourth state. It is the state that transcends the three states, and is known as samadhi.

It is the false or relative 'I' called *ahamkara*, or ego, or *jiva* that wakes up, dreams and sleeps. The waker, the dreamer and the sleeper are all changing personalities, they are unreal. The real Self, the real 'I', never wakes up, and it never dreams or sleeps. From the viewpoint of the absolute truth, no one wakes nor dreams nor sleeps.

Western psychologists hold that the subconscious mind operates even during deep sleep and that there is a little consciousness also in this state because one remembers after waking that one enjoyed sound sleep. This is not correct. The subconscious mind functions during dream only.

In the deep sleep state of sushupti, all the senses are at perfect rest and the mind does not function. It becomes involved in its cause; it becomes merged for the time being into the *karana sharira*, the causal body or the anandamaya kosha. In deep sleep only two things exist, prajna and anandamaya kosha. The jiva is called prajna in this state, and although prajna is conscious of and is enjoying the bliss of sleep, he is not able to express this bliss. The anandamaya kosha, the seed body, is functioning, yet there is a veil between the jiva and Brahman.

Samadhi is sleepless sleep

In samadhi the sage has no consciousness of the external world. He is drowned in the ocean of bliss and wisdom. Samadhi is a state of pure awareness or pure consciousness, whereas sleep is *jada,* an inert condition. When a person returns from sleep, he has no experience of the transcendental wisdom of the Self; he is heavy and dull. He retains the same mind, the same thoughts and samskaras that he had before he went to sleep. But when a yogi or sage comes out of samadhi, he is full of illumination, full of the supreme transcendental wisdom of Atman. He has equal vision and a balanced mind. He can clear away all one's doubts, inspire and elevate. He is Brahman himself.

If you wake up, the deep sleep state disappears. A changing state is illusory or unreal. But the samadhi of the superconscious state is the witnessing consciousness of the three states, waking, dreaming and deep sleep. It always exists; therefore, it is the only real state. In sleep the *vasanas* and *samskaras,* subtle desires and impressions, are in a very subtle state, but in samadhi they are burnt entirely by the fire of wisdom. Burn, therefore, egoism and vasanas, and the five senses, and enjoy the eternal bliss of the sleepless sleep of samadhi.

The difference between deep sleep and samadhi

As soon as you wake up, your dreams become unreal, and the waking state does not exist in the dream state. Both the dream and waking states are not present in deep sleep, and deep sleep is not present in the dream and waking states. Therefore, all three states of waking, dreaming and deep sleep are impermanent. They are caused by the three qualities of sattwa, rajas and tamas. Brahman or the Absolute is the silent witness of the three states, and also transcends these three qualities. It is pure consciousness. This is the difference between deep sleep and samadhi.

Deep sleep is the seed and the states of wakefulness and dream are the fruits thereof. Deep sleep is but very little removed in one of its aspects from samadhi or union with *Paramatman*, cosmic consciousness.

Turiya, the fourth state, transcends the above three states. The sage who has controlled the mind and the senses, who is above body consciousness and the three gunas, who identifies with the satchidananda Brahman, enjoys this blissful or superconscious state. This is the transcendental state or *moksha*.

12

Overcoming Obstacles to Samadhi

The aspirant will come across various obstacles when endeavouring to control the mind and enter into samadhi. You are not able to enter into samadhi because you are not able to practise meditation. You are not able to attain profound meditation because you are not able to fix the mind steadily or concentrate. You are not able to concentrate properly because you are not able to practise *pratyahara*, withdrawal of the senses from objects, thoroughly. You are not able to practise pratyahara thoroughly because you have not obtained mastery over asanas and prana through pranayama and are not established in yama and niyama, which are the foundation of yoga.

Mental inactivity, distractions, passion and the taste for pleasure will have to be conquered. The mind needs to be woken up. The mind is still not freed from *raga,* attachments, which are the seed of all its activity in the direction of external objects. Passions and subtle desires are still lurking within. The mind will have to be restrained again and again by right thinking and selfless service. One will need to practise rigorous meditation and samprajnata or savikalpa samadhi. Finally, one must rest in asamprajnata samadhi or *nirbija,* seedless, samadhi.

The aspirant who wants to attain samadhi should have patience like the bird Tittibha, which tried to empty the ocean with its beak. Once you make a firm resolve, God will come to your aid in the same way that Garuda came to assist Tittibha. Help invariably comes from all beings to those performing righteous acts. Even the monkeys and squirrels helped Rama to rescue Sita. One who is endowed with self-control, courage, prowess, fortitude, patience and perseverance, strength and skill can achieve anything. Never give up the attempt even if facing insurmountable difficulties.

Whenever desires trouble you, try to attain *vairagya*, dispassion. Withdraw the mind again and again from objects and fix it on the immortal Self or a picture of your Lord. When the mind attains a state of equanimity, when it is freed from distraction and mental inactivity, do not disturb it. Tossing of the mind, sleep, cravings, carelessness, indecision, subtle desires, disease, the happiness of savikalpa samadhi, doubt, spiritual pride, etc. are all obstacles to the attainment of deeper samadhi.

Habitual states

Laya is sleep. Do not mistake sleep for samadhi. When one returns from samadhi, one has transcendental wisdom. The mind that withdraws from sensual objects enters into deep sleep through the force of old samskaras of deep sleep. The aspirant should try to fix the mind on the Self and not allow it to pass into the state of deep sleep. One must be ever vigilant. If the sleep condition still persists despite vigorous efforts, find out the causes that induce sleep and then remove them. Then again practise meditation.

The mind that is withdrawn from sleep does not enter into meditation as a result of *vikshepa*, tossing of the mind. Vikshepa must be eradicated and then meditation practised again and again. The mind has the tendency to wander about in sensual objects as it finds it difficult to rest in the very subtle Atman.

When the mind is turned inside after eradicating laya and vikshepa, it still refuses to enter into deep meditation. Through the force of strong hidden vasanas or desires and strong attachments, it becomes attached to objects, and is drowned in sorrow. At this point if there is one-pointedness of mind, this state must not be mistaken for samadhi. This is *kashaya*, passion, this is *manorajya*, building castles in the air. Passion can be removed by adopting the same methods that you used to eradicate tossing of the mind or vikshepa.

Aspirants without absolute even-mindedness will never be able to attain samadhi, even though they may comply with all the formalities of sitting in a proper asana and offering salutations to Parabrahman.

As soon as vikshepa is removed the bliss of *savikalpa samadhi*, superconsciousness with the triad of knower, knowledge and known, manifests. The mind must be weaned away from the pleasure of savikalpa samadhi, known as *rasasvada,* as it is also an obstacle which prevents the aspirant from reaching nirvikalpa samadhi. Some aspirants have false contentment from attaining this happiness, stop their sadhana, and do not attempt to attain the nirvikalpa state. The bliss of this rasasvada is tantamount to the pleasure enjoyed by a person who has killed a serpent which was guarding a vast, hidden treasure. Killing the serpent represents eradication of vikshepa. Only when one takes the treasure can one enjoy the highest bliss. In the same way, when the aspirant tastes the bliss of nirvikalpa samadhi, he has reached the highest zenith or culmination point.

Important points for samadhi sadhana
1. Still the waves of the mind and hold it steady in nirvikalpa samadhi. This needs constant and protracted practice of meditation. There may be breaks in the meditation in the beginning, but practice can make one perfect, so that later one will be able to remain absorbed in meditation, merged in samadhi with a mind steady like a flame protected from the wind. Before attaining success in meditation, first achieve victory over the asana or posture. Sit with the steadiness of a rock for two or three hours. If the body is steady, the mind will also be steady.

2. Do not mistake a little concentration or one-pointedness of mind for samadhi. Simply because you have risen a little above body consciousness on account of a little concentration, do not think you have attained samadhi. Samadhi is obtained by practice for a long time with zeal and enthusiasm.
3. Samadhi is the highest goal that can be attained through meditation. It is not something that can be attained by just a little practice. To attain samadhi one should observe strict brahmacharya, dietetic restrictions and have a pure heart, otherwise there is no possibility of attaining that state. Only when these preliminary qualifications have been grasped well should one try to enter the portals of samadhi. No one can enter samadhi unless he is a great devotee of the Lord. Otherwise, the so-called samadhi becomes *jada*, without awareness.
4. If the subtle desires and attachment to the objects of the world vanish entirely and if one is in that immovable state, one has become a jivanmukta. One will abide in one's own self; one will rest in that non-dual supreme seat. The light of wisdom, *jnana*, will shine unobscured like the sun in the absence of clouds. There will be no attraction to any worldly object. There will be absolute freedom from delusion and sorrow. One will actually feel that the Self alone pervades and permeates everywhere in this world. One will shine with Brahmic effulgence, and possess equal vision and a balanced mind. There will be no longing for sensual objects because the mind will always be cooled by Brahmic bliss. The aspirant will be bathed in the cool ambrosial nectar that dribbles from a contented and quiescent mind.
5. When one enters into deep meditation, the pulse beats may become as low as thirty per minute. The breath may not come out of the nostrils, and an onlooker may not be able to perceive any breathing. In the jada samadhi of hatha yoga, the breathing and heart will stop entirely. In the initial stages of chaitanya samadhi the lungs and heart will be functioning very, very slowly.

6. During intense concentration many aspirants feel certain peculiar sensations as if an electric current is passing from mooladhara chakra. Out of fear they immediately disturb their practice and come down to physical consciousness. There is no need for fear; keep steady and allow the practice to move onwards.
7. Whether you call it rest, peace, perfection, freedom, fullness, nirvana, nirvikalpa samadhi or sahaja avastha, kaivalya or moksha, everyone is striving towards it unconsciously in all their activities, as the transient, mundane objects of the world do not give full satisfaction. Every movement of the feet is towards satchidananda Brahman. Even a rogue or a vagabond is marching towards that immortal city of Brahman though he is on a circuitous or zigzag path.
8. The aspirant will be tested to see whether he is free from ambition and passion. *Siddhis* or psychic powers are hindrances to samadhi, and have no proper place in spiritual life. Shun them ruthlessly even if they manifest during sadhana. If you run towards them, you will be caught in a maze and it will be almost impossible to escape from it. You will misuse the powers and fall hopelessly from your quest to attain samadhi.
9. Do not attach much importance to any experiences and visions that come and go during sadhana. They are either subjective or objective, your own mental creations or experiences on finer planes. They may be crystallizations of one's own intense thinking. Even a glimpse of Brahman will not give liberation. The highest goal or realization is profound silence or supreme peace, wherein all thoughts cease and one becomes identical with the Supreme Self. The final experience of the Supreme, intuition and direct knowledge, is the true one, so abandon all other visions, thoughts, melodious sounds and other small experiences that come. Discriminate well and avoid false contentment. Do not stop your sadhana.
10. Those who have not removed the impurities from the mind through selfless service, who have not practised the

yamas and niyamas and who have not developed the various divine virtues are not able to hold the divine light when it descends.

11. Some students do not take care of the body, which is a great mistake. There should be no infatuation with the body. Let them hear the conversation that went on between Prahlada and Lord Vishnu: "O immaculate Prahlada. Look after your body. Why do you think of abandoning your body at such a premature period as this? So long as you are not haunted by the sankalpa of attraction and repulsion towards objects, what does it matter whether your body exists or not? Now get up from samadhi. Administer justice in this world with this body of yours in the jivanmukti state, without groaning under the load of samsara."

12. Always take pure, sattwic food. Give up meat, fish, eggs, smoking, liquor, etc. Do not take heavy food at night, as it will disturb the evening and morning meditation practices. Take only milk and fruits at night to help focus the mind.

13. When the mind is tired, do not concentrate. Give it a little rest.

14. Steadiness and *paravairagya*, absence of attachment in any form, are needed to attain higher states in samadhi. The aspirant will have to cross a vast void and a region of darkness during spiritual life.

15. It is vitally important to always practise under the guidance of a guru. One will obtain radiant light. Be patient. Advanced students develop a new angle of vision, seeing the Lord in all beings and grasping the essence behind all names and forms. Those who make such tremendous progress must have nutritious food, frequent relaxation and ample rest. Glory to such dynamic yogis!

16. Never miss a day in sadhana. Be very regular in your practice, only then will you succeed. Regularity is of paramount importance.

13
Advice for Samadhi Aspirants

1. The raja yogi can acquire all the great powers called *siddhis* by spontaneous illumination, through purity in thought word and deed. Yet, siddhis are positive hindrances to the attainment of self-realization, and deter and obstruct the aspirant from marching directly towards the goal. They do not produce perfect non-attachment, which is the reason why Maharishi Patanjali, the author of *Yoga Sutras*, again and again advises the student of yoga to shun the desire to acquire siddhis.
2. Only when the mind is perfectly purified will the vessel or mechanism be fit to receive the descent of the divine light. It should be sufficiently strong to bear the pressure of a sudden expansion of consciousness or cosmic vision, which is above the mind, and which covers the whole of existence in one sweep of new exalted, magnanimous experience. Therefore, wait patiently if there is a delay in the descent of the divine light. Practise sadhana and grow in purity and strength.
3. Any effort in the direction of yoga never goes in vain; even a little yogic practice will bear fruit. If you have succeeded in the practice of the first three limbs of yoga, yama, niyama and asana, in this birth, you will begin your practice in the next birth from the fourth limb, pranayama. A vedantin who has acquired the first two means of viveka and vairagya in this birth will start his practice in the next

birth from the sixfold virtues. Therefore, do not be discouraged a bit even if you fail to attain *kaivalya* or independence or final asamprajnata samadhi in this birth. Even a little practice for a short period will give more strength, more peace, more joy and more knowledge.
4. Direct realization of the Self is a means to liberation. Even so, *Brahma jnana*, direct knowledge of Brahman, cannot be obtained without possessing the four means: *viveka*, discrimination, *vairagya*, dispassion, *shadsampat*, sixfold virtues, and *mumukshutva*, yearning for liberation. These qualifications can be acquired by *tapas*, austerity, and *seva*, selfless service, by propitiating one's *ishta devata*, chosen deity, and serving the guru. Even an avatar will not help unless you possess these qualifications.
5. Just as a person anxiously seeks the means of escape from the midst of a burning house, so also the aspirant should have a burning desire to free himself from the fire of *samsara*, the process of worldly life. Only then will he be able to enter into deep meditation and samadhi.
6. By gathering his mind, the yogi should retire to a mountain cave, a temple or a secluded place. He should not associate with anything through the mind, speech and action, for accumulation of and association with things causes misery to yogis. Indifference towards everything should be cultivated. The diet should be regular. Worldly gain should cause no pleasure, nor worldly loss any sorrow. He should look upon all with an equal eye, both those who censure him and those who bow before him.
7. When there is gain one should not rejoice, nor should one worry when there is loss.
8. An altogether different type of highly refined, extremely subtle force is necessary for the process that takes one across the barrier of the relative and launches one into the Absolute. *Dhyanavastha* is that subtlest of the subtle, most refined process that brings the aspirant face to face with the Supreme Reality, God-realization. It is the stage of yoga next to superconsciousness or samadhi, where

purusha, spirit, attains awareness of its own ever-free, independent, all-perfect nature distinct from *prakriti*, matter. And, therefore, it is only one step from the threshold of superconsciousness, Self-realization, aparoksha anubhuti. For that process, one can just imagine how subtle and how refined the mind has to be.

9. All aspirants commit mistakes in jumping after samadhi and dhyana without caring for ethical perfection. The mind remains in the same condition, although they have practised meditation for fifteen years. There is the same jealousy, hatred, feeling of superiority, pride, egoism, etc. Meditation and samadhi come by themselves when there is ethical perfection.

10. The mind becomes pure by cultivating habits of friendliness, compassion, complacency and indifference towards happiness, misery, virtue and vice. When one shows friendliness towards those found enjoying pleasures, the dirt of envy leaves. When one shows compassion towards those who are suffering and wishes to remove the miseries of others as if they were one's own, the dirt of the desire to harm others is removed. Whoever shows complacency towards those who are virtuously inclined has the dirt of envy removed from the mind. Whoever shows indifference towards the vicious and, adopting the middle path, does not take sides with those who are viciously inclined, has the dirt of impatience removed from the mind.

11. By removing the characteristics of the qualities of disturbing energy, *rajas*, and inertia, *tamas*, the characteristic of essential purity, *sattwa*, manifests. One becomes possessed of a very high manifestation of essential purity. The mind becomes inclined to restraint of the mental modifications, *vrittis*, because this enlightenment is natural to that state. If these moral qualities are not cultivated, the means cannot lead to steadiness. Therefore, the aspirant should be well established in *sadachara*, good conduct, in order to attain perfection in yoga. When one is perfectly established in good conduct, then samadhi will come by itself.

12. Self-realization is a transcendental experience. One can march forward on the spiritual path only by placing implicit faith in the words of sages who have realized the highest truth and have attained knowledge of the Self. The shrutis emphatically declare: '*Shraddha bhakti dhyana yogadvai hi* – Know Him by faith, devotion and meditation.' *Shraddha*, faith, comes first. Without faith, neither concentration nor meditation can be practised. Maharishi Patanjali says: '*Shraddha veerya smriti samadhi prajna-purvaka itaresham* – Samadhi comes through faith, energy, memory, concentration and discrimination of reality.' He has placed faith at the very beginning of this verse.
13. Nothing grand, meritorious and sublime can be achieved with a weak and wavering faith. The goal of life cannot be reached with a faith that flickers at every step. The summit of nirvikalpa samadhi cannot be ascended with an impotent and passive faith. One's faith must be as firm as the Himalayas.
14. Quiet, solitary places like Swargashram, Rishikesh and Uttarkashi have an indescribable charm of their own, which has to be felt and understood by the subtle discriminative intellect. A gross, worldly, practical intellect can never discriminate and understand the beauty and peace of such remarkable places, the supreme abode of rishis and sages. The spiritual vibrations present in these places can by themselves take one to samadhi without much effort. The Himalayan vibrations and the soothing and soul-elevating influence of the holy Ganges can turn an inveterate atheist and materialist into a staunch spiritualist. Live for three months in these holy places and realize the grandeur and benign influence of solitude.
15. There is no harm in mixing with congenial persons who are also devoted to meditation, study and other spiritual pursuits, for an hour daily, to discuss complex philosophical points. Being in the company of higher, spiritual personages who enter into samadhi will be highly beneficial. Instinct will speak aloud from within that such

and such company is elevating and such and such company is depressing.
16. Everything should be done gradually.
17. Dispassion, patience and perseverance must be developed to the maximum degree. There must be an unshakable conviction in the existence of God and in the efficacy of spiritual practices. One must have the strong determination to realize God in this very birth.
18. Attachment is the root cause of all the miseries and troubles in this world. Discipline the mind carefully. Old habits will creep in and must be rooted out. Leading a life of perfect non-attachment is the master key to open the realms of Brahmic bliss.
19. Learn to discriminate between the real and the unreal. Try to develop dispassion as much as possible, and avoid having any intimate connection with others. Lead a life of non-attachment to this world. Live like a lotus leaf in water. Do not bother a bit over the loss of petty things. Always think that the perishable objects of this world are worthless. Repeat mentally the formula, "All objects are perishable." One who has no attachment in this world is the happiest. He is God Himself. His joy is indescribable.
20. Karma yoga elevates a person to sublime, magnanimous heights. One should work patiently. Samadhi is not possible without preliminary training in karma yoga. To work without attachment is doubtless a difficult task, uphill work, but it becomes easy and pleasant for one with patience and determination. It will have to be done at any cost to attain final beatitude and immortality.
21. Train the mind daily in all dealings and actions. Develop intense internal dispassion by understanding the illusory nature of this world. Work cannot bring misery, but it is the attachment to and identification with work that brings about all sorts of worries, troubles and unhappiness. Understand the secret of karma yoga and work without attachment and identification. Slowly the mind will be weaned away from sensual objects, and it can be gradually

turned towards God-realization. Have recourse to the company of saints and devotees.

22. Extreme asceticism is not at all necessary for the attainment of perfection. What is wanted is strong mental dispassion born of strong discrimination. Not all bodies are fit to practise severe austerities. Do not spoil your health and body in the name of austerities, but maintain a strong, healthy body.

23. Peace is not to found in money, in the opposite sex or in eating. When the mind becomes desireless and thoughtless, the Atman shines and sheds forth eternal bliss and peace. Why search in vain for happiness in outside objects? Search within for supreme bliss in the subjective satchidananda Brahman.

24. Self-surrender is annihilation of the individual consciousness and the attainment of absolute consciousness. This is equal to nirvikalpa samadhi. The devotee flies to the state of the highest maha bhava and merges in God. The wave subsides in the ocean. The spark becomes one with the fire. The ray is absorbed into the sun. The mind merges in the Absolute. The individual soul loses itself in the Self. The devotee becomes one with God. All worldly consciousness vanishes into universal consciousness. Man becomes God and the mortal becomes the Immortal.

14
Guru, Disciple and Sadhana

From 1930 onwards, many earnest students with a burning desire to devote their lives to spiritual pursuits came to me for guidance. I also had a burning desire to serve the world. Those were the days when sadhus and mahatmas lived in pitiable conditions, without the necessary comforts and conveniences and proper guidance for spiritual evolution. Many tortured their bodies in the hot sun and in the Himalayan cold. Some were addicted to intoxicating drinks to induce the so-called samadhi. However, I never said or did anything to tempt people with promises of grand results like liberation from a drop of water or samadhi by mere touch. I emphasized the importance of silent sadhana, japa and meditation for systematic progress on the spiritual path. Invariably I asked all aspirants to purify the heart through selfless service to mankind.

Dear aspirants, always remember that you can march on the spiritual path only by placing implicit faith in the words of sages who have realized the highest truth and attained Self-realization. It is true that a personal guru is necessary in the beginning and that aspirants must live under his guidance until they are moulded properly. Know for certain that only he alone who is the guru of gurus can show the path to attain the highest samadhi, for this is a transcendental experience. Yet, realized gurus can guide aspirants to this experience provided the aspirants are in a fit condition to receive the light imparted by the guru and are prepared to surrender to him completely.

In the *Bhagavad Gita* (4:34), Lord Krishna says, "Know that by prostrating to the guru, questioning and service, the wise who have realized the Truth will instruct you in that knowledge of the Self." Surrender is a great force, it is the stream of spiritual life. Without surrender to the Lord, human life and spiritual life is empty. Without surrender, the sadhaka lives in vain. Self surrender liberates, destroys pain and gives supreme peace.

Spiritual progress requires intense and unswerving faith in the teachings of the guru, burning and lasting vairagya, yearning for liberation, adamantine will, fiery resolve, iron determination, unruffled patience, leech-like tenacity, clock-like regularity, childlike simplicity, and the ability to also grasp the Truth. The guru will only impart spiritual instructions to that aspirant who has subdued the passions and senses, who has a calm mind, and who can appreciate virtues like mercy, cosmic love, patience, humility, endurance and forbearance.

Initiation into the mysteries of samadhi will fructify only in those disciples who are desireless. It takes a long time for charcoal to catch fire, but gunpowder can be ignited in the twinkling of an eye. In the same way, it takes a long time to ignite the fire of knowledge in one whose heart is impure, but an aspirant with great purity of heart attains knowledge of the Self within the twinkling of an eye. Unless you are pure, you will not be able to realize the true greatness of a liberated sage. When he appears before you, you will take him for an ordinary man, and you will not be benefited. Even if Lord Krishna or Sri Shankaracharya were to come, they would not do anything for you unless you are ready to receive the spiritual instructions.

Dedication and sincerity

Personal contact with a realized soul is highly elevating, but the guru cannot do sadhana for the aspirant. He can inspire and guide the disciple, clear away his doubts, pave the way, remove snares, pitfalls and obstacles and throw light on the spiritual path best fitted to the aspirant, but the rest of the work will have to be done by the aspirants themselves. The disciple himself will have to place each foot on the spiritual path. The *Bhagavad Gita* (6:5) says: "Let a man raise himself by his own Self alone, let him not lower himself."

Guru's grace is needed by the disciple, but nirvikalpa samadhi cannot come to the student as a miracle performed by another. Lord Buddha, Lord Jesus and Rama Tirtha all did spiritual sadhana. Lord Krishna prescribed *vairagya* and *abhyasa* – dispassion and practice. He did not say to Arjuna: "I will give you liberation directly." The lower nature of the mind must be thoroughly regenerated. There is no magic pill for attaining samadhi, it is mere delusion to think so. Aspirants will need to practise yoga and meditation regularly and steady the body, purify the mind and calm the senses.

It is quite true that the mere grace of a guru, his touch, sight or sankalpa can work wonders. This does not mean that the disciple should sit idle and expect a miracle from the guru to push him directly into samadhi. The aspirant may say to his preceptor, "I want to practise sadhana. I want to enter into nirvikalpa samadhi. I want to sit at your feet. I have surrendered myself to you." Mere talk or discussion on samadhi, any amount of merely studying the yoga scriptures cannot help anyone in the realization of samadhi. Yoga needs to be practised with sincerity, eagerness and tenacity. But if you do not want to change your lower nature and habits, old character, behaviour and conduct so as to transform your lower nature, you cannot move forward towards your goal.

The aspirant will need to introspect, find out his weaknesses and remove them, have an intense urge from within, and be regular in sadhana and dedicated to it for an extended period. Many students, according to their own fancy, select their own method of sadhana without considering the consequences. Improper diet, wrong sadhana without a proper guide, hard and foolish austerities on a weak body, torturing the body in the name of tapasya, have entirely ruined many aspirants. Therefore, a personal guru is necessary to give timely instructions according to the change of season, circumstances and progress. The sadhana must be well-regulated and gradual. Then, in due course, the goal of samadhi is assured.

If you have no guru, take God, Lord Krishna, Lord Shiva or Rama as your guru. Pray to him, meditate on him, sing his name, remember him. He will send you a suitable guru, but do not expect a miracle from your guru to put you immediately into samadhi. To find a guru who can sincerely look after the interests of his pupil is a very difficult task in this world, but to find a disciple who will act sincerely according to the instructions of the guru is also a very, very difficult task.

Samadhi will come when you are ready, not before. There is always an inner unfolding from level to level in spiritual experiences. Wait patiently and continue sadhana with purity and courage. If negative thoughts enter the mind, substitute divine thoughts. Intensify vairagya and aspiration. Samadhi is beyond the realm of gross thought, but a pure, subtle and concentrated mind is fit to attain samadhi. Take the example of the lives of realized saints, who are compasses on the way to liberation.

The background thought of God

When one idea exclusively occupies the mind, it is transformed into an actual physical or mental state. Therefore, if the mind is kept fully occupied with the thought of God and God alone, blissful nirvikalpa samadhi will be attained very quickly. Have a background thought, either a concrete background of your ishta along with the mantra, or an abstract background of the idea of infinity with Om if you are a student of jnana yoga. This will help destroy all other worldly thoughts and take you to the goal. Again and again and again withdraw the mind from worldly objects and thoughts, then through force of habit, the mind will at once take shelter in this background, the moment you release it from worldly activities.

Identify with Atman

Step by step, you must climb the ladder of yoga towards the top rung, samadhi. One will have to advance step by step on the spiritual path; there are no shortcuts. But remember at each step, you are not the perishable body, your being is of the substance of Atman. Identify with the supreme soul.

Realization cannot come as a miracle done by the guru, so abandon the wrong notion that the guru will give you samadhi and mukti. The salt of sadhana is selfless service. The bread of sadhana is all-embracing love. The water of sadhana is purity. The sweetness of sadhana lies in devoted surrender. The perfume of sadhana is generosity. The fruits of sadhana are inner spiritual strength, perfect peace, realization and the bliss of samadhi. Strive, purify, meditate and realize.

Story of Markandeya

Markandeya was a great devotee of Lord Shiva. His father Mrikandu performed rigorous austerities to obtain a son. Lord Shiva appeared before him and said, "O Rishi! Do you want a good son who will die in his sixteenth year or a bad and foolish son who will live for a long time?" Mrikandu replied, "O my venerable Lord! Let me have a good son."

The boy learned of his fate and began to worship Lord Shiva wholeheartedly with intense faith and devotion. He entered into deep meditation and samadhi on the day decreed as the day of his death. Hence Yama himself went to take his life. The boy prayed to Lord Shiva for protection and embraced the linga. Then Yama threw his noose round the linga and the boy. Lord Shiva came out of the linga immediately and killed Yama to protect the boy. Lord Shiva was called Mrityunjaya and Kalakala from that day.

Then the devas approached Lord Shiva and said, "O Adorable Lord! salutations unto Thee. Pardon Yama for his mistake, O ocean of mercy, and bring him back to life." Then Lord Shiva brought Yama back to life at the request of the gods. He also conferred a boon on the boy Markandeya that he should live forever as a boy of sixteen years of age. He is a *chiranjivi*, one who has obtained eternal life. In South India, even now men and women bless a boy when he prostrates to them, "Live as Chiranjivi Markandeya."

Through austerity and meditation one can attain samadhi and become immortal, thus conquering death, and one can achieve anything in the three worlds. May you be established in samadhi through the grace of the Lord.

15
Jivanmukti and Videhamukti

The *jivanmukta* is a liberated sage, free from the trammels of birth and death. He is emancipated while living. He lives in the world but not of the world. He always revels in the eternal bliss of the Supreme Self. He has no identification with the body and senses, hence he has no idea of enjoyment or enjoyer when he exhausts the residue of his unalterable or *prarabdha karma*. He has no idea of action or agency. He roams about happily without attachment or egoism, with a balanced mind and equal vision. His state is indescribable. He is Brahman himself.

The jivanmukta is a liberated sage who lives in the knowledge of Brahman. For him the world has vanished forever; the Self alone is everywhere. He does not perceive plurality or even duality. He rests in the oneness of consciousness, in his own *satchidananda swaroopa*. He exists with a body as long as the prarabdha karma lasts; at its end he attains videhamukti and exists as the Absolute.

A jivanmukta is a great spiritual hero, an enlightened sage who has realization of the Absolute. He is pre-eminent amongst human beings. He is the conqueror of the mind, absolutely free from desires, craving, fear, delusion, pride, egoism, etc. For a jivanmukta there is no distinction between a rogue and a saint, gold and stone, high and low, man and woman, human being and animal, censure and praise, honour and dishonour. He beholds the one Self everywhere, seeing divinity in everyone. As he is mindless, all differences and barriers have vanished.

The state of jivanmukti is a state of consciousness, so it can be experienced even when the physical body is dropped. The jivanmukta of this physical world, with his physical body, is really in *Brahma loka*, the celestial sphere of Brahma, in his consciousness, though the body is in this world. This dual consciousness of the jivanmukta places him in a unique position. He has both the conditioned awareness of the world and the unconditioned awareness of the Self found only in the state of Self-realization. His realization of Brahman is irrevocable, and he cannot be shaken from supreme consciousness. Yet for the good of humanity, he engages a part of this consciousness to function in the worldly sphere. Lord Krishna is an ideal example who possessed this dual consciousness.

King Janaka asked a sage, "O venerable sage, how is it you do not perform the sandhya ceremony at daybreak, midday and sunset?" The sage replied: "O Raja, the sun of knowledge, *jnanasurya*, is ever shining in the chidakasha of my heart. There is neither sunrise nor sunset for me, so how can I perform sandhya? Further my old grandmother Maya is dead." King Janaka bowed his head before the sage and left silently. He realized that a real jivanmukta is one who is established in Brahmic consciousness.

The criterion of salvation lies in the *Shvetashvatara Upanishad* (1:2): "By knowing God there is a falling off of all fetters, all distresses are destroyed; there is cessation of birth and death; there is breaking up of individuality. One becomes Absolute, and all desires are satisfied."

Karma

The jivanmukta realizes that the whole universe is Brahman only. The individual consciousness of this jnani is powerful enough to maintain the existence of his physical body, but it is not capable of bringing him another birth as an embodied being. He has no feelings of *kartritva*, 'I am the doer', and *bhoktritva*, 'I am the enjoyer'. His actions are cosmic movements, not the instincts of the sense of egoism. But the desires he had given rise to during the time he thought that the objective world was real will not cease from demanding materialization as long as the momentum of their craving lasts. Hence, these desires keep up the physical body of the jivanmukta for some time even after Self-realization. The prarabdha karma, which has given rise to absolute knowledge, lasts as long as the momentum of past desires, which constitute the present prarabdha, lasts.

When the prarabdha karma is exhausted, the body drops off by itself and the sage becomes unified with the infinite Brahman. But even while living with a body, the jivanmukta identifies his consciousness with Brahman and is not affected by the pairs of opposites amid the forces of nature. The whole universe is his body for he is in tune with all the forces of nature, due to his transcending all phenomenal relativities and resting in Brahman consciousness at all times.

Though a jivanmukta identifies with all the bodies of the world, *samashti abhimani*, cosmic identification, yet he is aware that he has a little special connection with the particular body he is wearing, which is brought about by his own prarabdha karma. Prarabdha has to be worked out. Therefore, the body will be subjected to disease. The jivanmukta will not experience any pain. Onlookers may wrongly imagine that the sage is also suffering, but it is a serious mistake. Ramakrishna Paramahamsa had cancer of the throat, Buddha had chronic dysentery, Sri Shankara had piles, but they experienced no pain. When the doctors asked Ramakrishna Paramahamsa, "Why do you suffer like this? Can't you undergo an operation?" he replied, "I have given my mind to Mother Kali. How can I think of the body? How can I bring my mind back into the cage of flesh? I am always in bliss."

In a jivanmukta, ignorance is destroyed by the dawn of knowledge. *Sanchita karma*, the accumulated storehouse of karmas, depends upon *avidya*, ignorance. The current or *kriyamana karma* depend upon egoism. The prarabdha karma depend upon the physical body. The sanchita karma are burnt up by the fire of *Brahma jnana,* knowledge of Absolute Reality. He has no egoism, so kriyamana karmas, his current actions, are destroyed. From this viewpoint he has no body as he identifies himself with the all-pervading Brahman. Thus, it is said that the three kinds of karmas are destroyed when one attains knowledge of the Atman.

A jivanmukta is pure consciousness. He realizes that he is beyond the three bodies and five *koshas* or sheaths and that he is the witness of the three lower states of consciousness, the waking, dreaming and deep sleep states. He realizes the turiya state, which is peaceful, blissful and non-dual. He lives in the highest level of jnana, where the mind becomes Brahman itself. The expanded consciousness soars above the five sheaths and hails beyond the region of thought and intellect. He experiences the world and individuality only apparently and not in reality.

Every sage has his own prarabdha

The knower of Brahman shakes off good and evil and becomes freed from sorrow. He attains oneness with the Supreme Self and delights in the soul. The way of living for each jivanmukta differs. The sage Bhagiratha lived in a princely style, while another sage lives in a beggarly manner. One sage is always in a meditative mood, never works, never talks, and always lives in seclusion. Jada Bharata lived this kind of life. Another sage lives in a busy, crowded city, plunging himself into seva, talking with people, delivering lectures, writing books, etc. Sri Shankaracharya led this kind of life. This is due to prarabdha. Every sage has his own prarabdha. If all sages had the same kind of life and the same kind of prarabdha, this world would be like a prison. Variety in manifestation is the nature of prakriti.

The *Brahma Sutras* discuss the question of the possibility of a return of the liberated one to earth in a new existence. Sages like Apantaratamas, though possessed of the highest

Brahma jnana, return to bodily existence in order to fulfil a mission for the good of the world. When their mission is completed, they again exist as the Absolute. Lord Krishna says that though he has no form, birth or death, he assumes forms in every age for the upliftment of the world. Such incarnations are not the effect of prarabdha karmas; but rather conscious manifestations of the Supreme Absolute in the plane of relativity.

The Upanishads also indicate the free will of the liberated soul when they say that it acquires full freedom in all the worlds. Logically, the highest state of moksha is the merging of the individual consciousness in absolute consciousness. Eternal existence, infinite knowledge and immortal bliss is *moksha* or final liberation, nirvikalpa samadhi.

The jnani attains *sadyomukti*, immediate salvation. The jivanmukta, who has realized that there is nothing anywhere except Brahman, does not have any departure of the soul, as is the case with other individuals. Where can his Self depart to? There is no space where the Self is not, and hence it merges into itself.

He knows the secret of true bliss

The jivanmukta is not delighted by pleasures nor does distress cause pain. Even violent distractions cannot make him move away from the highest reality. He does not trouble anyone, nor is he troubled by anybody. He roams about happily, and speaks sweetly and nobly. He comes out of the net of distinctions and desires like a lion from its cage. Fear is unknown to him, and he is never helpless or dejected.

The love of the jivanmukta is universal. He loves all equally for his is transcendental love. He loves others because he loves his own Self. He alone exists. The jivanmukta feels the great unity of himself and the whole universe in the Supreme Brahman. He has abiding realization of the secret oneness of existence, which is the basis of universal love. His teachings are the outpourings of his inner life of glory, peace and blessedness, and his expressions bring peace, harmony, power and strength to those who hear him. He possesses tremendous power of attraction.

Teachings of a jivanmukta

When you sit before him, he will clear away all your doubts in a marvellous manner. You will feel great wonder and a peculiar thrill of joy and peace in his presence. Whatever a jivanmukta says will be impressed in your mind. Until the end of your life you will never forget your experiences with him.

Silence is his language and he teaches aspirants through this silence. He is very compassionate and free from selfishness, anger, greed, egoism, lust and pride. He is an embodiment of truth, peace, knowledge and bliss. He breathes and emanates joy and love to everyone. It is the love that does not expect any reward, return or recompense. Through his *satsankalpa*, perfect will, he works wonders. He always possesses an unruffled mind. Wherever he goes, he radiates spiritual currents to the different corners of the world. Such beings are the veritable emperors of the universe. What meritorious acts jivanmuktas must have done to become liberated sages while living! Adorations to such exalted beings.

The love of the jnani is real love. It is only the jnani that can serve and help the world in the best possible way, for he knows that all is the one Self, the great being of Brahman. Without knowing this, how can one be truly good and virtuous? The ideas of doership and enjoyership cannot be overcome without knowledge of the Self.

One who attains Self-realization is absolutely free from all desires because he knows everything in himself, and there is nothing outside himself for him to continue to desire. What can he desire who has everything? Brahman is *paripoorna*, all-full, and *nirapeksha*, self-contained. How can desire arise in the mind of one who has realized the Self, who beholds the Self in all beings and all beings in the Self?

That illumined sage whose mind is merged in his true nature of satchidananda, who has conquered the enemy ignorance, who is devoid of 'I-ness' and 'mineness', and who has rooted out pride, self-love, envy and hatred, revels in the ocean of boundless bliss. He is free from doubt, delusion, and limitation. He is free from the three knots of the heart: *avidya,* ignorance, *kama,* desire, and *karma,* action. He attains immortality and enjoys eternal bliss. He crosses grief and goes beyond good and evil.

His absolute consciousness, by its very nature of all-inclusiveness, attracts that part of universal existence where the objects necessitated by his personal existence lie. He does not make an effort to acquire any object that is limited in space and time; whatever he needs flows to him. The palms of his hands become his bowl, the sky is his clothing, his shoulder is his pillow, the earth filled with grass is his silken bed or fine green carpet, the stars are his lights, space is his cloth, and he sleeps blissfully beneath a tree. Embracing renunciation as his wife, he sleeps anywhere without any anxiety and enjoys supreme peace or unalloyed joy amidst his children, *jnana,* wisdom, *vairagya,* dispassion, and *uparati,* sense withdrawal.

All beings are the Self
Just as when you look at a picture which contains fruits, flames, knives, rivers, etc., you think that they are false, so also when the jivanmukta or liberated sage looks at the world, he feels that all forms are false. The seer does not see death or sickness or distress. The seer sees only the All, and obtains the All entirely. He delights in the Self, sports in the Self, keeps company with the Self and has bliss in the Self. He is autonomous; he has unlimited freedom in all the worlds.

For a jivanmukta who beholds the all-pervading, immortal, indivisible, self-luminous Atman everywhere, there remains nothing to be attained or known. He has attained perfection, highest bliss and highest knowledge. The jivanmukta is a transcendental actor. Whatever he does is righteous, moral and ideal, for his actions are the expressions of the Absolute itself. He leads the divine life and moves in the free flow of the law of eternal existence. He has no war between the body and the spirit. His external actions are just like those of an ignorant worldly person, but the greatest difference lies between their minds, the desires and vasanas. One no longer desires and the other is immersed in desires.

The mind of a liberated person is pure sattwa; it is no mind at all. He is established in the Self unimpeded by phenomenal laws. He rejoices in the infinite being and lives in the world like a happy bird, being fully illumined with transcendental wisdom. Just as camphor melts and becomes one with fire, so also the mind of the jivanmukta melts and becomes one with Brahman. He sees the Atman in the Atman.

To one who sees only oneness everywhere, where is delusion and where is grief? The experience of secondlessness is achieved through finding his Self in each and every being, including the wicked and the ungrateful. Such an expansion of the Self leads to the glory of the manifestation of the real essence of the being of all beings, where one finds oneself in truth, where the lost Self is recovered, as it were, with unbounded joy.

Beholding existence as undivided, he walks on the earth unknown and unidentified. No one can find out whether such a person is learned or ignorant, virtuous or vicious. He lives in the great silence of the Self, and whether active or at rest, does not link his ego with his act. He does not see duality even when he is awake to the world. He is a representative of the Supreme Brahman, appearing before human eyes.

Nothing more to learn or do
A jivanmukta or sage becomes aware that he is free. He realizes that rebirth is exhausted. He realizes also that he has fulfilled all his duties and that there is no further return to this world. He further realizes that he has obtained everything, that all his desires are gratified, that he has nothing more to learn and that he has obtained the highest knowledge. The world has vanished for a jivanmukta.

He does not instruct or give orders to anybody, for he is the essential being of everything that he may have to deal with. He has reached the climax of perfection and the whole universe is a part of his body. He does not feel or say, "It should have been like this, it should not have been like that," for he realizes the absolute validity and perfection of all movements of nature in accordance with the eternal law.

The sage keeps a cool mind even when assaulted, and blesses those who persecute him. He beholds only his own Self everywhere. The perfected condition where thought reaches the freedom of immunity from being misled by the external forms of the universe is liberation, even if the forms persist in coming within the sphere of the vision of the jnani. He controls them; they do not control him. His individual consciousness is in harmony with the universal consciousness.

He beholds only Brahman everywhere. Even if the world comes back again, it is no longer the same world of pairs of opposites, pains and sorrows, not the prison of miseries and afflictions. The world of troubles and sorrows has changed into *satchidananda*, existence, knowledge and bliss absolute.

He has rendered his mind completely quiescent by identifying himself with Brahman. Delusion has vanished. The sense of want is annihilated once and for all by the ineffable experiences of Self-realization. His only delight is in the Self, for he is truly conscious of living, moving and having his being in the divine existence. The transcendental intuition which has brought him the realization of his oneness with Brahman also gives him the realization of the same Brahman in all beings. His life, therefore, becomes one of service in the light of knowledge of the one Self in everything. He performs *jnana yajna*, sacrifice of the self in the knowledge of Brahman. Brahman is offered in Brahman by Brahman through the act of Brahman. It is a joyous suffusion of oneself in Brahman and the exact nature of this experience is one of immediate directness of being and cannot be understood, thought, felt or talked about.

Just as you feel that a pair of worn-out shoes is hanging loosely to your feet and that you are distinct from the shoes, a jivanmukta will feel that a worn-out physical body is sticking to him and that he is Brahman himself in reality, quite distinct and separate from the body. A jivanmukta who is intoxicated with Brahmic bliss is not aware of his body. Even a jivanmukta will experience pain, but his feeling is entirely different from the experience of a worldly person.

A jivanmukta sees the whole universe existing in himself and sees the All as one soul, as Atman, as the self-luminous 'Light of lights'. 'I am that.' 'There I am.' The liberated sage says, "I am the earth, I am in the earth. I am the water, I am in the water. I am the fire, I am in the fire. I am the air, I am in the air. I am the flower, I am in the flower. I am the tree, I am in the tree. I am the woman, I am in the woman. I am the intellect, I am in the intellect. I am the ocean, I am in the ocean. I am the manifested *Virat* (macrocosm). I am the immanent *Hiranyagarbha* (golden womb of creation). I am Brahman or the transcendental Self."

The jivanmukta says, "I enjoy in all bodies. I suffer in all bodies. I see through all eyes. I work through all hands. I hear through all ears." 'I am the All', 'I am all in all.' He identifies with Brahman. This whole world is hanging or floating in Brahman, so he feels 'I am the All'. "All names and forms are inseparable from my thoughts. Thoughts are again inseparable from 'I'. Therefore, it is proper to say 'I am the All'." This is the jivanmukta's feeling of cosmic identification. You need not study many books. Just dwelling on the above ideas constantly will lead to Self-realization soon.

To whom should I offer my salutations or respects, when I am Brahman myself? When there is nothing save myself, who is to respect whom? Who is to salute whom? I know that mighty Purusha, who is resplendent like the sun and who transcends all darkness (ignorance). By knowing Him alone, one conquers death. There is no other way for salvation.

I see a world in a grain of sand,
A heaven in a wild flower,
Infinity in the palm of my hand
And eternity in an hour.
In me the universe had its origin
In me alone the whole subsists,
In me it is lost – this Brahman
The timeless, it is I myself.
Shivoham. Shivoham. Shivoham.
I am neither this body nor the mind.
Chidananda roopa Shivoham.
Shivoham – I am Shiva – I am Shiva –
All-blissful and all wise.

Kinds of jivanmuktas

A *jivakoti* jivanmukta is one who has realized the Self through gradual evolution and by his own efforts. He has released himself from jivahood to Brahmanhood by meditation. He has taken many births. He has managed to free himself from the round of births and deaths. He can help a few people; he cannot elevate many people. He can be compared to a bullock-cart on the road which can carry four or five people, or a plank in the river.

The eternally free *Ishwarakoti* jivanmukta was born in the world to establish dharma, to protect the virtuous and to do good to humanity. He does not practise any sadhana or meditation in this birth. He is an *amsha* or part of the Lord. He is a born siddha, illumined from his very childhood. He can elevate many people. He manifests, then disappears when the *lokasangraha* work of uplifting society is over. He can be compared to a train which carries a large number of people or a big steamer in an ocean. Sri Shankara was an Ishwarakoti, and Sri Vamadeva was a jivakoti jivanmukta.

The jivanmukta is of two kinds, kevala and siddha. The *kevala jivanmukta* is one who is not able to help the world much, but who has obtained Self-realization for himself only.

He is like a star which only glitters at night. He is not known to the world at large, but the world needs people rich in intuition.

The *siddha jivanmukta* is a glorious person who shines like the sun in the world. He is a jivanmukta and a yogi combined. He can help the world immensely. Sri Shankaracharya was a siddha jivanmukta. Madalasa was a kevala jivanmukta. Awakened souls such as these, who have attained illumination, are a blessing to the world. They will guide people on the path of righteousness and help them to cross the ocean of ignorance and attain immortality and eternal bliss.

A jivanmukta who lives in the highest level of consciousness cannot do any action in the plane of earthly consciousness. Those jivanmuktas who wish to uplift humanity have to come down to lower states of consciousness in order to be useful to humanity. A little rajas is necessary to perform any kind of action.

The pure sattwic state of the highest kind of jivanmuktas is completely devoid of rajas, and hence is unsuitable for working in the world. The very existence of such a blessed being will give solace to the whole world. His life is the most supreme teaching. Wherever he is, he spreads such a force of conscious equilibrium of being that those near him are easily transformed. The satsankalpa of the jnani is beyond all powers of the greatest siddhas and he works through his mere Self, which is in all. He is the ocean of knowledge and power and nothing is impossible for him.

The jivanmukta rests with an unshaken mind in the all-blissful Brahman. He is free from all the modifications of the mind. His heart is pure like the Himalayan snow or the clearest crystal. He is free from the distinctions I, he, you.

Videhamukti
The jivanmukta is like a person sitting on a wall. On one side is the conditioned existence in awareness of the world. On the other side is the unconditioned awareness-whole which is found only in the state of self-realization. A person sitting on

one side of the world cannot see what is on the other side. A worldly person cannot have knowledge of Brahman.

A *videhamukta*, whose individuality is absolutely merged in Brahman, cannot have awareness of the world which is non-existent to him. If his body is to be maintained, it has to be fed and cared for by others. The videhamukta is thus not in a position to engage himself for the good of the world. However, we have to make a distinction between two kinds of videhamuktas. There are those who are on the verge of absolute experience, and those who have actually merged in Brahman.

A visitor once asked me, "Swamiji, what is the difference between jivanmukti and videhamukti? As long as the body lasts how can there be videhamukti?" I replied that jivanmukti itself is videhamukti, but there is a slight difference. A jivanmukta has slight body consciousness in the form of mental retention or *swaroopanasa* of the mind. In him rajas and tamas are destroyed but the sattwic frame of mind remains. On account of this sattwic mind a jivanmukta is able to implement the cosmic will as a detached agent. He is able to feed himself and attend to his bodily needs mechanically due to the force of prarabdha, and previous samskaras.

A videhamukta is a *turiyatita*, one who has transcended *turiya*, the highest consciousness. He is ever absorbed in samadhi. In a videhamukta there is no form of mind; even sattwic qualities are not present in him, so he is unable to perform even as an instrument of the cosmic will. He has to be fed by others. A videhamukta will cast away his body in seven to twenty-one days after attaining that state. Jada Bharata, the late Mouni Swami of Kumbakonam, and the late Akalkot Swami were all videhamuktas.

The jivanmukta has a consciousness of the body in the form of a samskara; the videhamukta has no consciousness of the body. When all the desires lodged in the heart are cast off, then the mortal becomes immortal. Herein he attains Brahman. Sage Vasishtha tells Rama that a videhamukta need not necessarily dissolve himself in the absolute Brahman.

If he so wishes, he can merge in the being of satchidananda. Also, if he wishes to remain as an individual merely as a sport, he may shine as the sun of a universe or rule like a Vishnu or become a Brahma or a Shiva.

He may become a universal individual like Krishna or Vishnu who are identical with Brahman, but still assume bodies for the solace of the world. If at any time he does not wish to remain as an individual, he may exist as the Absolute whenever he pleases to do so. The liberated state is not bound by or limited to indivisibility and changelessness alone, for the Absolute is unlimited and is free to assume any form. But that formative will is not like the unconscious will of the jiva which involuntary binds it to individuality. The conscious formative play of the Absolute is completely a free and voluntary act. The videhamukta is Brahman himself and hence lives and acts as the Absolute.

16
A Sage's Experience

I am ever free. I alone am. I am taintless, spaceless, and timeless. The world appears like a mirage within me. I am infinite, imperishable, self-luminous, self-existent, self-contained. I know neither pleasure nor pain, nor joy nor sorrow, nor happiness nor misery.

I am beginningless. I am endless. I am decayless. I am birthless. I am deathless. Never was I born. I am ever free. I am perfect. I am pure. I am independent. I am tranquil. I am pure knowledge, transcendent. I am above good and evil, virtue and vice. I am one. I go nowhere. I come from nowhere. I abide in myself. I pervade the entire universe. I am all-permeating and interpenetrating.

I am Absolute. I am non-dual. I am pure wisdom. I am pure consciousness. I am the limitless, infinite ocean of consciousness. I am Atman, impersonal and all-pervading. I am Atman, the Self of all beings. I am the substratum, support, source for everything. I am the nectar which is knowledge absolute. I am beyond the reach of the mind, the intellect and the senses. I am unattached. I have renounced both action and inaction. I am not the doer, *akarta*. I am not the agent. I am not the enjoyer. I am the silent witness, *sakshi*.

Free from subject and object am I; satchidananda Brahman am I. The one, the taintless, transcendental Truth am I. Ever stable, peaceful, immovable, immutable, invulnerable, imperturbable Truth am I. The nectar of immortality am I. The immortality-giving knowledge am I. Ever blissful Shiva am I. I am the taintless nirvana. I am *turiya*, the fourth stage of consciousness. I am being-ness.

I am freedom absolute. I am supreme transcendental peace. I am supreme stupendous silence. There is neither space nor time in me. I am infinity. I am eternity. First I abandoned desires, then attachment. Now I abide in eternal peace. I do not mix much. I do not move. I meditate. Now I abide in everlasting peace.

The world is an illusion. Brahman is the only reality. Knowing this, now I abide in the peace that passeth all understanding. I am all-pervading, immortal Atma. Knowing this, now I abide in immortal peace.

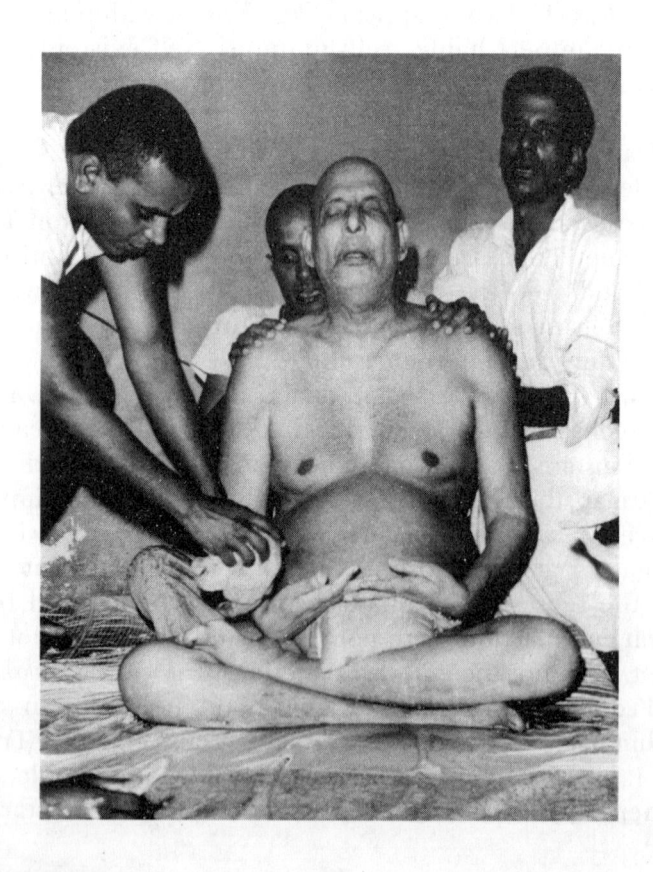

Cup of Bliss

Sorrow touches me not, pain affects me not,
All joy, all bliss I am,
Eternal satisfaction I am.

The silvery moon, the brilliant sun are my eyes.
The rivers are my veins, the stars, mountains,
Herbs, trees and plants, the Vedas and Devas,
Are my expression, my breath.

My exhalation is this universe,
My inhalation is dissolution,
The world is my body, all bodies are mine.

All hands, ears and eyes are mine,
The fire is my mouth, the wind is my breath,
Energy and time proceed from me,
All beings throb in me, all hearts pulsate in me,
Causation I am, all quarters I am,
Quarters are my garment.

All time is now, all distance is here,
I fill all space, where can I move?
No space to move, infinite I am,
Unconditioned I am,
Bhuma I am, Bhumananda Swaroopoham.

Samadhi

From the teachings of Swami Satyananda Saraswati

Showers of Samadhi

When serenity and equilibrium prevail,
Not only ideas but dreams also come true
And sleep is converted into samadhi.

Generally, the mind is dull and dissipated,
Sometimes it goes in for higher things
But then returns to its lower field.

It is by persistent sadhana and vairagya
That ekagrata, savikalpa samadhi, dawns
And the mind loses its separateness from self.

Freed from its usual patterns of samskaras
Mind is fashioned in the divine pattern,
Then the showers of samadhi descend.

At this juncture true knowledge arises,
This is samprajnata samadhi, let me call it darshan,
But it takes time to become permanently established.

Soon after its first emergence
There is a revival of vrittis
And the sadhaka returns to his usual state.

Therefore, even after darshan
The sadhaka has to plod on,
Let him not slacken his usual zeal.

He must establish the state of samprajnata
Through effort, serenity and detachment
In order to enter the regions of nirvikalpa samadhi.

There he is permanently established in his own self,
When the mind has ceased to exist
How can it tune in with the vrittis?

Just as water does not wet a rock smeared with oil,
Likewise the incoming sensations of day to day life
Leave no trace of effect on the mind of such a yogi.

—Rajnandgaon, 1960

17

Samadhi

Samadhi is the culmination of yoga, the culmination of meditation. *Samadhi* means supramental awareness. Sensual awareness comes first, then mental awareness and above that is supramental awareness, awareness of one's own self. Awareness of the senses is awareness of forms, sounds, touch, taste, smell. Mental awareness is awareness of time, space and object. Supramental awareness is not a point, but a process, a range of experience. Just as the term 'childhood' refers to wide span of time, in the same way, samadhi is not a particular point of experience, but a sequence of experiences which graduate from one stage to another.

Raja yoga

In the *Yoga Sutras*, Patanjali classifies samadhi into three main categories. The first is *savikalpa samadhi*, samadhi with fluctuation. It has four stages: *vitarka*, reasoning, *vichara*, reflection, *ananda*, bliss, and *asmita*, 'I-ness'. The second category, *asamprajnata*, is samadhi without any awareness, and the third category, *nirvikalpa*, is samadhi without any fluctuation.

These names only indicate the particular state of one's mind during the samadhi experience. After all, the erosion of normal mental awareness does not take place suddenly or come to an abrupt end. There is the development of one type of awareness and the erosion of another. The mind is not a static substance. Even the brain is subject to evolution. Evolution means change, progress and movement. When we are fifty, our brain is not the same as it was when we were nine. Everything has changed, and therefore we should allow ourselves to change according to the laws of nature. The normal consciousness fades and higher awareness develops; there is a parallel interaction between the two states.

Where does meditation end and where does samadhi begin? It cannot be pinpointed. Where does youth end and old age begin? The same answer applies. It is the same in samadhi. Where does savikalpa samadhi end and asamprajnata begin, and where does asamprajnata end and nirvikalpa begin? The whole process occurs in continuity, each stage fusing into the next and transforming in a very graduated way. This seems logical when we consider that it is the same consciousness which is undergoing the experience.

Tantra

According to tantra, samadhi can be achieved by awakening the kundalini. The awakening of kundalini in tantra and the samadhi of raja yoga is the same experience described in two quite different languages. When Patanjali is discussing the various states of samadhi, he is actually referring to the evolution of spiritual consciousness, or kundalini. In tantra, sahasrara is the highest point of awareness, and in Patanjali's raja yoga the highest point of awareness is nirvikalpa samadhi. If we compare the descriptions of sahasrara and nirvikalpa samadhi, we will find they are the same. And if we compare the experiences of samadhi described in raja yoga with the descriptions of kundalini awakening in tantra, we will find they are also the same. It should also be noted that both systems talk about the same types of practices.

Raja yoga is more intellectual in its method of expression and more in tune with philosophy; tantra is more emotional in approach and expression. That is the only difference. Kundalini awakening and samadhi are the same thing. Buddha and the other great saints and teachers have also talked about the same experience but in different languages.

Duality

When the body is transcended in sadhana, when matter is also transcended, at that time the object within is illumined. Duality ceases to exist. The experience alone remains and that experience is *nirvana* or enlightenment.

There are two realities within us, time and space, and they are categories of the mind. As long as time and space are apart there is external awareness. When they are brought together, there is a moment when they unite. The moment there is union between time and space, individuality is lost, awareness of the limited 'I' diminishes and the greater experience dawns. It may be the experience of light, or the experience of truth, or the experience of divinity, or the experience of eternity. During the instant of this experience there is no experience of duality, no notion that 'I am experiencing'.

Right now, there is duality. However, when one goes inside oneself, duality becomes feeble. There is duality: 'I am experiencing imagination, I am experiencing a feeling, I am experiencing a vision', but it becomes very feeble, and is not very significant. As we go on purifying the ego, that is the notion of duality, ego awareness becomes increasingly fainter and dimmer, until there is a very rare moment that can come in our life, although it does not come to every individual. That is a rare moment when the ego is completely fused and lost. At that time there is only experience, not the experiencer of the experience. Such an experience is known as homogeneous experience or absolute experience.

Darshan

This experience has various names. Some say transcendental experience, or nirvikalpa samadhi; some call it *nirvana*, emancipation or salvation, *moksha*; some call it *adwaita anubhuti*, the non-dual experience. In tantra it is called darshan. *Darshan* means to see, but not with the eyes. Every great yogi has had the experience of darshan. Without it one cannot be a yogi; one cannot become a guru. One who does not hold time in one hand and space in the other and then has the experience of putting them together in one pocket cannot be a yogi.

Only when the duality of time and space is non-existent can one have darshan of the true self. When the eyes are shut and the senses have been closed, when the mind retires and the ego has been locked permanently, at that time there is a vision which is more real than this. At that time you are face to face with what you call God. You are face to face with what you call your *guru tattwa*, the very essence of yourself.

In India, for thousands of years, the great people have told us that if one has darshan of that inner being, nothing in the world is needed anymore because darshan is the wealth of all wealth. It is not for a monkey, a donkey or a dog to have darshan. Only man has the evolution of inner vision; it is for him alone. Darshan is the fulfilment of human destiny.

Darshan means jumping out of the mind, kicking off matter. There is no fire, but the fire is there. There is no external light, but still one sees the light. There is nobody making a sound, but still the sound is heard. There is no substance for life, but still one is alive. What does it mean? It means enlightenment, it means illumination, it means nirvana, it means samadhi. It has nothing to do with the body, mind, senses and emotions.

Samkhya

The totality of existence is divided into two external realities, matter and consciousness. Tantra calls them Shiva and Shakti. The Samkhya system of philosophy calls it *purusha* and *prakriti*, consciousness and matter. Scientists also use the terms matter and energy. Matter is the lower and empirical substance, and consciousness is the higher and transcendental substance. In our existence both are interacting. Purusha and prakriti are both interacting. In yoga, purusha is looked upon as the highest manifestation of consciousness, free from the vrittis and from any entanglement with prakriti. One has to withdraw oneself from prakriti and become aware of purusha, consciousness. That is called *kaivalya*, non-duality, final liberation, nirvana.

Definitions of samadhi

A good definition of samadhi is found in the *Katha Upanishad* (111:10): "When the five senses of perception together with the mind are at rest, when even the intellect has ceased to function, that, say the sages, is the supreme state." This is the state where there is complete absence of both external and internal mental modifications; all that remains is awareness. Samadhi brings self-realization.

The *Bhagavad Gita* (2:53) says : "When the intellect, having been perplexed by hearing the words of the scriptures, stands immovable in samadhi, then you shall attain self-realization."

The most bland definition of samadhi is given in the *Yoga Chudamani Upanishad* (111–113): "Twelve (protracted rounds) of pranayama lead to pratyahara. Twelve (extended durations of) pratyahara lead to dharana. Twelve such dharanas lead to dhyana and twelve such dhyanas result in samadhi."

Focus the entire personality

Samadhi is focusing all the senses, all the thoughts, concentrating the entire personality on one point. That point can be the void, *shoonya,* light, a circle, gods and goddesses, God, guru, a word, a pulse, a shiver or a thought; whatever the mind can be fixed on is called *pratyaya*, the base of the mind. The mind needs a base to be focused. It is said in the scriptures, "Wherever the mind is fixed, there is samadhi."

Total awareness

In samadhi, one is aware of awareness but of nothing else. Names and forms die, time dwindles into nothing, space is annihilated, and there is total awareness. That is the existence of *atman*, the self, and when that has been reached, one has obtained the fruits of dhyana and samadhi.

Sahaja samadhi

In the state of samadhi one is completely unconscious of the external world but fully awake in the internal world. Externally one is asleep, but internally one is awake and has full inner knowledge. This is a very high stage. There are some saints and yogis who remain wide awake externally as well as internally. This is called *sahaja* or spontaneous, natural samadhi.

Jada samadhi
Jada means unconscious, inert, dead or lifeless. When jada samadhi is developed, the consciousness enters into an unmanifest state, *avyakta*. Many spiritual aspirants throughout the world practise jada samadhi, never realizing that they have made a mistake, because jada samadhi leads one astray from the spiritual path and into the kingdom of *tamas*, darkness, inertia. Tamas is one of the three *gunas*, the inherent characteristics of the material substance of the world.

The essence of existence
Behind the flesh, pranas, mind and subconscious there is something in us which is all-powerful and all-pervading. That something is Purusha. It is known as Ishwara, Rama, Atma, Govinda and is the essence of all that is known variously.

The essence of existence, of creation, is in us. The essence of your existence is enveloped by ignorance, desire, karma, impurity and similar other mental cloaks. This atma, which we are, has the first cloak of *avidya*, ignorance, the second cloak of *bhrama*, illusion, and the third cloak of *samskara*, impressions. This atma, which we are, becomes manifest either in our guru or our ishta devata as soon as the sadhaka has united with the same. This atma, which we are, becomes manifest in that state wherein all cloaks have been torn asunder, aptly known as samadhi.

The last point of our earthly pilgrimage
As long as we remain within the confines of the individual mind, we cannot understand the universal mind. Through meditation practices, however, we begin to go beyond the individual mind and experience or perceive the cosmic mind, the total mind. This total mind is the experience of samadhi.

The books call it trance, but it is not trance. They say that there is no thought in samadhi, but there is thought. In samadhi awareness of the total mind emerges and in realization of the cosmic mind, the birth of inner vision takes place.

Just as a virus cannot be seen with the naked eye and requires a microscope, just as the radiation of electromagnetic or radioactive energy cannot be seen without the correct instruments, in the same way, there is an internal experience which cannot be known unless one has been able to understand and develop awareness of the universal mind.

To do this, the barriers of individuality have to be broken down, just as scientists have overcome the limitation of matter. Only then can matter assume the form of energy. In the same way, when you meditate and go beyond name and form, and gradually merge the individual limited consciousness, there comes a point of experience, of homogenous awareness, of total absorption, where there is existence but *you* are not there.

At this point of experience, consciousness tries to annihilate itself; the trinity of the experience of meditator, the meditation and the object of meditation also falls flat. The boundaries of individuality are broken down and at that time the principles of life and existence are affected. The 'I' is completely dissolved and 'self' no longer exists. That is the area of expanded awareness where one enters the domain of samadhi. That is the highest point of human evolution. It is called samadhi, nirvana, emancipation; it has no name and it has every name. It is the last point of our earthly pilgrimage. It is enlightenment, and the permanent goal.

Samadhi is our nature
Samadhi is an experience, darshan is an experience, para bhakti is an experience, dhyana is an experience. It is not a practice, it is just an experience which we realize. Dhyana and samadhi are our nature. Swami Sivananda and all the great souls have said so. Samadhi is our dharma, our

swabhava, our prakriti, our swaroopa, our essence, our fundamental nature. The experience we are trying to achieve does not have to be developed or processed, it just has to be realized. The barrier between oneself and that experience is just a very fine veil or covering of ignorance. That veil is not real, it is just psychological, and it must be removed.

Therefore, to merge the individual or gross consciousness with the universal and cosmic consciousness, one must do exactly those practices by which meditation becomes an experience. The state of samadhi that we are trying to experience is very close. It does not have to be developed or created or evolved, just as the result of taking LSD or ganja is instantaneous and does not have to be developed. Samadhi is just an experience that one realizes. We just have to remove that veil, and that is the purpose of sadhana.

18
Realms of Superconsciousness

According to the *Yoga Sutras* of Patanjali, samadhi is not a static point, but a field of superconsciousness composed of three separate domains: savikalpa samadhi, asamprajnata samadhi and nirvikalpa samadhi.

Savikalpa samadhi

The first domain is *savikalpa samadhi*, a relative state, in which the mind is still functioning with a slight vibration. Patanjali has charted the territory of savikalpa very thoroughly and has left us a good road map. Savikalpa begins with the state of dhyana yoga in which a smooth, unfluctuating flow of concentration is maintained towards the object of meditation. As the samadhi becomes deeper and deeper, the aspirant enters finer and finer realms of consciousness, and the object of meditation becomes subtler and more cosmic, until finally it disappears entirely.

Within the broad region of savikalpa samadhi, there are several progressive states. The first state is *savitarka samadhi*, where there is only thought and nothing else. Here the object of meditation is represented by words, knowledge and sense perceptions. Then comes *savichara samadhi*, a state of reflection which is devoid of language and thinking, in which only imagination and vision are functioning. Next there is *ananda samadhi* where there is a feeling of total bliss. Finally, *asmita samadhi* is reached where complete awareness and knowledge of the self is attained.

During these four progressive stages of savikalpa, various experiences of a psychic nature can occur, such as the experience of light entering the body, the experience of scents, of lightning, fire, the sun and the moon, and the experience of angels, devas and divinities. Many people mistake these psychic experiences for the ultimate experience, but it is the small remnant of ego in the mind that is experiencing all these things. Therefore, such experiences come in the category of savikalpa samadhi.

Asamprajnata samadhi

The second domain of samadhi described by Patanjali is *asamprajnata samadhi*, the intermediate state. It is an unconscious yet very dynamic state. Here there is no experience of the self, of any events, or even of the unconscious, but still the consciousness is functioning in a very dynamic way. Just as fish can swim unseen and unknown under the surface of the water, the inner awareness can be active underneath the surface of human consciousness.

Asamprajnata samadhi is a temporary state in which the consciousness is trying to evolve to a higher dimension. It is like leaving your car at the airport and waiting in the transit lounge before boarding the plane. In order to reach the third and highest domain of samadhi, the great barrier of asamprajnata must be crossed. This state of vacuum is also known as *shoonyata* or the void. At this point one becomes totally unconscious, totally helpless; it is not within one's power to move or think in any way. One's karma, sadhana, spiritual life, connection with the inner guru and the lightness of one's soul alone determine one's movement during this intermediate state of shoonyata.

It may be possible to come out of this void into the highest stage of samadhi, or the aspirant may return time and again to savikalpa. When one is in this state of unconsciousness there is no experience. Only when the aspirant returns, does he know that he went into it and came back out again. The experience of savikalpa can be noted, it can be known, but not the void experience of asamprajnata.

Nirvikalpa samadhi

After crossing the uncharted area of asamprajnata, one enters the third stage, *nirvikalpa samadhi*, the domain of infinity. This is a totally subjective state in which there is only experience but no experiencer. It is the essence of what is, not what can be seen or known. Here, one is no longer a participant in the drama of life but a creator. One is not watching the drama, one is the drama. Neither Patanjali nor anybody else has said much about this tenuous state. All that can be said is that it is a perfect, absolute dimension of the Self, where one becomes free from the effects of karma and further incarnations. One has total knowledge and nothing more remains.

It is important to note that savikalpa can be attained by most people, but to reach this stage of nirvikalpa samadhi is not a matter of personal or individual effort. It is impossible to say what decides success or failure in the final attempt to attain this ultimate samadhi.

Many people wonder what happens to life after the experience of nirvikalpa samadhi. Of course, it will vary according to the different stages of attainment. At one stage there seems to be an aversion to desires, while at the next and higher stage there is acceptance, but with an understanding of desire in relation to a greater life rather than in relation to oneself. At a certain stage of evolution there is no care for oneself, but immediately after that, at a higher stage, there is greater awareness of this body, not as an individual unit separated from everything else, but as part of the cosmic body.

At a certain level in spiritual life one may feel like renouncing all possessions as useless, but then at a higher level start accumulating again just as one did in the beginning as a householder. At that time things were collected instinctively, without being clear about their purpose or meaning, for the aspirant was almost completely submerged in ignorance. When one becomes enlightened, however, property, friends, knowledge or desires are still accumulated, but with an unselfish purpose. Compassion develops for all living things, not only one's own family. Things remain the same, but the background changes, the vision is completely purified. One learns to live as part of the cosmic being and to combine this greater awareness with daily life.

According to all canons, samadhi is the state where one's total being can operate. That is why samadhi is the ultimate of life. If you had only one leg to walk on, but a surgeon made it possible for you to walk with two legs, just imagine what a great relief that would be. Or if you were blind and could not see the beautiful world and a surgeon restored your eyesight, can you imagine the happiness and bliss? In the same way, the experiences of the senses, mind and emotions are also limited, but when samadhi lights up the soul, infinite fulfilment, satisfaction and bliss are experienced. That is why people everywhere are taking up the practices of yoga in order to attain samadhi.

How can we achieve samadhi?

Samadhi is a state of perfect serenity of mind in all states. When the mind becomes free from all activities, when one feels at peace with everyone, when the mind has attained the state of peace even while the body and organs are functioning in different spheres of the world, then it is said one is entering into the state of samadhi. No time limit can be fixed for the sadhana of samadhi. It all depends upon the sincerity and efforts of the sadhaka. The more sincere and earnest one is, the quicker one's progress will be.

The ancient authors described samadhi as a state of higher awareness where the mental body does not function. The spiritual vehicle alone functions in that state; there is no need for a *pratyaya*, contents of the mind or basis for knowledge. We may define samadhi by saying that in that state the aspirant arrives at the pointless point of consciousness beyond which no consciousness remains. It is reaching the deepest level of consciousness where even the sense of individuality does not function. Samadhi is the goal of yoga.

There are, in all, five spheres of consciousness: *annamaya kosha*, the gross body, *pranamaya kosha*, the pranic body which is finer, and manomaya, vijnanamaya and anandamaya koshas, which are even finer. *Anandamaya kosha* is the finest sphere of consciousness, which is nothing but bliss, there is no physical content. Beyond these five spheres of consciousness there is ultimate awareness, known as atman or purusha.

Samadhi begins only after consciousness has become free from the physical sphere. The boundary line of the sense world, or maya, ends where pure awareness begins. If one is able to withdraw the physical as well as the pranic sense of awareness, but remain aware of mental awareness, that is the beginning of samadhi. This samadhi begins when the consciousness has gone deep into *manomaya kosha*, the mental body, where there is no trace of physical or pranic awareness. There are three spheres of mind, manomaya kosha, vijnanamaya kosha and anandamaya kosha. Atman is subtler and finer than all of these. Atman is not a sphere, but pure awareness.

Samadhi is achieved when the consciousness goes deeper and deeper into finer states and transcends the spheres of object, motion, thought, instinct and ultimately reaches the sphere of awareness. In this process the consciousness frees itself from the physical, pranic and other spheres. The five spheres of consciousness are entangled with prakriti, but when the consciousness reaches anandamaya kosha, it becomes practically free from the clutches of prakriti.

The whole range of samadhi is classified under two categories: *sabija*, with seed, and *nirbija*, without seed. Sabija is the lower state and nirbija is the finer state. Thus samadhi is a particular range in which the spiritual aspirant begins with minimum pratyaya, minimum objects on which to rest the mind. Gradually one goes deeper and deeper and there comes a time when the pratyaya are discarded. Even the last basis for consciousness to rest and dwell upon is dropped when the mind becomes free from pratyaya. In the beginning one has the japa mantra or symbolic form as the pratyaya for meditation, but later on that is dropped. Thus one may have a chakra, a lotus, a sound, a mudra, a pranayama, a smell, a sensation in mooladhara, a light in bhrumadhya, or one's own guru for the pratyaya, but when ultimately the pratyaya is thrown away through a process of refinement of consciousness, one reaches the state of samadhi.

Is it at all possible to describe one's personal experience of nirvana or samadhi?

The direct reply is no. Philosophers say that beyond the mind there is the self, atma, which is higher than the mind. That atma is more capable and complete than the mind, which is very limited. The ten senses have their terrible limitations, but in comparison the mind is much more capable. Higher than the senses is the mind. However, in comparison to the self, the mind is limited.

The experiences of the mind are limited to the information conveyed by the *indriyas* or senses. If the senses have not conveyed the information, the mind cannot experience it. Therefore, to operate through the mind seems to be a great limitation for us. Philosophers say that we should develop the self. Animals have senses, man has the mind and now we have to develop the self, atma or supermind, or whatever one may call it.

The atma has no limitations in the field of experience. When that perception is developed, one can be aware of external as well as internal experiences. This inner experience is called experience of the self, *atma anubhava*. *Atma* refers to the inner self, *anubhava* refers to the experience which originates from within. Knowledge comes from outside; this is the difference between knowledge and experience.

When self-awareness or higher awareness is developed, then the experiences are from within. After this, there is another state called nirvana. In nirvana, in moksha, in higher stages, the mental awareness, the sensorial awareness and even this self awareness is completely withdrawn. There is complete and total homogeneity of experience. The barriers that limit the mind, time and space are not experienced for the time being or for a long time. Those who have been able to go deep and experience this state remain dumbfounded when they come out because they do not know how to express what they have experienced.

When one goes into the state of nirvana or moksha, one must really understand that one is not attached or related to the body, to the mind and senses, even to the self. Intuition is not final. What people call intuition is a product of the self, the atma. Prophecies are the product of the atma, but when nirvana is attained, the experience at that time, they say, is as if one is the whole universe and everything is happening within.

19

Samadhi in a Nutshell

The culmination of hatha yoga and raja yoga is samadhi. The word *samadhi* is made up of two roots, *sama*, which means equal, and *dhi*, which means to hold. The word samadhi does not indicate liberation, but it is a field of awareness comprising supraconsciousness. It is the result of total one-pointedness of mind and expansion of consciousness from mundane perception to cosmic awareness. It is the final experience of every human being towards which we are all evolving. Through yogic and tantric practices this process is accelerated. Just as scientists have developed the means to release nuclear energy from the uranium atom, similarly the yogis found this scientific system to release energy and consciousness from the bindu within the body.

Samadhi is the experience of that which exists beyond the influence of nature. It is a timeless state beyond birth, death, beginning, end. Samadhi starts with total concentration on the object of meditation, with no other thought, not even awareness of the witness remaining.

Progressive stages
According to Patanjali's *Yoga Sutras* there are six stages of savikalpa samadhi: savitarka, nirvitarka, savichara, nirvichara, ananda and asmita. They are names of very subtle fluctuations taking place before the superior samadhi – nirvikalpa.

Samadhi is neither trance nor ecstasy. Samadhi is that state of consciousness in which there is no fluctuation. A thought is a fluctuation, objective awareness is fluctuation, subjective awareness is fluctuation, a dream is fluctuation, a spiritual vision is fluctuation, psychic forms are fluctuation. The knowledge of 'I' in the depth of meditation is fluctuation. In deep meditation, when one becomes unconscious of everything, that is also fluctuation. It is called *sankalpa/vikalpa*, thought and counter-thought, awareness and counter-awareness. Even in the deepest mental states the sankalpa/vikalpa keep on taking place, but when sankalpa/vikalpa dies, then a state emerges that is called samadhi.

Samadhi is either savikalpa or nirvikalpa. *Savikalpa* is samadhi or supraconsciousness with *vikalpa*, counter-awareness, *sa* means with. *Nirvikalpa* is samadhi without any vikalpa, or counter-awareness. In savikalpa samadhi one experiences higher awareness, but the four main types of vikalpa continue. These vikalpas are not like passion or fear, but they are very slight modifications termed vitarka, vichara, ananda and asmita by Patanjali.

When samadhi begins, the consciousness moves beyond the awareness of the physical and pranic sheaths, *annamaya* and *pranamaya koshas*, and abides in the mental sheath of *manomaya kosha*. Later, the awareness develops into *prajna*, meaning intuition, or the higher mind in *vijnanamaya kosha*, then transcendental awareness in *anandamaya kosha*, and then beyond that. Samadhi is progressive, transcending the spheres of object, motion, thought and instinct.

Savikalpa and nirvikalpa samadhi

The entire range of samadhi is classified into two divisions: savikalpa, which is also known as *sabija*, with seed, and nirvikalpa, also known as *nirbija*, without seed. The unfoldment from vitarka to asmita is part of sabija or savikalpa samadhi because the consciousness still has the trace of ego, a base support or *pratyaya*. Consciousness operates within the koshas and is therefore still entangled with *prakriti*, nature.

Nirbija is beyond that, devoid of consciousness. Rather, it is conscious unconsciousness. It is without vibration or movement, there is complete stillness of everything.

Each stage of sabija has a positive and negative aspect. Positive samadhi is *samprajnata*, with higher consciousness. Samprajnata indicates that there is consciousness of the object of meditation, or pratyaya. *Asamprajnata* is negative samadhi, which means there is unconscious awareness of the object. It is called *virama pratyaya*. It is not complete absence of the symbol. The symbol of concentration is in the mind, but there is no awareness. It is a dynamic state which intercepts vitarka/vichara, vichara/ananda and asmita/nirvikalpa. It is a state of shoonya or laya, characterized by the presence of samskara, but the dropping of object or pratyaya. It is an impermanent state preceding the ascension into a higher or subtler state of samadhi or the descent into a grosser state.

Savikalpa samadhi

In the first stage of savikalpa samadhi, *savitarka,* also known as *vitarka samprajnata*, the mind is absorbed in the object, subject and sense of perception, or 'known, knower and knowing', but there is no distinction between the three. *Chitta* or memory exists and confuses the subject, object and idea, so they appear to be one. In this state the concept still exists in language and gross form.

When knower, known and knowing become unconfused and memory is free of any past impressions concerning the object, it is *nirvitarka* or *vitarka asamprajnata*. The gross form of the object and knowledge of it shines in the mind, but there is no awareness or language. The faculty of memory is checked.

The second stage of savikalpa samadhi, *savichara* or *vichara samprajnata*, begins when the subtle layer of the object appears. However, in this state the mind is still not totally fixed on the subtle object, *sukshma artha*, because of association with time, space and idea. In savichara there is infusion and awareness of each aspect (knower, known and knowing) separately. *Vichara* is direct reflection without the basis of language. It is *pratyabhijna*, illumined knowledge, which guides all the processes in the deeper states of supraconsciousness.

When time, space and idea (knower, known and knowing) are removed, and the essential nature of thought remains, it is *nirvichara* or *vichara asamprajnata*. At the culmination of this samadhi, the chitta is illumined and intellect ceases.

Nirvichara develops into ananda samadhi when chitta has penetrated beyond the subtle existence of the object and there is only awareness of the existence of the vritti 'I am', *Aham asmi*. It is sattwic *ahamkara* or ego, a state of pure existence and awareness without word or idea.

Ananda becomes asmita when there is no differentiation between the object of consciousness and the consciousness. Awareness and consciousness are absolute, but there is still the seed of ego. It is the highest sattwic state of consciousness.

Nirvikalpa samadhi

At the end of savikalpa samadhi there is a state called dynamic samadhi. Before making a jump from savikalpa to nirvikalpa, there is a gap, which is complete *shoonya* or void; there is no experience. The self is dynamic potential, and it is after this gap that nirvikalpa samadhi dawns.

However, before nirvikalpa there are a few other samadhis, one of which is known as dharmamegha samadhi. *Megha* means cloud, and *dharma* means virtue. *Dharmamegha samadhi* is the emergence of a consciousness where the virtues pour down. The virtues are not religious, but all the good qualities automatically come because it is very necessary before nirvikalpa. If the dawn of virtue does not take place, then one will enter nirvikalpa samadhi with all the rubbish that one carries in life. In order to remove that dirt, it is necessary to achieve dharmamegha samadhi, and then one can enter nirvikalpa samadhi.

Nirvikalpa or nirbija samadhi is the disappearance of the last trace of samskara and vikalpa. Individual consciousness is eliminated just as a fire which has consumed its fuel dies out. From dharmamegha samadhi onwards, there is complete freedom from karma and the five *kleshas* or afflictions: ignorance, egoism, attachment, aversion, clinging to life. There is no desire to become liberated, but nevertheless, nirvana, kaivalya or moksha ensues. That is timeless, changeless – the supreme samadhi.

What is samadhi with seed?

The object on which one meditates is *bija*, or seed, or *pratyaya*, the basis of support for the consciousness. Finally, when the consciousness becomes concentrated in the form of that bija, they become one, like salt merges with water, and the subjectivity of the mind is lost. The mind loses itself in the seed and vice versa, but then there is a stage where even this consciousness should be eliminated.

Asmita consciousness is the last, the highest stage of consciousness. In that state neither the consciousness nor the object of consciousness is lost, but they are in dependent existence with each other. There is no differentiation. After this, the awareness of asmita is to be eliminated. Thus the consciousness as well as the seed is to be removed. It is just like evaporating the water from a mixture of salt and water. The very process of awareness is eliminated, which is difficult indeed.

The whole process of samadhi from vitarka to asmita is sabija. There the superconsciousness has a basis to rest upon. After this comes nirbija samadhi. The arrow is one's personal consciousness going through the planes or *lokas*. In each loka first there is development of the positive and then of the negative. First there is savitarka and nirvitarka; language for the basis of awareness, then it is in the form of reflection, and after that it is simple experience. There is no word, no idea, nothing. It is just awareness.

What is the difference between samprajnata and asamprajnata, and between sabija and nirbija samadhi?

There is a misconception created by intellectuals regarding these states of samadhi. Nirbija samadhi is the highest samadhi; both samprajnata and asamprajnata are varieties of sabija samadhi. We should remember clearly that at every depth of sabija samadhi, samprajnata samadhi is intermixed with a state of asamprajnata samadhi.

When the spiritual aspirant departs from the field of dhyana and enters into samadhi, that particular state is known as vitarka samprajnata. If it is perfected, it will be followed by asamprajnata. The next stage is vichara samprajnata, which is again followed by asamprajnata; similarly, with ananda and asmita samadhi. Asmita samprajnata samadhi finally culminates in nirbija samadhi.

Pratyaya means the content of mind. Our consciousness has something to dwell upon during concentration. That support, which may be a symbol or a particular idea, gross or subtle, is called pratyaya. When you meditate on Aum, the form Aum is the pratyaya for the mind; similarly with other symbols. It is sometimes argued that no symbol is necessary because the supreme being is formless, but this is simply a kind of theological and philosophical confusion created by individuals. It is true that God or the supreme being has no form or shape, but the aspirant's mind must have something to rest upon during the process of meditation.

In asamprajnata samadhi there is no awareness of any symbol. This is called *virama pratyaya*, the cessation of awareness of a symbol, but the mere absence of awareness of a symbol does not mean asamprajnata. Asamprajnata has behind it a dynamic state of consciousness. This state of *laya*, or dissolving, which comes between vitarka and vichara, vichara and ananda, etc. is not free from samskaras; the consciousness is not static there. Although there is absence of the symbol, even during the laya state there is an underground dynamism called samskara. When the samskaras are completely finished, the consciousness is completely dissolved. That state is nirbija samadhi because there is no need of consciousness.

Thus in asamprajnata there are two distinct characteristics: dropping of the pratyaya and the presence of samskara. In vitarka samadhi, the aspirant is aware of the chosen object only, without there being an awareness of anything else.

When this practice continues, the consciousness of this object or symbol also ceases and that is the state of laya, which we call asamprajnata. From asamprajnata the aspirant is either thrown up into the next higher state, or may again revert to a state of awareness of the symbol. It may even happen that one reverts to the state of dhyana or dharana. From it, one may either ascend to a deeper state of consciousness or one may revert back to a grosser state. This is very important.

It is important to note that when one steps into the asamprajnata stage, the personal conscious willpower stops functioning and the entire range of operations is held by samskara; that is the dynamic consciousness which carries the aspirant further on. It is this same dynamic consciousness which may again bring the aspirant back to the state of dhyana or dharana.

The word *samskara* may be translated in English as latent impression, or dormant or past impressions, but this is perhaps not the most correct meaning. Samskara is the seed of consciousness which survives up to the state of asmita samprajnata samadhi. After that state it comes to an end, giving rise to nirbija samadhi, a state devoid of awareness. According to yoga, consciousness or awareness is in the form of motion or vibration, but nirbija samadhi is not a state of motion or vibration. It involves stillness.

Asamprajnata samadhi is there when only samskara remains and awareness of object drops, due to practice, *abhyasa*. A confusion prevalent amongst scholars who do not practise samadhi but only look at it intellectually needs to be cleared up. The confusion lies in the belief that the objective consciousness, samskara, is ultimately dropped, but actually it is not. Consciousness of the object does not vanish completely; it only changes layers of our past experiences. We usually experience the symbol through these layers, but when they are dissolved through practice, the object can be clearly seen. This is what happens as a student passes from vitarka to vichara, etc.

In dharana the object appears as the formulated pattern of gross consciousness; in dhyana there is the concentrated pattern of consciousness; in vitarka samadhi there is a supramental pattern of consciousness; in vichara it is a contemplative pattern; in ananda it is the bliss pattern, etc., but pratyaya remains until the end. It only drops intermittently, which is called virama pratyaya. In asamprajnata samadhi, the pratyaya or awareness of the symbol drops, but only temporarily. It again revives itself, but not in the same state of awareness; rather the state of awareness becomes either subtler or grosser. Asamprajnata samadhi is like the period between alighting from a car and boarding a plane. It is a transient period, the going over from one plane to another.

It may be said that most practitioners do experience the vitarka and other stages as well and therefore also experience the intervening asamprajnata stage, but the only difficulty is that these stages are not stabilized; they are fluctuating. So one should never give up the object or symbol, whatever it may be – a cross, or a shivalingam, or any object for that matter. One should, through continued practice, try to go to deeper states until at last the nirbija state is reached, but that is indeed extremely difficult.

20
Stages of Samadhi

SAMAPATTI

Samapatti means complete absorption. That state of samapatti precedes samadhi. According to Patanjali, "Samapatti is a state of complete absorption of the mind (which is free from the vrittis) into cognizer, cognized and senses, just as polished crystal takes the colour of that on which it rests." (*Yoga Sutras* 1:41) When the three states of knower, knowing or known merge as one experience, that one-pointedness of mind becomes the state of cosmic or universal consciousness. When the three perceptions exist, there is the individual mind. The mind has to become subtle and as clear as crystal so that it reflects the *paramatma*, supreme spirit, not the *vrittis*, mental modifications, or *vasanas*, subtle desires.

Samapatti is the end result of dhyana. Until total absorption is attained there can be no experience of samadhi. One cannot go into the state of meditation unless the mind is clear. If the mind is clear, the state of meditation can come as easily as sleep comes to an ordinary person. For this, the vrittis must be diminished or weakened, which can be achieved by various techniques of steadying the mind. It is like sleeping in a train. In that state there is awareness of people coming and going and of the stoppages of the train, but not full awareness like in the waking state.

When the fragmentary consciousness of the vrittis also fades away, the mind becomes as pure and clear as crystal, and can be applied totally to any object. This is samapatti. The moment the vrittis are removed from the mind, it starts to function like crystal, which gives rise to a purely objective consciousness of the object upon which the mind is cast. When trataka or meditation is practised on an object like a shivalingam, the vrittis diminish slowly and, ultimately, there is a sudden flash of consciousness when the mind fuses completely with the object. The three facets of the object: name, form and meaning, can be experienced separately.

There are six types of fusion, called respectively savitarka, nirvitarka, savichara, nirvichara, ananda and asmita. They are the stages of fusion of consciousness in relation to the object of meditation and, finally, a time comes when the object vanishes. It should be remembered that only when the object disappears from consciousness has something been achieved. When there is fusion, the modifications of consciousness or vrittis are almost annihilated from consciousness. This is *ekagrata* or one-pointedness. During that state, all three components: meditation, its object and its consciousness, become one. As long as samapatti is not attained, there is simultaneous awareness of these three vrittis. In samapatti these three types of awareness fuse into one single consciousness so that nothing is seen except the form. Only the form of meditation shines in that state.

SAMPRAJNATA AND ASAMPRAJNATA SAMADHIS

Samprajnata samadhi is that transcendental state where there is knowledge with awareness, *prajna*. According to Patanjali, "Samprajnata is knowledge with awareness in association with reasoning (*vitarka*), reflection (*vichara*), bliss (*ananda*), and the sense of individuality (*asmita*)." (*Yoga Sutras* 1:17) In samprajnata samadhi the mind is taken beyond into a state where there is continual, constant awareness linked with knowledge. The phases are vitarka, vichara, ananda and asmita. Samprajnata alternates with asamprajnata and culminates in nirbija samadhi.

Asamprajnata samadhi is the transitional state which is experienced between the different states of samprajnata samadhi. According to Patanjali, "Stopping the content of the mind (*virama pratyaya*), whereby the mind remains in the form of traces (*samskara*) is asamprajnata."(*Yoga Sutras* 1:18) It is not a permanent state, but only an intermediate state in which the consciousness is trying to transcend into a different plane. Asamprajnata samadhi is the process of reversal from one state and entrance into the next where the traces or samskaras become active according to their intensity. Every depth of samprajnata samadhi is intermixed with a state of asamprajnata samadhi. Both are varieties of *sabija samadhi*, samadhi with seed.

SAVITARKA SAMADHI

According to Patanjali, savitarka is the mixed state of mind due to the consciousness alternating between word, true knowledge and sense perception. (*Yoga Sutras* 1:42) Samadhi is not a particular state, but covers a whole range of awareness comprising a field of superconsciousness. Just as the waking state can also be described as a field of consciousness, as it includes many activities such as talking, walking, laughing, etc., in the same way, samadhi includes various states. As the samadhi becomes deeper and deeper, the aspirant goes into finer and finer realms of consciousness. The first state of the superconscious mind is called *savitarka*, absorption with reasoning, or *vitarka*. In savitarka the mind keeps moving between word, knowledge and sense perception. Thus our knowledge about an object is confused or mixed up.

When we think of a rose, we think of many qualities such as colour, weight, smell, structure and so on. Our knowledge of these qualities is mixed up in our idea of the rose. When the mind goes beyond these qualities and becomes one with the object without reference to particular qualities, it is the state of samadhi.

Mixture of elements

In the first state of savikalpa samadhi, called savitarka, there is a mixture of three elements: shabda, artha and jnana. *Shabda* is the word which indicates the object, or *artha*. We know that the word shivalingam and the object shivalingam are quite different. Furthermore, the knowledge, *jnana*, that arises in the mind while meditating upon the shivalingam is also quite different; it is the pratyaya arising in the mind, and is called jnana.

These three elements are necessary aspects of the process of concentration. In savitarka they are mixed up. Sometimes there is simultaneous awareness of word, object and knowledge, and sometimes only awareness of them one at a time. These states keep on changing. If one is concentrating on a particular form, the form remains but the continuity of that awareness goes on changing. For example, sometimes there is awareness of the shivalingam, sometimes of mantra, sometimes of the lingam, etc. There should be continuous awareness of a single factor, but this does not happen and the elements become mixed up. This is due to *bija*, or seed. This seed has different layers; the outermost layer is just the husk, the innermost layer is the essential part. Due to this husk, or impurities caused by past experiences, the elements of knowledge become confused.

Seed means a basis for the mind. It is the awareness of the support which the mind takes. When we meditate, we first visualize the form, which is like taking off the outer layer. Then the deeper qualities can be visualized and, finally, the innermost layer can be visualized. Savitarka is the outermost layer of the seed in samadhi, and below it are the layers called nirvitarka, savichara and nirvichara, etc. Or we can say that the sense consciousness is the outer layer of the seed. When consciousness transcends pratyahara, dharana and dhyana, savitarka samadhi and the other finer states, ultimately it sees the finest entity, called drashta or atman.

Consciousness cannot function without a seed, which in yoga is called the *pratyaya*, basis. A symbol is needed, for example, the shivalingam. In savitarka they are mixed and cannot be separated. Those who practise japa and meditation with mantra and form should remember that after having seen the form in meditation, the consciousness should alternate between shabda, artha and jnana. Shabda is mental reasoning, a thought process in the form of words. Artha is the object, such as the shivalingam. *Artha* also means the ultimate purpose, and that is very difficult; it is real knowledge of the object, jnana, inner sense perception.

Samyama

By attaining samadhi through a particular symbol, one has complete control of the awareness of the object on which one is meditating. This happens in samyama, which includes the threefold processes of dharana, dhyana and samadhi. *Samyama* means holding the object completely in one's awareness and keeping the awareness of the object under full control. The result of samyama, of complete absorption or fusion in different objects, is different for each object.

It is absolutely meaningless to say that you get only one thing from meditating on different objects. For example, if you hold completely the awareness of cotton, the result will be altogether different from the one you obtain when you do samyama on something else such as physical strength. During the process of samyama the ultimate purpose is there, although one may not know it in the beginning. The purpose has to be arrived at by separating it, and the separation takes place spontaneously.

In savitarka samadhi the awareness is free from imperfections. There is absolute peace and tranquillity, no alternating oscillations and waverings of the mind. It is important to note that there is already in us a fragment of achievement of the superconscious state, but it lasts only for one or two moments.

The three aspects of the object of meditation should be visualized separately, alternating name, form and meaning. One should try to see one's own awareness on the basis of those elements, then try to see them as one. There should be awareness of the name, form and meaning together. Ultimately one tries to see them separately. This progression is one of the most important methods of concentration.

NIRVITARKA SAMADHI

According to Patanjali, "After the purification of memory, when the mind is as if devoid of self-awareness and the true knowledge of the object alone is shining within, that is nirvitarka." (*Yoga Sutras* 1:43) *Nirvitarka* is samadhi without reasoning or argumentation, without any confusion of the three aspects of an object, name, form and meaning. There is neither subjective awareness of the object, nor of the word. Memory becomes absolutely free of past impressions and associations.

Purification of smriti, memory
In the nirvitarka state, purification or clarification of memory, *smriti*, takes place when what we are looking at is seen in its real form without the superimposition of our own idea. Usually our memory is not clear, but constitutes a collection of past impressions. Smriti is an independent awareness in which the impressions are embedded, and even if everything of the past is cleared up, the smriti remains.

On the tablet of smriti there are past impressions which appear in deeper states. In the waking state this is brought about by conscious thinking, but in samadhi they come up on their own. Sometimes in this deeper state of consciousness, impressions from early childhood are seen, but even if these impressions are cleared up, the memory does not disappear, because memory is different from the impressions. It is as if the brain is different from the mind or thought. Similarly, the vritti known as smriti is different from past impressions.

Smriti is awareness of one's self. However, when smriti becomes purified through the practices of sadhana, it becomes *swaroopa shoonya eva*, a state of self-awareness where it appears as if everything has become void but actually it is not. The word *eva* means 'as if', and is used to show that although one is not aware of the object, the object is there. When the past impressions of the object, such as the shivalingam, are gone, one is not aware of it.

It appears as if the mind becomes absolutely devoid of the impressions of the shivalingam, but it is not so. Smriti does not become free of the impressions of the object. The impressions permeate the entire structure of one's awareness. In this state the mind loses its subjective awareness. It loses the knowledge of the object although the awareness and knowledge are still present. You remember that you are concentrating on the shivalingam, then next there is only the shivalingam and you do not remember that you are concentrating on it. The whole mind appears to have become completely void, but it is not. It is because the mind is completely permeated with the memory of the object and thus the object cannot be known separately. This is known as *parishuddhi*, purification of memory, which is the cause of swaroopa shoonya eva, the mind being devoid of itself.

True knowledge of the object

It is important to remember the subtle point that if the memory is not purified, the mind will slip into blankness, but if the memory is purified, then the object will permeate the whole consciousness and become one with that state of mind. The awareness and the object become one. The mind and the memory of the form become inseparable. Memory does not exist separately. At that time there is a momentary experience of void, *shoonya*, in which the consciousness of memory, of the object, merges completely in the mind. For a moment the mind blinks and sleeps, and memory is not present. At that point, the true knowledge of the object shines within. This is the difference between nirvitarka samadhi and laya, or asamprajnata samadhi.

In nirvitarka true knowledge of the object is revealed. The object may vanish, but behind that a bright light may be seen. In dream the experience is very intense, but in nirvitarka samadhi it is far more intense. It is necessary to be aware of the real knowledge or real form of the object of concentration, whether it is a shivalingam or a rose, etc. Otherwise one may be misled, because here the subjectivity of the mind is completely lost, the difference between the inner and outer state is completely lost, due to the absence of memory.

A state beyond

The state of nirvitarka is different from normal consciousness due to the absence of memory. Therefore, one cannot remember the experiences of this state because the normal consciousness does not function here. When you enter nirvitarka, a different awareness takes over.

Various purushas conduct the mind to deeper and deeper states of superconsciousness. The conscious purusha stops working and a second purusha takes its place. This state continues up to a certain point, and stops. Then the third purusha comes and takes one further. In this way one may progress through different planes of consciousness. It is not even the mind which dreams, remains aware of the dreams and remembers in the morning; it is a different state of mind. If at all one has achieved this blessed state, it may not even be possible to remember it due to the absence of the same memory, due to the absence of the mind. If one remembers the experience of meditation, samadhi, either one has not achieved meditation, or one's normal consciousness is of a very high order.

Summing up, the nirvitarka state involves purification of smriti, the vritti of memory, which gives rise to true knowledge of the object of concentration.

SAVICHARA, NIRVICHARA, ANANDA AND ASMITA SAMADHIS

After nirvitarka there are four more stages: savichara, nirvichara, ananda and asmita. In savitarka and nirvitarka, the samadhis before savichara, there is awareness of an object, its name, form and qualities. These three either alternate or, as in nirvitarka, the essential nature of the object is perceived. So it is said that in savitarka, the process of awareness is limited more to reasoning, whereas in savichara the process takes place through deep reflection, *vichara*; there is no form present.

The process of reflection has no association with knowledge, word or symbol. There is no thinking in language or words. Language is present during the states of savitarka and nirvitarka, but when thought is devoid of language, it is called vichara, reflection. In savichara there is only awareness in the form of vision, which is still filtered through to the lower mind. Here the mind alternates between time, space and object. There is no fusion of these three; there is absolutely pure awareness of each separately. Either there is awareness of time and one forgets about space and object, or there is awareness of space and one forgets about time and object, or there is awareness of object and one forgets about space and time.

Awareness of time, space and object is vichara. It is not thinking. Here one aspect remains, which is experienced by the lower mind in the form of vision. The consciousness is flowing without the basis of language. There is pure awareness which is independent of any other association or link. The object of concentration is seen in the form of a vision. In this experience there is total absorption and natural, spontaneous one-pointedness. This process is effortless because here no language or process of understanding is required.

When the reasoning of the mind in the form of a particular language has been taken out, that is the state of savichara. The consciousness in savichara is called *pratyabhijna*, illumined knowledge. It guides all our processes in the deeper states of consciousness. In *nirvichara samadhi*, absorption without reflection, one-pointed absorption on a single aspect of the space, time, object continuum disappears. Behind that, however, something else remains, and that is known as the essential nature of thought or reflection. Again this is followed by a stage of shoonya from which we move into a different dimension. We have moved from the dimension of reasoning to reflection. We then enter the state of shoonya in asamprajnata samadhi before moving into ananda.

Ananda and asmita samadhi are the subtle stages of samadhi in which the object of fusion is bliss and awareness respectively. In ananda samadhi there is the feeling of absolute peace and absolute bliss, but that bliss is not associated with any form of reasoning and reflection. It is experienced at a deeper level of consciousness where there is total absorption in the feeling of bliss. In asmita samadhi, the awareness is absolutely pure, there is no thought, there is no awareness of time or space, and there is complete understanding or realization of that awareness.

According to Patanjali, "After becoming absolutely perfect in nirvichara samadhi, the spiritual light or illumination dawns. The eternal and transient nature of the self is then known and the superconsciousness becomes full with cosmic experience." (*Yoga Sutras* 1:47–48) Nirvichara samadhi is the highest form of superconsciousness. This spiritual illumination comes to the mind in the last stage of nirvichara samadhi. After that there is an end of consciousness where intellectual functioning ceases completely, and a different consciousness overtakes the aspirant. It has been said in many Puranas that after the death of the jiva, one is conducted by different beings to different *lokas*, planes or worlds. The concept of death here means the death of the intellect, not the death of the body.

There is a stage in spiritual meditation when the consciousness which is pervaded and permeated by the intellectual consciousness completely dies out. In the same way, the intellectual consciousness gives rise to other kinds of consciousness. That stage is achieved by self-realized persons, perceivers of the Self. That is a special instrument, a special form of consciousness, which is called *atma drashta*. When the nirvichara stage is perfected, a different aspect of awareness is born.

NIRBIJA SAMADHI

Nirbija samadhi means absorption without seed. It is the innermost or finest state. In nirbija samadhi there is no pratyaya, no object, no seed, but only pure awareness. Nirbija samadhi is not a state at all; it is devoid of awareness, devoid of consciousness. This is the final state of total dissolution. According to yoga, consciousness or awareness is in the form of motion or vibration, but nirbija samadhi is not a state of motion or vibration. It involves stillness.

After meditation in savitarka, nirvitarka and asamprajnata, savichara, nirvichara and asamprajnata, ananda, asamprajnata and asmita asamprajnata, nirbija samadhi starts. Up to this point it has been samadhi with seed, *sabija*. Nirbija is the final state of samadhi in which there is absorption without seed.

The seed has the quality of becoming many. It is to be burnt so that it does not divide and produce. Even this samskara of the seed in the form of purusha, Shiva, Aum, etc. will have to be eliminated. For that one needs a different consciousness called *ritambhara prajna*, full of truth, and that does all the work. This is a different consciousness when the seed that is the basis of upasana is destroyed. Unless it is eliminated, samadhi without seed cannot arise. Whereas other samskaras multiply their effects, ritambhara prajna gives rise to the seedless state.

Seeing, hearing, feeling, etc. are all seeds of consciousness. Even the study of the *Yoga Sutras* is a samskara. It has multiplied like a seed and one will feel like reading the Upanishads and other texts. However, in the final stage all samskaras, such as the shivalingam, or Aum, are eliminated through ritambhara prajna. This is because the limits of the intellectual boundary are crossed and the aspirant attains a state of bliss. The form is finished.

That state of shoonya is dynamic, not static; it is transcendental stillness. It appears void in the dynamic aspect only. The ultimate state is peaceful, yet dynamic. There is the light of purusha which illumines the whole consciousness. That particular light which was illuminating the objects is withdrawn; that is the only process. It is withdrawn from the outer world and goes inside, and while it goes inside, it keeps on illuminating the inner chambers of vitarka, vichara, ananda and asmita. It is very difficult to explain. It is not possible to explain the exact nature of nirbija samadhi because one who knows it cannot express or convey it.

21

Dharmamegha Samadhi

Patanjali states that when there is no interest even in the highest meditation, dharmamegha samadhi develops due to complete discrimination. (*Yoga Sutras* 4:29) When the state of *vivekakhyati*, discriminative awareness, is completely established and the impressions causing interruption are also subdued, meditation culminates in the finest type of samadhi, called dharmamegha samadhi. Here the yogi develops an aversion even for enlightenment. There is complete *vairagya* or desirelessness even regarding vivekakhyati, and the yogi becomes free of the desire to attain kaivalya. So far, one has been guided by the ambition for kaivalya, but now even that is left behind. Once the culminating point is neared, the thirst for reaching that point is completely lost.

The yogi gives up the idea of gaining anything through meditation. Ambition and interest are left behind. Sadhana is practised, but there is no idea of achieving anything. The urge for kaivalya, which guides the aspirant from the lowest point of consciousness to the development of supreme consciousness, is automatically given up just at the time of attaining kaivalya. This gives rise to dharmamegha samadhi. In that state all the seeds of past impressions are completely burned, every karma is finished and the gates of reality are opened up.

In dharmamegha samadhi nectar drops of immortality are showered through knowledge of the supreme consciousness. In this context *dharma* does not mean religion or duty, but the inherent property or characteristic function, and here refers to *sat*, *chit* and *ananda*, truth, consciousness and bliss, which are universal characteristics or functions of the higher consciousness. *Megha* is a technical term meaning a mystical condition, which may be described as a very superior state of drowsiness through which we have the experience of satchidananda. In Sanskrit *megha* means a cloud. It is a cloud which showers on the yogi a very high state of homogeneous experience of satchidananda. It cannot be described in words. This becomes possible when the last stage of nirbija samadhi is reached. The great experience in dharmamegha samadhi is the last moment before liberation. It brings about an end to all efforts, all the sadhana, meditation or samadhi.

Freedom from kleshas

Only after attaining dharmamegha samadhi are the seeds of the *kleshas*, or afflictions, completely burned, not before. Until kaivalya there is every possibility that the seeds may again become active. A spiritual aspirant will find that for many years the vrittis do not trouble him and sometimes he thinks that he has finished with every samskara and klesha, but suddenly one day he has an unexpected failure due to the presence of the seed of the kleshas in his mind.

When the yogi attains the state of satchidananda through dharmamegha samadhi, he is no longer affected by kleshas and karmas. These two instruments of bondage, which keep the jiva tied down to the world of experience, are completely dissolved by the influence of dharmamegha samadhi. Once these twin instruments are destroyed, yogic sadhana ends. It should be understood that the immediate purpose of yoga is to eliminate *avidya*, ignorance, and the kleshas. Realization of kaivalya is not a direct effect, but an indirect effect through removal of the kleshas. We do not have to develop it. It is only discovering a state that is already there by the very nature of *purusha*, pure consciousness.

Jivanmukti, liberation in this life, is the state of freedom from the clutches of *prakriti*, the manifest universe, and the three gunas. The province of prakriti begins with avidya and ends in jivanmukti, which is a state beyond the realm of prakriti where the jivanmukta experiences eternal bliss. The jivanmukta can look at prakriti from outside because he is not in its fold. He has a practical understanding of both prakriti and *mukti*, liberation, at one and the same time. Though it is true that the ultimate state of mukti is already in us, it must be understood that it is hidden by layers of avidya and the impressions of past actions. When these layers are removed through yoga, the state which is already there is discovered anew.

So the spiritual aspirant should never give up his sadhana until he has finally achieved the experience of bliss, by virtue of the elimination of prakriti and the three gunas. He should continue on the path of yoga until he becomes a separate centre of pure consciousness in the supreme reality and becomes completely separate from prakriti. After achieving dharmamegha samadhi, the kleshas and karmas become non-existent and no longer bind the yogi.

The process of mukti is twofold: individual mukti (jivanmukti) and cosmic mukti, *prakriti moksha*. The latter is the liberation of prakriti and purusha as a whole. When an individual becomes free from kleshas and karma, they exist somewhere in prakriti, although for him they come to an end. When there is the end of a vast cycle, everything merges into prakriti; that is prakriti moksha. A rich person in an air-conditioned room while the heat of summer is everywhere outside may be compared to a jivanmukta. The elimination of heat from every corner after heavy rains may be compared to prakriti moksha. So mukti has two aspects: individual and universal.

Practical liberation

The efforts made by individuals are for individual liberation. Prophets like Christ, Buddha and Shankara are also examples of individual liberation. Universal liberation cannot be brought about by any single individual, but one can practise intense sadhana so as to bring about liberation for oneself.

There are two approaches to liberation: escapist and practical. The approach of a yogi should be practical, not escapist. The practical liberated jivanmukta works for the good of humanity; he does not escape into the realm beyond prakriti even when he is liberated. He works to bring solace and peace to the suffering. Thus he remains in dharmamegha samadhi and does not escape into kaivalya, although that is just at hand for him. When he feels that he has done his job, he goes beyond into the state of kaivalya.

Individual liberation is not liberation at all. Of course, academically it is liberation but in practical terms it is not. The liberated individual has to continue his fight against pain and misery, their causes and so on. So he goes on spreading the message of good living on earth. Ultimately, when he feels he has shown a way to the millions who are suffering, he transcends the realm of prakriti and becomes a *videhamukta*, liberated from the body.

Infinity of knowledge

Through *abhyasa*, constant, repeated sadhana, *vikshepa* or mental dissipation has already been eliminated. Dharmamegha samadhi removes two more things: the veil or covering of knowledge and all impurities.

It is said in the Upanishads and other scriptures that darkness and fear do not leave an individual until the light of knowledge rises on the horizon of the superconscious. After dharmamegha samadhi, the great event of the removal of impurities and the veils of knowledge takes place and the yogi realizes that little remains to be seen or known, won or desired, or known or fulfilled. This becomes his personal nature. However, until this enlightenment he has to make steady progress through rigorous discipline and constant sadhana.

He is a seeker in the beginning. When he becomes established in sadhana, he is called a *sadhaka*, but when he attains dharmamegha samadhi, he becomes a siddha. His thirst for knowledge, steadiness and peace is quenched by the showers of the cloud of dharma. Anything and everything becomes known whenever he desires it because there is no veil or covering for his knowledge. He comes to experience the *mahavakyas*, the great sayings, in his personal life: (i) *Prajnanam Brahma*: the ultimate truth, the cosmic reality is Brahman, (ii) *Aham Brahmasmi*: I am Brahman, (iii) *Tat Tvan Asi*: Thou art That (Brahman), and (iv) *Ayam Atma Brahma*: this individual soul is Brahman. These four immortal utterances are to be understood not only intellectually but in actual experience and realization, and that is possible only in dharmamegha samadhi.

After attaining dharmamegha samadhi, the purusha remains in its own form and nature. It is freed of the superimposition of the vrittis of the mind. By attaining dharmamegha samadhi, nothing remains to be achieved. The process of change in the mind and the gunas also comes to an end. The law of cause and effect comes to an end with the law of change, so far as the yogi is concerned. The entire process of the gunas has one object, that of creating experiences for the purusha and ultimately bringing about liberation. Both these purposes being fulfilled, the gunas retire.

The final point of transformation

There are five states of change or transformation: (i) from unmanifest to manifest, (ii) from mineral to vegetable, (iii) from vegetable to animal, (iv) from animal to human, and (v) from human to superhuman. In these different classes there are also various stages of evolution. We do not usually notice the individual changes from stage to stage because they are not very pronounced. When we meet a person after ten or twenty years, we can see a change. That change was actually going on every moment, but we cannot know it separately every moment. The end of this body becomes apprehensible only at the end of the process of death.

The process of death is taking place constantly, yet, it can be known only when it is complete for this birth. But it does not stop there because the moments of transformation are immediately succeeded by another form of existence. Things go on becoming old every moment, but we call them old only after the end of the process. It is true of everything that is a product of the three gunas, because the gunas go on changing every moment. Only the soul or purusha is beyond the scope of these transformations.

This process of change comes to an end in dharmamegha samadhi, which is the final point of transformation of the three gunas. With this, there comes the end of transformation, so there is no rebirth after moksha is attained because the transformations in the physical and mental realms also stop thereafter.

Liberation means breaking off, and dharmamegha samadhi is the ultimate point of the aim of yoga abhyasa. After it is reached, the yogi enters into a new field of existence and activities.

22

The Attainment of Kaivalya

Kaivalya means absolute. It is an outcome of samadhi. According to Patanjali, kaivalya is achieved by equalizing and purifying the illumination of purusha and chitta. (*Yoga Sutras* 3:56) Kaivalya comes about when the whole structure of *chitta*, individual mind or consciousness, is completely purified and its superimposition on the *purusha*, pure consciousness, is removed.

When there are distractions, then the chitta is full of impurities. When the purusha acts through the mind, intellect and sense organs, it is not free. It becomes affected by the senses and the intellect. It is the purusha in bondage. The external world is reflected in the impure chitta in a distorted fashion, but when the chitta is purified it shows everything as it is, including the purusha. When the awareness of ultimate reality increases in the framework of chitta, then we can say that chitta is being purified or illumined. This is like cleaning a mirror so that it shows the reflection very accurately, without distortion. In that state the purusha is free of the influence of prakriti. It is the state of kaivalya. There is a process of division and discrimination; it is a progressive and a gradual realization.

The purpose of yoga is to give a method of involution by which the purusha functions in isolation, independent of the chitta or prakriti. The realization of their difference comes gradually. At different stages of psychic achievement, the purusha can see without eyes and can act without the medium of the senses. Therefore, kaivalya is achieved when the chitta is purified and the purusha is made free from the binding or colouring effect of the chitta.

When this process of illumination in the sphere of chitta and in the sphere of purusha is attained through sadhana, purusha becomes completely isolated from the sphere of prakriti. That is not emotional isolation but spiritual isolation, in which the subjective consciousness in an individual can function at all stages without any hindrance due to chitta or the external world. That state of kaivalya is the goal of yoga.

Purusha is restored to its natural form, pure consciousness

The state of kaivalya is defined in two ways: in terms of involution of the gunas and in terms of the purusha. This is because in nature a twofold process can take place: evolution and involution. In the process of evolution or manifestation, the objects of experience manifest through various stages, such as *asmita*, feeling of 'I-ness', *tanmatra*, subtle perception, *bhootas*, elements, etc., for the enjoyment of the purusha.

The process of involution is the opposite, where objects merge into their cause progressively, so that ultimately the gunas remain in an undisturbed condition. This happens when the purpose of the gunas: *bhoga*, experience, and *kaivalya*, liberation of purusha, is achieved. Thus kaivalya can be defined as involution of the gunas by fulfilment of their purpose, *purushartha*. The process of involution of the gunas ends in kaivalya of the purusha.

According to the other definition, kaivalya is the state of purusha in its own pure nature of pure consciousness. The individual tries to purify consciousness through various sadhanas such as meditation, samadhi, samyama and so on. Due to this, the veils covering the real nature of the purusha are removed until at last, through dharmamegha samadhi, the consciousness becomes extremely pure and attains its real nature, *swaroopa pratishtha*.

The culmination of yoga

Self-realization can only take place when the chitta vrittis cease their activity, when the mind or chitta is no longer affected by the play of the three gunas and varying moods, and there is no longer a feeling of identification with the objective world. With our very limited understanding, we are not able to know or understand the state of kaivalya, self-realization, or even begin to comprehend the higher states of consciousness which unfold in samadhi.

Realization comes from within and cannot be comprehended by our present level of awareness of the mind, coloured and conditioned as it is by likes and dislikes, false beliefs, erroneous conceptions, false thinking and so on, which are our usual patterns of thought and which are all related to *asmita*, the ego or 'I' principle. Purity of mind, complete sense-control, desirelessness and so on are all necessary before one is competent to reach the goal of yoga, which is kaivalya or self-realization. The word *avasthanam*, established, is indicative of the restoration of the ego to its original state – *Tada drashtuh svaroope avasthanam* (*Yoga Sutras* 1:3).

Kaivalya is thus the highest point of the combination of all sadhanas. This is the belief of yoga as well as of the Jains, but there are some other thinkers, such as those rishis to whom the Upanishads were revealed, who believe that kaivalya is only a stage in the unfoldment of consciousness. We do not know how much more of the consciousness remains unfolded and remains beyond the point of realization.

More veils may remain

Lord Buddha has also written that kaivalya is reached when veil after veil of ignorance is removed through the practices of dhyana, etc., but even then it is possible that some veils remain to be lifted. It seems for the time being that kaivalya is the highest stage so far as we are concerned and, therefore, the whole of yoga sadhana is said to be directed towards this goal, directly or indirectly. Yoga is thus a means and not an end in itself.

23

Planes of Consciousness

To attain samadhi the mind has to be transformed and transcended. Up to the point of savikalpa samadhi the mind has to be transformed, and when one wants to go from savikalpa samadhi into nirvikalpa samadhi, one has to transcend the mind. In science there are laws of determinacy and laws of indeterminacy. For example, scientists were able to mathematically describe the movement of electrons and molecules under most conditions, but at certain times these particles moved randomly in a very illogical and erratic way and standard mathematics could not explain it. Then the scientist Eddington said that in order to understand the behaviour of the electrons one has to transcend the mind, because a different state of mind is needed to understand it.

In the same way, transformation of mind takes place up to the point of savikalpa samadhi. Of course, the altitude is very high and the subtlety is greater. The mind is not gross in savikalpa samadhi, it is very quiet, sensitive and refined, but it is definitely bound by the senses. Nirvikalpa samadhi does not belong within this boundary. Names and forms no longer exist there and one is no longer separate; one is all.

The mind must be finished with
The mind or consciousness has to be divested of all its forms so that the consciousness remains nameless and formless. This is the ultimate aim of yoga. It is not only cessation of

the outside world which is a part of yoga, a point which is misunderstood by many aspirants who close their eyes and ears, forget all the outer sights and sounds and then see wonderful visions inside. They think they have arrived at samadhi, the final goal of yoga, but even those visions must be destroyed. Anything that is of the nature of mind must be finished with. Therefore, before starting to practise yoga for the attainment of samadhi, the significance of what we are going to do must be understood.

Sometimes we are told to withdraw our consciousness, but what is consciousness? We withdraw our consciousness from outer sounds, but we cannot withdraw it from sleep because we do not even believe that sleep is a mental condition. Yoga says that sleep is also a mental condition. Patanjali says that even samadhi is a mental condition which has to be thrown out. The lower savikalpa samadhi is also a *vritti*, a modification of mind, and has therefore to be transcended.

The ultimate goal of samadhi is a refining process of all the *vrittis*, mental conditions or modifications. For this purpose Patanjali has carefully classified all that we see, hear and experience, all that the vrittis do through the mind and the senses, into five groups: *pramana* or right knowledge, *viparyaya* or wrong knowledge, *vikalpa* or imagination, *nidra* or sleep and *smriti* or memory. These five modifications form the three dimensions of individual consciousness. Every mental state is included in these five modifications, such as dreaming, waking, looking, talking, touching, beating, crying, feeling, emotion, action, sentiment, and so on.

In the states of dharana, antar mouna, dhyana, the aspirant imagines certain objects and qualities. They may be unreal and fanciful notions in the ultimate analysis, but they are very helpful in the beginning and a student of yoga must use their assistance until he goes forward to master the deeper states. Many great thinkers have declared that up to nirvikalpa samadhi, the different experiences an aspirant goes through are nothing but the planes of one's mental consciousness.

Phases of consciousness

The individual has four phases of consciousness: sense consciousness or *jagrat*, subjective consciousness or *swapna*, dormant consciousness or *sushupti*, and superconsciousness or *turiya*. Beyond this is *turiyatita* or transcendental consciousness. Yogis have witnessed these phases.

When consciousness is realized through the medium of the five gross senses, it is gross body consciousness. Here the mind, intellect and memory are working. The second plane of consciousness is the astral body, *sukshma sharira*, psychic consciousness, or the subconscious body. When we practise meditation, our awareness travels deep inside, and in that inner meditation we begin to see beautiful visions and dreams. When meditation becomes deeper and deeper, the state of void or *shoonya* comes. There is no awareness, external or internal. It is the experience of the dark night of the soul, like midnight, formless, sightless, where there is no awareness of 'I'. That is the third body, the causal body, the *karana sharira*, or the unconscious body. In the Vedas it has been called *hiranyagarbha*, the golden womb.

Experiences and motions of objective consciousness depend upon the senses and mental activities. Perceptions of subjective consciousness are reflective projections dependent upon objective experiences. They can be experienced within our own selves because of the subtlety of mental vision. Even the biggest objects can be seen within in a very subtle form. Dormant impressions, *samskaras*, are projected and reflected upon in dreams. Dreams are manifestations of samskaras. Samskaras are born of experiences. Experiences are born of actions, *karmas*. Thus the numerous impressions of previous incarnations are also manifested in dreams, so we see hitherto unseen things as well.

Subtler than dream consciousness is the sushupti stage. The individual consciousness becomes dormant and is temporarily suspended because of the inactive conditions of the senses and mind. However, it does not lose self-consciousness even at that stage. It becomes free from sense experiences just for some time. It contains in it the seeds of reincarnation. It maintains in itself the usual link of individuality. There is no loss of the seeds of objective consciousness in this stage of individual consciousness. There is every possibility of the revival of continuous individual consciousness.

The fourth level of consciousness is transcendental. In the third and fourth levels of consciousness, awareness of the external world is absent. There is no awareness of one's old name or form, but there is experience of the eternal self, *akhanda swaroopa*. This fourth level of consciousness is called turiya. Turiya is samadhi. It is that fire wherein all impressions dormant in an individual are burnt entirely. Not only total merger of the mind and its vrittis, but total annihilation of every superimposition also takes place during samadhi or turiya. No possibility of remanifestation or reincarnation of individuality is allowed to exist. The yogi gradually awakens his inner consciousness. He tears away the first veil of sense consciousness. Veil after veil is rent asunder. Phase after phase of individual consciousness is transcended. The yogi soars high, taking mystic flights from bhu loka to bhuvar loka, then to swah loka, maha loka, jana loka and tapo loka, until he reaches *satya loka*, the land of reality.

Satya loka is the aim of all yogas. It is reached through yogic concentration, meditation and samadhi. It is only here that the purusha stands separately in his divine glory and divine power, and exclaims, "I am bliss absolute; I am knowledge absolute; I am Shiva; I am all." It is here that he really abides in his own self. This is the supreme abode. This is the ultimate experience of all yogas. It is the stage where consciousness is devoid of all dualities and erroneous notions.

What is meant by inner experience?
When the word consciousness is used in association with external experiences, it is called the ego. When external perceptions are withdrawn from the mind, then it becomes

atma, the pure spirit or the self. Consciousness then evolves through seven stages. There are seven higher planes of consciousness as well as three lower planes of consciousness.

We experience the three lower planes of consciousness every day. During waking, dreaming and sleeping, the experiencer is not the body, not the senses or mind, but the higher self. The self is experiencing everything through the body, senses and mind. This self or atman is like the master and the body, senses and mind are like servants. That is how the higher self experiences the waking state, dreaming state and sleep state. But when one withdraws oneself from the external world and shuts down the mind completely, then it begins to experience within.

This inner experience is also called spiritual experience and divine experience. When the outer doors and windows are closed, when the mind is stopped, the senses are disconnected and the body is immobile, then inner experience begins. This inner experience is again divided into seven stages. In yoga it is called *sapta bhumika*, seven landings.

So when we say divine experience or inner experience, we are talking of a very broad spectrum, not about a point. Inner experience refers to a range of experiences, not only inner experiences but also all the external experiences. There are ranges or stages or dimensions or levels.

Consciousness first experiences one range and gradually other experiences come. All ranges are experienced, but when the last experience comes, then there is no experiencer. Both the experiencer and the experience become one. In the Bible, when the divine angel came, the saint asked him to remove the veils. The angel replied, "You couldn't bear it," but the saint persisted, so the angel removed the first veil, and there was light. In the same way the second, third, fourth and fifth veils were removed. Then, when the angel removed the sixth veil, the saint saw nothing. That is the ultimate experience, when the experiencer and the experience both become one. This is the quality of higher experience where there is absolute unity.

What is the difference between extrovert, introvert and inner consciousness?

The mental condition at the awakening of sense perceptions may be termed extrovert consciousness. The mental condition during the processes of concentration and meditation may be termed introvert consciousness. The pure condition during samadhi may be termed inner consciousness. Again these may be called sensations, mind or thoughts, and *jnana* or knowledge, respectively, in other words conscious, subconscious and superconscious.

Extrovert consciousness is the condition of the mind when experiences take place through the medium of the ten senses, the fourfold mind and the five pranas, nineteen components in all. This consciousness is responsible for experiences in the waking condition. It does not have the capacity to be in tune with subtle thought radiations. Technically it is known as *bahirmukha vritti*, the outgoing tendency of the mind. Experiences of the extrovert consciousness include seeing, hearing, tasting, touching and the rest of the ten kinds of experiences we have during the waking condition, as well as thinking, desiring and wishing as we experience them every day. The whole of life is an expression of extrovert consciousness.

Introvert consciousness is the condition of the mind when sense perceptions and mental activities are united in one thought current, and when the mind experiences irrespective of the presence of gross objects. This state is materialized in true concentration and achieved fully in deep meditation. At that time it is not receptive to gross perceptions. It is a state wherein mental sensations are in full swing, and there is but one idea, one form and one sound. Technically it is known as *antarmukha vritti*, where the mind is turned inward and withdrawn from objects.

In the beginning, there are distractions and one is also aware of external perceptions. Gradually the external objects diminish. The form, name or idea of one's ishta becomes clearer and clearer. There are rare moments when one lands in blankness. At times there arises a strange feeling of ananda, or lights of various colours are visualized. The form of one's ishta is also experienced, either glowing with light or fusing into a flood of light. There are moments when the surrounding space of the ishta is covered with numerous flowers of various colours. Then again melodious, enlightening and unsounded Aum may be heard.

At a certain stage, men and women, places and things might be visualized which one has never seen or even thought of before. This state is just a glimpse of one's previous life. But such experiences are rare and usually one cannot remember them after returning to normal extrovert consciousness. There are other experiences too. And there comes a stage when physical passions are troubling and lower temptations try to assail the aspirant. There is also a tendency to revolt against these practices.

Inner consciousness
Inner consciousness is the condition of mind when no sense perceptions, no mental sensations and no idea, name and form remains. At that time it is not in tune with gross sense perceptions. It is a state where suprasensual intuitive radiations, light and sound are experienced. This state is a direct culmination of dharana and dhyana. It is here that knowledge dawns. This is also known as *atma chetana*, or samadhi.

There are no more sensations. Only the form remains, and this form is in tune with that inner consciousness. Now this form becomes what is called conscious form or *chinmaya vigraha*. All other experiences cease; one forgets even oneself. This stage is a culmination of faith, sincerity and love.

At first, the experiences of this stage are not remembered at all when one reverts to sense consciousness, but gradually they become vivid even during the gross condition. At this stage, wisdom dawns, power is achieved and light perceived. This pure consciousness is God or atma, which was called jiva because of its tendencies to perceive externally. No sooner is it introverted than it shines in its original glory.

Here the lower self is completely transformed and the mental screens or fluctuations are torn away. Joy and ananda become boundless. The mind becomes calm, quiet and serene. The power of magnetism grows intense. The voice grows sweet. One's prayers are fulfilled and one's questions answered. Beware not to exploit this achievement for personal and petty ends. Pure atmabhava dawns. The sadhaka becomes a siddha, master of the mind, senses and body. Knowledge through revelation after revelation emerges spontaneously. One becomes powerful, full of wisdom, a *kalpa vriksha*, able to materialize what is needed, and a receptacle of *Brahma anubhava,* absolute experience, the final goal.

24

Transformations in Consciousness

When samadhi is attained, consciousness has undergone a definite state of transformation, and that change takes place in the realm of consciousness. According to Patanjali, *nirodha parinama* is that state of transformation of mind where it is permeated by the moment of suppression which appears and disappears between incoming and outgoing samskaras. (*Yoga Sutras* 3:9) *Parinama* means transformation or change.

In samadhi or even in the preliminary sadhana, the mind undergoes transformations, which take place in different degrees and at different points. The whole range of transformation is classified into three stages. Here nirodha parinama describes the transformation in the form of suppression. There are also two other forms: transformation in the form of tranquillity, and transformation in the form of concentration. Thus the mind undergoes these three changes after attaining samadhi.

Three transformations

When you have started the practice of samyama, the mind undergoes transformation in three stages. The first stage is samadhi parinama, the second is ekagrata parinama, and the third is nirodha parinama. *Nirodha* is suppression of the object of meditation. When samyama is practised, for example, with Aum as the basis, you first try to be aware of it and nothing else. All distractions are overcome, even guru, or God, or any other idea except Aum. That is called *samadhi parinama* and thereby the state of tranquillity is attained.

When that stage is finished, then Aum becomes clear and there is a continuous flow of it in the mind. If this continues for half an hour, Aum will be in one's awareness every moment. In this process, one Aum is followed by another and there is continuity. In that state, the mind undergoes a transformation, which is called *ekagrata parinama*. When you go ahead, suddenly another idea comes; that is called *vyutthana*, which is just the revival of the previous consciousness. Then there is suppression of it and again Aum emerges; that particular period of suppression is called nirodha.

The aspirant should know how to remove the *pratyaya*, content of the mind, completely. In nirodha parinama, the pratyaya of disturbing factors is suppressed. There comes a period when the mind undergoes the second state of transformation in ekagrata parinama. Then, after that, for the third type of parinama, instead of concentrating on Aum, one will have to concentrate on the intervening period and try to remove that Aum from the mind.

It is very difficult to remove the pratyaya from the mind because the moment you try to make your awareness objectless, *shoonya*, Aum will come again. It has to be removed. Again it will come and again it has to be removed. With practice, the intervening period will go on increasing, and the pratyaya will ultimately disappear. Then there will be an absolute void. This is the period of nirodha parinama.

Yoga first tries to remove one thorn with another thorn and when the thorn is removed, the other thorn is also thrown away. Yoga tries to bring about transformation in awareness by introducing one particular pratyaya or symbol and then discarding it. So nirodha parinama is dropping of the pratyaya which one might have cultivated for years.

Dynamic samskaras

Vyutthana and nirodha, manifestation and suppression, are the two kinds of activities of consciousness. These two kinds of dynamic samskaras are the impressions of consciousness which are responsible for the stage of suppression and manifestation. These two states of suppression and expression come and go, and with them, the pratyaya comes and goes. Thus, even when there is a single pratyaya coming into awareness, time and again there is nirodha, but that pratyaya is also to be suppressed eventually. There comes a condition of complete void, and then the pratyaya comes up again.

Laya is different from nirodha. Sometimes while practising meditation, there is momentary blankness in which everything disappears; that is *laya*, not nirodha. It is involuntary. Nirodha is voluntary suppression, which is different from laya. Transformation in the form of voluntary suppression is the last transformation of the mind. The physical body also undergoes transformation; for example, childhood, youth, old age and death. The mind undergoes a similar transformation from dharana to samadhi, through the three transformations or stages called samadhi parinama, ekagrata parinama and nirodha parinama.

In samadhi parinama, you try to establish the pratyaya and diminish other thoughts. In ekagrata parinama, you try to continue that pratyaya because there are few distractions now, the mind is quiet. In nirodha parinama, you try to diminish the pratyaya which you have established and now try to establish shoonyata. Thereby you transcend the field of *sabija samadhi*, absorption with seed, and go into *nirbija samadhi*, absorption without seed.

Fruits of nirodha parinama

The final state of transformation of mind becomes tranquil and powerful by practising it again and again; then that state is not interrupted by any disturbance of the pratyaya. This is a very crucial point. If nirodha is practised before ekagrata parinama or before samadhi parinama, you will enter laya, or darkness, and those who follow the path of *nirakara*, the formless, will enter into double darkness. So this particular state of suppression should never be tried before ekagrata parinama has been finalized. Just as milk comes first, then curd, then butter, similarly samadhi parinama, ekagrata parinama and nirodha parinama should follow each other.

While you are practising deep meditation, the impression breaks sometimes and this breaking point is called nirodha. This will only come when there is practically continuous awareness. When awareness becomes continuous and then in between two impressions suddenly there is blankness, shoonya, this is called nirodha. Suddenly your consciousness emerges into the next plane of one-pointed concentration, then there is a break again, there is no impression at all; hence it is called nirodha. Hereafter the whole pattern has to be changed.

Once the pratyaya becomes continuous, without any intervention, you have to wait for some time until there is a voluntary suppression. Then the pratyaya of the symbol, such as Aum, becomes clearer and then suddenly there is a break again. This is again nirodha; there is continuity of impression and suddenly after a few months of practice you find a break. Afterwards, suddenly the impression appears. Again, by force it should be broken. It disappears and automatically Aum will appear again. The moment it reappears, one should try to break it.

When you have come to a particular state where nirodha, suppression, increases and vyutthana, expression, decreases, then samadhi comes, so you undo what you have already done. Therefore, yoga is called *viyoga*, separation. We try to bring about a transformation in the mind in three stages. It is not an imaginary circle, but an actual change in the molecular structure of the mind. Even the brain is changed. This particular transformation in three stages is again subdivided into many stages.

Do pratyayas still arise in samadhi?
According to Patanjali, "In between the state of discrimination (*viveka*), other pratyayas arise due to past impressions (*samskaras*)." (*Yoga Sutras* 4:27) After the yogi achieves the state of *vivekakhyati*, discriminative awareness, it so happens that he cannot maintain the conditions of unfluctuating consciousness of viveka because the relaxation of effort is followed by an intervening pratyaya. Even after the mind becomes full of *vairagya*, non-attachment, and, leaving the sphere of prakriti, starts being pulled towards the state of kaivalya, there are intermediate stages when it reverts back to places from where it had entered the plane of nirbija samadhi. This is due to traces of ignorance, *avidyaklesha*, which are nothing but traces of past samskaras which break through the state of viveka. Here the pratyaya stands for the last trace that has been left after complete scorching of the karma and samskaras. However, this condition is not constant; it only intervenes between the flow of viveka.

When a yogi is established in the highest form of meditation, the meditation is broken up only slightly and temporarily before he reaches the point of final experience, but that interval does not take him to a lower stage once he establishes himself firmly in it in the highest stage. Just as when we sleep during the night there may be short periods when we are awake or half-awake, similarly, in the case of the mind which is being attracted towards kaivalya, the traces of impressions break through viveka, but viveka again continues. There should be no misunderstanding about this point.

Some people feel that when a yogi finally attains the ultimate state, he is not able to look back and he merges completely, but it is not so. As long as the seeds are present, they give rise to *vyutthana*, expression, from the state of viveka, but this does not cause any disturbance because the seeds are almost scorched or burned.

Eventually this process of the revival of previous consciousness must be stopped completely. This is done by removing the pratyayas arising due to traces of personality like the *kleshas*, afflictons. The kleshas are removed by understanding their nature and their relation to karma. The pratyayas in samadhi are also due to the past karma and its impressions. These impressions are rooted in the kleshas and the kleshas are rooted in avidya. This is how these pratyayas are to be traced back to their root.

When avidya is removed, the kleshas vanish, the power of discrimination evolves and due to past impressions the conscious pratyayas also arise. Just as kleshas are removed through meditation and through making the vivekakhyati state more stable and firm, similarly, the pratyayas during vivekakhyati can also be removed through making the vivekakhyati very firm and unshakable.

What is the difference between samadhi and sleep?

When we compare the sleep we have every night with the state of samadhi, the highest spiritual state, they appear to be more or less the same, but of course sleep is not samadhi. The appearance is the same, but the contents are very different. Many scholars have compared the state of samadhi with sleep, but their assumptions have been based on misunderstanding and misinterpretation. They suppose that samadhi is a state of absolute unconsciousness whereas it is the opposite. They say there is no awareness in sleep and samadhi. However, in sleep there is no knowledge, no internal awareness, while in samadhi there is total knowledge, absolute internal awareness, clear awareness of the self, the atman; there is no trace of sleep in samadhi. It is very important to understand this because if we are able to analyze the sleep state of the mind, we can easily understand the state of samadhi.

Sleep is a condition which hides or conceals knowledge of the external world because it is characterized by no awareness, no consciousness or unconsciousness. When we go into deep sleep, the mind is dissolved. There is total dissolution of consciousness. We do not even know we are sleeping. For the time being, the ego is almost dead. At that time the mind functions very slowly. Studies have shown that when the brain frequencies are lowest, when delta waves are most prominent, one has perfect sleep.

Sleep is a *vritti*, a pattern or modification of the mind, which is distinguished by the absence of mental contents for its support. Yet, in order to experience superconsciousness, in order to experience samadhi, one must be able to control this vritti. However, this does not mean that you should not sleep. It means sleep is a mental condition and you have to maintain perpetual awareness of sleep just as you are now aware of objects and know that you are aware.

Sometimes when you dream, you know that you are dreaming. In the same way, when you sleep, you must know that you are sleeping. In fact, you must become a witness of all the states of mind: waking, dreaming, and sleeping. The seer is the self, the spirit, but it identifies itself with these three states of mind. In order to experience these states as distinct from the self, you have to separate yourself from these objective or subjective experiences.

In the *Mandukya Upanishad*, it is said that in sleep one does not desire anything, nor is there dream or any other perception. All the vrittis of the mind are concentrated together and the energy process fuses into one. The capacity of the faculty of perception is introverted. Outer objects are not seen or heard, nor is there any feeling whatsoever. Sleep is an unconscious state of mind.

Mind has no sense or mental experience

Patanjali says that in sleep there is no object before the mind; it does not see, hear, touch or feel anything. Every form of knowledge, every content of mind has become silent. When we have a mental experience of an object, that experience is called a *pratyaya*, a content of the mind. We can have a pratyaya with or without the senses coming in contact with an object. We can, for example, see a rose inside our mind either in the form of a vision, a dream, or an ideal. The content of mind in all these states is called pratyaya. When the very idea of an object, the very content of mind is removed through a certain process, the mind becomes supportless. But remember that sleep is a vritti in which the content of the mind is absent. In this state there are thoughts but they are not present before the mind, so the mind does not see, touch, think, hear, feel or have any sense or mental experience.

Psychologically, in that state of sleep the brain and the mind are disconnected and thoughts are temporarily suppressed. Similarly, in dhyana we sometimes become unconscious when the activity of the mind stops. In this respect the state of sleep is comparable with the state of samadhi, as in both there is an absence of consciousness of the external world.

The only difference between sleep and samadhi is that in the latter state the notion of 'I' persists to a certain extent, whereas in sleep there is no awareness of the 'I' notion. In the state of samadhi, the awareness of separate existences and qualities, such as an individual's nationality, one's own name and form, ceases completely, yet a kind of awareness still persists. When one is inside in samadhi the inner experience of the self, the atman, is as effulgent, as true and as absolute as the experience one is having here, right now.

25

The Supreme Being is Changeless

When yogis vividly perceive the various spheres of *chitta*, individual mind, during different states of samadhi, it becomes a subject of perception and knowledge, but the *purusha*, the supreme being, is changeless. The moment the mind is introverted and it transcends the limits of the senses, one is aware that purusha, pure consciousness, is other than chitta. Here chitta does not mean the ordinary mind, but a higher expression of consciousness. The purusha illumines the chitta. According to Patanjali, chitta is not self-illumined because it is the subject of knowledge and perception. (*Yoga Sutras* 4:19) Just as the sun shines of its own accord but the moon is not self-illumined, similarly, the soul is self-illumined but not the chitta.

The purusha is not realized through the mind. For its realization, the mind as a whole is completely separated and is thrown out of the field of experience. While an ordinary person depends on the senses for knowledge, or a scientist on instruments, the yogi depends upon the highest faculty of self-knowledge. Only after the changing instrument of knowledge, chitta, is eliminated can the purusha be realized. Therefore, the supreme being or purusha is not the subject of knowledge through the mind, but the subject of knowledge by itself. The whole process of yoga sadhana is not so much the awareness of purusha, as the elimination of the lower forms or vehicles of awareness. Though the purusha illumines itself, it is not perceptible by the chitta.

Gaining knowledge of one's self

Cognition through chitta depends on different levels of consciousness, because the consciousness assumes that particular form of *buddhi*, higher awareness, through which the mind is passing. When the consciousness assumes that pratyaya in which one's experience does not pass from one level to another, due to absence of the mental vehicle, then cognition of the self takes place. Thereby the knowledge of one's own nature is obtained. This has a connection with the state of purusha called swaroopa avasthanam. That state comes into being when the chitta assumes pratyaya which is a product of *ritambhara*, full of truth, in which the experience does not change. So long as meditation continues in the field of the mind, experiences go on changing.

When the mental awareness is evolving or becoming subtler and subtler, the experiences also go on changing. The mind is not steady, it is ever developing, changing. The psychological and physiological structure of the mind keeps on changing. The inner structure of the mind undergoes a tremendous change in meditation. The experiences in meditation are not ultimate because there is constant change.

In the final stage, when the chitta has a constant, unchanging pratyaya, there would be no change. There is a stage of samadhi where the process of experience stops and there is no longer the possibility of transcending the limitations of chitta. Then the seer accomplishes his own form, *swaroopa avasthanam*. In the beginning there may be different forms such as a shivalingam or Aum, but in the final stage there is only one form which does not change. This is called *tadakarapatti* and belongs to the last category of samadhi.

This final state is described in the Upanishads and in the *Bhagavad Gita*. It is the state of pure consciousness which has the attributes of *sat*, *chit* and *ananda*, existence, consciousness, bliss. It gives a homogeneous experience which is not limited by the mind. It comes when one transcends the limits of chitta and establishes oneself in unfluctuating pure consciousness which is absolutely homogeneous and static. In that state there is *swabuddhi samvedanam*, complete knowledge of one's inner nature. Knowledge of the body, senses and mind completely stops and there is only the unchanging knowledge of *swaroopa*, one's own form.

The knowledge of buddhi is the knowledge of one's inner nature. Here buddhi means awareness, not intellect or mind. In yoga, buddhi means intellect as supreme awareness. It is said in the *Bhagavad Gita* that supreme reality is beyond buddhi or self-awareness, but here we are using the word buddhi for that state of supreme awareness. It is there when one is not functioning through the medium of the mind but rather through the medium of supreme awareness. Just when the level of consciousness stops fluctuating, a single unchanging awareness of one's own inner nature arises. Then there is supreme knowledge of the self.

We know that in the highest state of samadhi the consciousness becomes static, and does not change. In that state the difference between the seer and the seen is known perfectly. Moreover, the vasanas which constitute the general structure of mental consciousness are not the end but just the means. Therefore, the ultimate purpose of the mind is to transcend itself.

Heading to kaivalya

When the yogi acquires the highest state of consciousness of the self, he can make a distinction between prakriti and purusha by which he is able to see purusha consciousness as different from prakriti consciousness. There arises then the sankalpa to retire from awareness of the self. This happens when one becomes aware of prakriti and purusha with their distinction, when one wants to transcend even this consciousness. Atmabhava is the finest point where the mind as an entity dissolves itself. It is here that awareness of the self is transcended. At this stage there comes the experience of kaivalya.

When the yogi realizes that even *atmabhava*, awareness of the highest point of the self, is also inadequate for realization of the absolute and becomes determined to cast off even the highest features of the mental factors, then he develops a peculiar unconscious sense of renunciation of the bliss and knowledge which is born of the higher spiritual plane. When the perfected state of samadhi is attained, then he forgets everything about himself and around himself, but at the same time he is able to visualize the entire range of consciousness which he has transcended.

At that time, the entire movement from the lowest to the highest spiritual point comes before him. He remembers all the spiritual experiences he has had from the beginning of his spiritual life. Then he is able to create a sense of distinction between experiences of different dimensions. He then realizes that all of them, including meditation and even bliss, are relative, not absolute.

It is said that the bliss and jnana born of the supreme consciousness is unchanging and permanent, but during periods of sadhana, over many births, the quality of experience changes. Even the quality of samadhi and consciousness of the self and supreme knowledge are not absolute. As such, the aspirant feels that all those experiences should be transcended because they are inadequate.

If you sit down quietly and look back over your life, you do not remember how your physical body has been developing. You remember only how you have been progressing materially, academically, socially and politically. You take just one of these and start thinking about it. When the mind is introverted, the whole continuity of experiences will be seen. You can just feel the experiences. However, if you compare the last one with the first one, you can always see the difference. Then you see the developing factors. Practise this with the mind. You can then transcend the whole path of the mental sphere, and then come to know that all these experiences were on the plane of prakriti.

This is the point of purusha. Until it is achieved, all the experiences are within the range of prakriti, even the finest ones. It is the plane of mental consciousness, sensual consciousness. It includes the supramental consciousness as well as visions, subtle currents, vibrations in telepathy, clairvoyance, clairaudience and so on. The whole thing forms a continuous process, starting from the grosser plane and going down to the deeper planes. Here the mind is inclined towards viveka through discriminatory analysis and sees all the happenings in the past with a bird's-eye view. The consciousness has a tendency to gravitate towards kaivalya. This is described by the wonderful word *kaivalya-pragbharam*.

We know from physics that everybody is gravitating towards the centre of the earth and so we have heaviness or weight. In the same way, during the final stages of sadhana, the mind is drawn towards the centre of gravity, kaivalya. Thus, when all the superfluous agents of consciousness are taken away, the purusha becomes filled with absolute consciousness and is drawn towards the state of kaivalya by a force or pull.

26

The Absolute Experience

It is said that there is no creation at all, no dissolution, no doomsday. No one is bound. No one is a sadhaka, no one is a seeker of liberation. There is no moksha. This is the absolute definition of the entire creation. When I was a child of eight, I used to wonder what was beyond the sun and the moon. Today I also wonder. The only answer I get is that there can be no answer. But there is an absolute existence.

As we experience this universe now, it is so vast that we can only understand that there is something beyond the sun and something beyond that and something beyond that again. Scientists have told us that there are endless creations, hundreds and thousands of suns and solar systems, and this universe as matter is expanding. In the scriptural texts we read about endless universes and endless creations, their distances from each other, and how many suns, moons, solar systems and endless galaxies there are. This is just man's concept of the universe, which is perceived with this gross and limited mind. Physics has also taught us about the relativity of creation, the relativity of the universe. Yet, everything has to be understood in its absolute form.

Relative, illusory and absolute experience
The relative universe and the absolute universe are not the same. The relative universe is the experience of the relative mind and senses. What can we say about the laws of the

universe? We have a relative mind which is composed of time, space and matter, and that is the ultimate boundary of this mind. It is true that the mind cannot think or operate beyond these three. When you try to think about anything, even about God, paradise or samadhi, you are thinking within the limits of time, space and matter, nothing beyond that, although God, or paradise, or samadhi are all beyond.

We know about the laws of nature related to this body and the world around us. The great scientist Einstein used to speak about relativity and absolutism, as part of his scientific philosophy. The Upanishads, written many thousands of years ago, also talk about three forms of existence: relative, absolute and illusory. One type of experience is through the senses and the mind, by coming into contact with an object. It is dependent on the quality of the mind and senses, and on the nature of the matter with which the mind and senses come in touch. That is called relative experience.

In dream the experiences have nothing to do with the senses or environment; they are products of the archetypes stored in the unconscious mind, and are illusory. If one takes drugs like ganja, hashish and LSD, the experiences are illusory, not relative and by no means absolute. The third type is absolute experience. In relative experience there is no homogeneity, everything is a combination of many things, but in absolute experience there is total homogeneity, it is not made up of components.

The law of nature here and now is relative. As long as we are operating through the mind and senses, all our experiences are relative. Therefore, our knowledge about nature is also relative. This nature is of two types. One is the lower, empirical nature and the other is the cosmic nature. This empirical nature is composed of eight elements: earth, water, fire, air, ether, mind, intelligence and ego. Do not mistake this nature for forest, rivers, valleys, hills, dales, rivulets, pastures, gardens, sky, clouds, sun and moon. That is not nature in this sense; that is a product of nature.

Prakriti

Prakriti is the philosophical term for nature. Prakriti is twofold, empirical and cosmic. I prefer to remain silent about cosmic prakriti. Empirical prakriti is composed of eight elements. It is permanently present in each and every substance. Human beings are no exception and in no way superior. The earth, minerals, vegetables, animals, humans, all visible and invisible beings, each and every thing is composed of this eightfold prakriti.

Throughout creation this eightfold prakriti is in constant motion, never static. However, when the whole cosmos is disintegrated, when there is no life anymore, no substance, no matter, no object anywhere, when time, space and matter contract into one nucleus and there is no creation, as it was in the beginning, at that time prakriti is static, there is no motion. When there is motion in prakriti, there is creation, existence, growth, death, birth and rebirth. Each and everything is growing from one form into another, and as prakriti takes a forward leap, thousands and thousands of human beings begin to experience the awakening of kundalini. This prakriti is something very fundamental and basic, something of which we are all composed.

Two eternal realities

There are two eternal realities, although the monistic schools of philosophy which believe in non-duality do not agree. Adwaita Vedanta says that consciousness is the only reality, that nature is produced by reality. Monistic philosophy says there is one God, nothing else. But this is not totally logical or scientific. According to samkhya philosophy, yoga and tantra, there are two eternal realities, known as purusha and prakriti, cohabiting with each other, interrelating with each other, moving with each other, interspersed with each other.

Purusha means consciousness, soul, spirit or atma; no name, no form, no house, no address, no identity, nothing! Consciousness is here, there, everywhere; it is in you, in me, in everyone; it is far and yet also near. The other aspect of reality is *prakriti*, primordial nature, out of which two things can be seen, called matter and energy. Matter and energy are both produced by nature. Nature is the creatrix of matter and energy. Matter and energy are one aspect of reality and consciousness is another.

In tantra, through various paths of yoga, we are moving from material, gross, sensorial consciousness to the field of energy, kundalini shakti. When we have arrived at and realized this energy, then we have to make the leap. We have to go beyond this, because awakening kundalini and realizing this energy is not the ultimate experience. It is not even the ultimate destiny of everyone. The ultimate destiny is to realize this consciousness which is beyond prakriti. Therefore, the law of this world, of this empirical nature, starts with prakriti and brings us closer to consciousness or purusha.

Is the atma present in samadhi?
The self, the individual soul, has no name or form, no such empirical limitations. It is the light, the energy, or something which cannot be limited to the area of definition. We can't define it; we don't even know what the spirit is. We only know about the possibility of the higher immortal spirit, *atman*, the soul, because the wise people who had intuition told us, and we believe them because they had purified body, mind and soul, transcended the limitations of maya and ignorance and brought us deeper, greater and unlimited vision. It is just a matter of belief. But through inference also we can come to the conclusion of the possibility of the individual soul.

There is a constant awareness that flows through our soul, our existence, and that unbroken awareness feels that the idea 'I am' is a spirit. At night when you sleep, you are completely unconscious. You don't know anything, not even if someone opened the door, came into your room, picked up something and left. But in the morning if you are asked how you slept, you say, "Oh, I slept so well." "How do you know you slept so well?" "I slept very well and I did not know anything."

The knowledge that 'I did not know anything' means you knew that you did not know it. From this we infer the possibility of a witness, even in the depths of sleep. That is called atman, the witness of waking, the witness of sleep, the witness of dream, the witness of sorrow and agony, the witness of time and space and the witness of the mind. It knows that you know that you know. That witness is present in samadhi.

In samadhi, that witness is completely bereft and devoid of all limitations. We call it full of *jyoti*, full of light. That self which is in the form of light, in the form of enlightenment, is immortal and does not die. The nature of the soul does not change; it just migrates with the karma. Once the karmas die, the desires, cravings, passions and attachments, which are the motivating forces for karma, wither away gradually.

When we are completely disillusioned about our relationships with this world, then liberation takes place because then the spirit has nothing to hold on to. There is no reason why we should be born, no reason why we should be manifesting ourselves. This is the religious idea of liberation. Buddhists call this nirvana, when the lamp is extinguished. As long as the lamp of attachment and existence is burning, life goes on, but when the light is extinguished, nothing is there. In raja yoga this is called *kaivalya*, which means the state of total oneness, onlyness. Vedantins call it *moksha*, freedom. When butter becomes free from milk, when energy becomes free from matter, that is moksha. This is the general idea.

The self is not confined

If you go on analyzing and trying to understand, you will find that the deeper you go in dhyana, the deeper you go within your own self, within the dimensions of total equanimity and samadhi, the clearer it becomes that all you have been thinking and experiencing about yourself does not exist. There you are a different person altogether. The experience of that 'I' and the experience of the present 'I' are totally different.

The experience of this present 'I' is covered with notions of duality and multiplicity; there is no unity. As long as you have the experience of the present 'I', you cannot experience unity. You can only experience duality, and therefore conflict. Multiplicity and diversity do not bring unity. Unless you experience unity, you cannot experience love. Love is a much misused and abused word. Love is the highest experience in life. But you have never experienced it. When saints say 'God is love', they do not mean the lower form of love that we know, but the experience which is a result of unity, born of the experience of the self, when you have become completely devoid of the lower ego. This experience of *aham*, the cosmic 'I', emerges when we go deeper and deeper into our own self, not into our body, mind or personality. This self is not confined to this body, even as energy is not confined to one particular point. Energy is universal. Spirit, atma, the cosmic self, are universal.

By mistake, you identify that self with this body because you know this body as your self, but the spirit, the atma, the cosmic self, is not confined to this body. It is beyond the body. The body is in the self, because the body is limited and the cosmic self, the atma, is not limited. The cosmic self is the finest experience of human life. It is the ultimate experience, and therefore we call that experience of the cosmic self *atma jnana*. *Atma* means cosmic self, infinite self, real self, total self, not the little, egotistical, physical or mental self. *Jnana* means awareness, knowledge, experience, samadhi. This is the ultimate of yoga. It is the destination we have to reach sooner or later, and throughout the world, hundreds and thousands of people are working, irrespective of religious faith and political ideology, to achieve this greatest experience of life.

It is said that samadhi is like death. What happens to the consciousness after this death?
St John of the Cross said, "By God, I swear I die every night." The same idea is reiterated in the *Bhagavad Gita*. What is this death that takes you into samadhi, into spiritual awareness?

What happens after this death? What happens to the consciousness?

When the senses are withdrawn, the sensual experiences stop. There is no more seeing, smelling, hearing, feeling or tactile consciousness. And when the mind stops, the process of thinking ceases. That is death. By the practices of kriya yoga in particular, and by the practices of yoga and meditation in general, we trigger off a process of total withdrawal of sensory and mental consciousness for a moment of time, say ten minutes, five minutes, one minute, a split second – that's long enough. Now, after this death takes place, the light shines.

After the senses have been withdrawn, the mind has been withdrawn and your individual ego has been withdrawn, at this point of death, the inner awareness becomes effulgent. Your inner awareness becomes clear and it can follow two paths. One is the path of illumination, of inner experience, of total experience. This is the path which is developed by the practice of yoga. However, many aspirants who are able to withdraw their senses and their minds sometimes enter into the path of darkness.

There are two paths: white and black, illuminated and dark. It is the practice that is responsible for one's inner experience. That is why tantra says that the way should be illuminated. When the eyes are closed, when the mind is closed, when there is no external experience taking place whatsoever, then inner experience must become full, rich, complete and total. One should not enter into a state of rigor mortis or suspension of awareness. This is the most important result of yoga.

What does it mean to have direct experience of the atman?
The word atman is used synonymously with *Brahman*, the supreme reality; there is no difference. Atma vidya, Brahma vidya, adhyatma vidya are philosophies related with these terms. Anyone can understand and explain these terms by reading the books, but experience is very difficult to obtain.

This experience is not possible through the mind, senses or intellect. It is living experience, which is the experience of the soul. The path of living experience is very difficult. Only a few walk that way, and of them one or two reach half way; very rarely does someone make it to the end. It is a state in which everything is seen by direct experience, *aparoksha anubhuti*.

You may read an entire book about America, Russia or the atom bomb, but you have not experienced it. Similarly, the experience of the soul is called *atma vidya* or *Brahma vidya*. That living experience has many names: the vision of God, self-realization, moksha, kaivalya, samadhi and so on, and those who have lived them have not been able to express them ultimately, just as nobody has been able to describe the taste of cyanide.

There is a story about a man who took cyanide as an experiment in order to be able to describe its taste, but before he could spell it out, he passed away. In the same way Kabir has also said,

> *No one returns from beyond.*
> *To whom could I run and learn of the path to God?*
> *All depart from here with load after load*
> *of accumulated baggage.*
> *My master comes from beyond*
> *with knowledge profound and pure;*
> *He pilots the battered boat of seekers*
> *and ferries them to the opposite shore.*

So the question remains, what is that state? The Upanishads say it is like fire, like an explosion, like space, like wind or like infinity. They go on hypothesizing until in the end they have to say, *Neti, neti* – 'Not this, not this'.

Everyone should move on the path to realization because it is a special path. The path of sannyasa, no matter how the world interprets it, is the path to the knowledge of divinity, the path of Brahma vidya. The aim of a sannyasin is *atma vidya*, realization of the highest self, not by commentaries, thinking or reflection, but by direct experience, aparoksha anubhuti. That living experience is independent of the mind and senses. It cannot be accomplished in one life; one has to struggle for it life after life. First you have to find the path and then you have to walk it. When you are walking on the path, it is not that you don't fall, you do fall. After all, you will become tired after walking and walking, fall ill and think of turning back and putting an end to that journey. That happens because the path is not straight, nor is it easy to follow. You fall because it is your destiny.

Everyone has to come to this path one day, whether they wish it or not. If you find someone who can give you the living experience, then a start can be made, because this experience does not happen automatically. The experience is effortless, but to reach it requires effort and you have to make the effort yourself. The experience of samadhi itself is transcendental, beyond logic, beyond the mind. Therefore, the Upanishads say, "Neither speech nor mind can enter into that domain."

27

Transcending the Realm of Duality

Liberation remains impossible within the confines of duality. Dual experience, the twofold nature, inherently causes struggle. The individual consciousness is mainly made up of ego, *ahamkara*. Due to the ego we are aware of dualities. Duality exists because of the ego, which is constantly present in the individual, and we will have to transcend it some time or other. As long as there is duality there cannot be samadhi. As long as you remember yourself, you cannot get out of yourself. There is always some sort of holding on to your own karma and personality. Although there is experience of trance, at the various chakras, there is no merger of the individual ego with the cosmic ego. Throughout you find that you are trying to assert yourself behind all the experiences you are having.

It is very important to understand what is meant by transformation and by total metamorphosis. When matter is transformed into light, matter is not seen, it is completely transformed. In the same way, one has a quantum of individual consciousness, and there is individual awareness, better known as 'I'. Every morning after the night's sleep, that individual awareness is revived and linked with the individual consciousness. This individual consciousness must be transformed.

When union between ida, pingala and sushumna takes place in ajna chakra, then one loses oneself completely, not in a state of unconsciousness, but the awareness expands and becomes homogeneous. With the expansion of awareness, individual awareness falls away. At this moment one completely transcends the realm of duality.

A little above ajna chakra is the centre known as *bindu visarga*, the centre of ambrosia. When union takes place between individual and cosmic consciousness, bindu visarga is affected and divine or ambrosial nectar begins to flow and becomes mixed up in the body. The whole system functions in a completely new way. The force of maya becomes completely weak.

Dreaming and awakening

Most people are under delusions. Whether we talk about love and attachment, hatred and jealousy, tragedy and comedy or victory and defeat, the way we look at things is a complete illusion. Our fears, jealousies and attachments are unfounded, but they are still there. Our mind is functioning within a limited area and cannot get out of it. In a dream we feel that someone is beating, shooting, killing or loving us and we respond in the dream by crying or becoming happy, but when we come out of the dream, we understand that it was only a dream. Just as we wake up from a dream, there is also a process of waking out of this dream in which we are at the moment.

Dream is a state of mind, so this waking experience is also a state of mind in as much as the experiences of the waking state are also relative. In comparison to this state, that state seems to be very coarse. But when you are dreaming, you do not remember this state. In dreams you may roam about as a beggar, hurt your body, acquire a lot of property or be looted or murdered, but you do not think at that time that it is, after all, just a dream, because of the relativity of the states of mind. Some states of mind are higher than others.

When ajna chakra awakens, then the experiences of this life are thrown back to relativity. They do not appear to be false, but it seems they are only relative and therefore your whole philosophical attitude to life changes. Life does not affect you adversely at all. You participate without being involved. The experience in one state of mind does not necessarily affect another state of mind and therefore it does not affect you.

From mundane to higher consciousness

We are now enclosed and entrapped in a particular state of mind in which death means death, love means love, loss is loss, injustice is injustice, suffering is suffering. If we want to change the very interpretation of experience, we will have to transcend this state of mind. There is no way out of suffering unless we change the mind and the vision. That happens when ajna chakra wakes up. Gradually the individual awareness withdraws and higher awareness takes its place.

Man has always been trying to enter a state where the ego will be extinguished. He has tried different methods such as soma or homa in the past, drugs such as hashish and LSD in the present, methods of laya yoga, and the possibility of suspension of consciousness. Man wants to know how to dissolve his consciousness, and at the same time he wants to be in tune with existence, both relative and absolute. However, he has never been able to do it because when he opens his eyes, he sees the mundane worldly existence outside and forgets himself, and when he looks within, he sees himself but forgets his link with his external existence. Therefore, he has not been able to create a link between internal and external existence.

The transition from mundane consciousness to higher consciousness happens when one wakes up in ajna chakra. Then one is no longer following the flow of events, but begins to monitor the movements of consciousness. *Ajna* means order, or command. A higher consciousness evolves at this point, which monitors the senses, the body and all the functions related to daily existence.

The only problem the aspirant faces is that the physical body is standing in the way. The body is made up of tamasic elements. It is a composition of five tattwas: ether, air, fire, water and earth, the permutation and combination of which is responsible for the composition of the body. Therefore, this body is gross. There is no question of its divinity and its transmutability. All we can say is that this body dies and is finished. But is it possible to transmute this body? When one wakes up in ajna chakra, the quality of the physical body is also changed. It becomes full of light particles, and if we want to, we can transform the whole body into light.

Enlightenment – I am that

Enlightenment is the nature of every being. Man is very fortunate that he is able to realize this supreme state. All beings in the world are permeated through and through by the divine principle, but they are not aware of it. Only man has become aware, and he has been developing this awareness from the beginning of civilization.

What is the real form of enlightenment at the point of realization? Some would say light and others knowledge, but the best term is experience of totality, experience of one without a second. Just as salt merges and becomes one with water, in the same way when the experiencer experiences the non-empirical experience, he no longer exists as an ordinary experiencer. The knower of Brahman, or God, becomes God. He loses his individuality, his limitations. That is the divine experience which man has when he becomes purified.

Enlightenment is like a state of becoming. You become that, you live that, you are that. You are not a seer, a knower, or a witness of that experience. That is why many saints have lived like fools. People either call them mystic visionaries or crazy people. There are many names for enlightened people. In the West they are even known as cynics, and in India they are called avadhootas.

In yogic terminology the divine experience is known as samadhi. Samadhi is a state of subjective awareness, beyond time and space, where the mental body no longer functions. The state we are experiencing now is not samadhi because there is simultaneous awareness of many things. We see, taste, smell, listen, feel, think and know. These mundane experiences are an expression of the interaction between the senses, mind and object.

Experience takes place because of duality, and ego creates this duality. Transcending duality is the main purpose of spiritual life. Duality does not refer to only two, but more than two – multiplicity. It means perception after perception, where the experience, experiencer and experienced are all taking place concurrently. Many people have fantastic experiences which they mistake for divine experiences. For example, being able to hear music clearly without the aid of the ears is an experience, but it is not the ultimate experience. As long as there is experience and experiencer, there is ego, and where there is ego, there cannot be the absolute.

Journey of the ego

Ego is a very subtle principle of life which follows the soul like a shadow follows the body. Throughout the mineral, vegetable and animal kingdoms, the same ego migrates in different names and forms. At the time of death the ego withdraws itself from the manifest state to the unmanifest. It enters into the causal body as dormant potential, and the moment you are born from your mother, the ego manifests. With the additional experiences and impressions which accumulate in the course of one's daily life, the ego becomes more and more fixed.

In yoga, the ego is known as *asmita* or 'I-ness'. It is the normal self-awareness by which you know yourself as an individual. It is the ego which brings you back each morning from your death-like sleep. Because of this principle, dreams are broken and sleep is disturbed. In pratyahara, although the mind is disassociated from the sensory nerve channels, the ego is still present. In dharana, when concentration takes place and you begin to see visions, there is still ego, otherwise there would be no awareness, no knowledge of the experience.

Ego remains throughout the early stages of samadhi. There is a point when samadhi begins and a point where it is full. Between these two points there is a large range of human behaviour, and at one stage different emotions of human life become very keen. Fear comes out, the ego becomes terrible, sexual fantasies become immense. There are references to these experiences in the lives of Buddha and Christ. It is said that Christ was tempted by Satan, and Mara, or the devil, came to Buddha and troubled him the whole night.

From the yogic point of view these references describe the stage after the awakening of enlightenment, when the samskaras and karmas quickly burst out. The last vestige of the animal comes out, and passion, anger, greed, ego, attachment, vanity, pride, jealousy, neurosis, fear of death and many other things may appear. For that reason it is recommended that when the awakening begins, and up to the time it becomes stable, the aspirant should cut himself off and go into seclusion, otherwise it will create chaos. That is also the rule when there is awakening of kundalini; the sadhaka should go into seclusion and minimize worldly activities.

Due to the play of Satan many yoga practitioners develop very big egos. Such people should seclude themselves from social interactions for a while and perfect their samadhi. When one is steadfast in spiritual awareness, then one becomes fully illumined. When samadhi becomes stable, virtues automatically bloom forth and the behaviour is divine. Such a person will never criticize or abuse others. He will have innate humility, and will not only show love, but will have love for all.

When kundalini reaches sahasrara, is that enlightenment?
Enlightenment is experienced due to the awakening of kundalini. Kundalini resides in mooladhara chakra in a dormant potential state. When it wakes up and rises through the chakras, there are various experiences which are not transcendental or final, but at the same time they are indications of the evolving nature of consciousness. It is not

until kundalini reaches sahasrara that the experience of enlightenment takes place.

From mooladhara up to ajna chakra, the awareness is experiencing higher things but it is not free from ego. The ego is a very subtle substance which follows the individual from incarnation to incarnation. Knowledge takes place only because of the ego. The ego carries the total stock of karma from one life to another, and so individuals keep on incarnating and having experiences because the ego is the seed of existence. One cannot transcend ego at lower points of awakening, but when kundalini reaches ajna chakra, transcendence of the individual from ego to cosmic consciousness begins. The experience in ajna chakra is the death of the individual ego. Once the individual consciousness crosses ajna chakra and reaches sahasrara, the ultimate experience in the form of nirvikalpa samadhi dawns.

The first stage of transcendence is savikalpa samadhi. The second is death, and the ultimate and final one is nirvikalpa samadhi. In the state of savikalpa samadhi the ego exists in some form or another. All the chakras below ajna chakra are centres of relativity and pertain to savikalpa samadhi. In ajna chakra, the ego is disintegrated. In nirvikalpa samadhi there is no movement, no existence of the mind, no experience of duality. Consciousness experiences the absolute state. There is no knowledge of time, space and object.

Relative experiences are dependent on one's karma. What is in the psychic body is experienced upon awakening. A mistake is often made when you have some fantastic psychic experience. You may even think that you have achieved the ultimate state, but a vision is not total enlightenment. One can have hundreds and thousands of experiences during meditation practice, but they are all parts of savikalpa samadhi because you are experiencing them.

When there is an experience, there is an experiencer. If there is an experiencer and an experience, then it is a process of duality. If there is duality it cannot be absolute. When you say that you had a very nice experience in meditation practice, it proves there was duality. Furthermore, you are able to remember it now, which means your mind was also present, otherwise how could it know that it had an experience? When you dream at night and remember it in the morning, it is the mind that remembers it. The mind saw the dream, therefore, the dreamer was the mind. All the visions you remember are experiences of the mind, not experiences of the supreme self.

The important difference between savikalpa and nirvikalpa samadhi is that there is no experiencer. Here, nirvikalpa samadhi is the experience. It is a state of being; it is what you are, not what you see or know. You are what you are. You are not seeing the drama, you *are* the drama. The Upanishads say very clearly, "One who has the experience does not know that he has had the experience, and one who has not had the experience says that he has had it."

The final awakening is not the subject matter of the mind. Christ was crucified, and died on the cross. Every individual soul has to be crucified. Everybody who practises kundalini yoga has to die on the cross, has to fix their individual consciousness on ajna chakra and then transcend it. The cross is here in this worldly experience, but that death is a painful experience because one's ego is attached to that life while at the same time one wants spiritual enlightenment. The pull is equal and opposite. Therefore, enlightenment has to come gradually.

Why do so few attain the last stage of samadhi?

The state of samadhi is divided into two stages, savikalpa and nirvikalpa. In savikalpa there is vibration and countervibration, movement. The ultimate stage of samadhi is known as nirvikalpa. In nirvikalpa everything is still, there is no movement. *Nir* means without, *vikalpa* means vibration or process of thinking.

Before coming into savikalpa samadhi, there must be one-pointedness of mind. The mind is only capable of visualizing one object at a time. If I am talking to you, one idea is flashing across your mind and intercepting it. The awareness of one object is not accepted by another idea. The state of meditation is one-pointed awareness, and when awareness of one point, one item, one person or one form becomes totally and absolutely continuous without any other thought intercepting, this ultimately leads to savikalpa samadhi.

In meditation one object is the centre or stuff of your awareness, but in samadhi that does not happen; the stuff falls down and there is only awareness. However, even in that awareness certain motions and movements go on, something very deep is going on. It is extremely difficult for everybody to reach the last stages of samadhi.

Very few have attained nirvikalpa samadhi, the last stage of transcendence. Amongst others, they include Ramakrishna Paramahamsa, Anandamayi Ma, Swami Sivananda, Ramana Maharishi, Swami Nityananda of Gyaneshwari, and Mahavir, the Jain prophet. They did not explain what the state was, but during that state when the bliss is experienced, they exclaimed something wonderful, and some of this has been noted down. Ramana Maharshi usually did not speak to any one. Anandamayi Ma only spoke a few words here and there. Sri Aurobindo gave darshan only once a year. Swami Sivananda also did not speak very much in the last few years. He did not indulge in intellectual discussions. He used to say frankly, "I know nothing – I know only God's name – that's all."

It is said that the nirvikalpa state is as if one is intoxicated from drinking too much wine and does not know one is drunk. It cannot be described exactly. The experiences of samadhi have been written about in *Taittireya Upanishad,* in the *Ashtavakra Gita* and also in the *Avadhoota Gita*. Read those books if you are interested in the subject of samadhi.

Freedom from Vrittis

We can live freely within the essence of nature
Or stay in the confines of individual consciousness.
Our mind is modified by right and wrong knowledge,
Fancy, sleep and memory.
Neither right nor wrong knowledge brings wisdom.
Fancy is not based on reality.
Sleep fails to release awareness.
Memory clings, giving no freedom.

Some of these things are painful,
Some are not painful
But burn them altogether and find peace.

Each day watch the colours of your mind
Until the light shines clearly
And you see straight through
The cravings of the senses.
Thus you will win freedom from experience
Which carves you to its form,
Release from desire which eats you from within.

Becoming whole and still
You can reflect
The world within your own self,
And like the mountain lake, spontaneously reveal
The beauty of snow-capped peaks, the sun and the moon,
Yet, still be filled with
The living waters of bliss.
Though saints are born in samadhi
All can work towards this goal
With faith, strong will, intelligence.

If you want this very much
We will be together soon.
If the urge within you continues to grow
We will unite in samadhi.
By devotion to the Lord
We will be one.

God lives above the causal world
Untouched by actions and consequences.
In Him is the seed of infinite omniscience.
He is the Guru of all gurus,
He is Aum.

Live in the meaning of Aum with each breath,
Thus your awareness throws light
On the inner consciousness.
When this is done,
What problem remains?

28

Yogic Preparation for Samadhi

There are no special practices to materialize the samadhi experience because it is a gradual state to perfection. However, if there are latent problems lurking in the mind, if the personality is tossed hither and thither like a shuttlecock, or if the consciousness is moving this way and that like a pendulum, then the experience of higher consciousness is not possible. You may sit for visualization and meditation, but without preparing the mind, you will only enter into a state of deep autohypnosis.

Raja yoga and hatha yoga
If you want to practise raja yoga, you have to perfect the eight systematic steps of mental purification for samadhi: (i) *yama*, self-control, (ii) *niyama*, self-discipline, (iii) *asana*, a steady and comfortable posture which can be maintained for one, two or three hours without moving the body, (iv) *pranayama*, which does not mean breathing in and breathing out, but the gap, the period of retention, between inhalation and exhalation, (v) *pratyahara*, delinking the brain from the senses, (vi) *dharana*, pictorial conception or visualization, (vii) *dhyana*, total awareness of the object of visualization, and (viii) *samadhi*, a living experience of the object. Each step is a preparation for the next and requires a different type of training in order to be perfected.

Those not in a position to practise the yamas and niyamas should practise the hatha yoga cleansing practices, and not worry about the mind or the preparations. If the aspirant continues with the practices, something will happen in the course of time. For strong people the yamas and niyamas come first, but for those with weak willpower, the hatha yoga shatkarmas come first.

If you want to practise hatha yoga, there are no conditions, except that the nadis, the digestive system, the breathing system, the elements in the body, must be purified by the six cleansing practices, which include neti for the nose, dhauti and nauli for the stomach, basti for the anus, kapalbhati for the brain and trataka for the eyes. The benefits of this purification will be felt when asanas and pranayama are practised. Guru Gorakhnath advised his disciples to begin with the hatha yoga shatkarmas, as due to the changing times, people have forgotten self-control and moderation and find the yamas and niyamas too difficult. When the hatha yoga kriyas have been completed, then the steps of raja yoga: yama, niyama, asana, pranayama, pratyahara, dharana and dhyana will take the spiritual aspirant to samadhi. The scientific way begins with gross matter, the body, and culminates in the finest samadhi.

Yama and niyama
After the cleansing practices, the practice of asana and pranayama lead to awakening of the chakras, mild psychic experiences and the awakening of sushumna. By this time the body has been purified, the mind receives the effect and the yamas and niyamas can be practised. The five *yamas* or self-controls are *satya*, truth, *ahimsa*, non-violence, *brahmacharya*, continence, *asteya*, non-stealing and *aparigraha*, non-accumulation. These practices make the mind calm and peaceful, otherwise it will be disturbed twenty-four hours a day. Stealing someone else's property will lead to fear, which will manifest during concentration and disturb the mind. A spiritual aspirant should have the minimum of possessions, otherwise the mind will be thinking about them all the time. Brahmacharya is very important because a

disturbed sexual life and sexual relationships act upon the nervous system, hormones, emotions and conflicts.

The five niyamas or personal disciplines are *shaucha*, cleanliness, *santosha*, contentment, *swadhyaya*, studying the mind every day, *tapas*, penance or austerity, and *Ishwara pranidhana*, surrender to a higher power. By nature, people are always dissatisfied, with their wife or husband and children, job and money, physical body and mind, and with the political system. A spiritual aspirant must understand that this dissatisfaction will ultimately disturb meditation. Austerities can include sleeping on the floor, eating little, living a simple life, trying to endure heat and cold, fasting from time to time, keeping the mind fixed on one point. Avoid behaving like a monkey or a shuttlecock. Don't be kicked around by your desires. The truth is definitely beyond what you think. Once you can practise the yamas and niyamas, even to a small degree, your concentration will improve.

Other yogas

There are other sadhanas for the different types of people wanting to attain the state of samadhi or excellence. If the mind is like a monkey, does not agree with what you are doing and creates a lot of obstacles, then practise bhakti yoga. Kirtan is one of the best ways of practising bhakti. Karma yoga, bhakti yoga, hatha yoga, raja yoga and the other forms of yoga all have their own preconditions. Some yogas say one should not eat meat, drink or smoke, and should observe brahmacharya. Many people cannot follow this path, so they have to find a path where they can easily proceed and make progress towards the perfection of human life, samadhi.

How is laya yoga related to samadhi?

All yogas should lead to a higher state where the dissolution of lower consciousness takes place. Whether pranayama or kriya yoga or meditation on God or guru is practised, when individual consciousness merges into superconsciousness, it is in a state of dissolution, *laya*. In that case every yoga is laya yoga, although laya yoga is still a yoga by itself.

Superconsciousness or samadhi is the ultimate aim of every individual, the ultimate in the continuing process of evolution. In a superconscious state one does not become unconscious, or lose individual consciousness, but remains completely aware of all that is happening inside and as well as outside. On the path leading to superconsciousness the aspirant has such alertness that the individual consciousness does not become suspended or dissolved. However, in the practices of laya yoga the individual consciousness is made to lose contact with the internal as well as the external.

There are two paths of self-illumination: the path of expansion and the path of total dissolution. The first path includes many spiritual practices and is taught by most yoga teachers. The second path is laya yoga, the direct route, which is taught by very few. St John of the Cross said, "By God, I swear I die every night." What is death and this night? When the mind is withdrawn to the source, the mind and pranas hibernate and the body remains as if dead. That is laya yoga samadhi. The only difference between the final stage of laya yoga and the death experience is that after death one does not come back into the same body, whereas after experiencing the laya state one returns to the same body and mind and resumes life as the same individual, without any change. There will be no spiritual change.

Total dissolution

The word *laya* means dissolution, of something into something. When one enters the state of laya, firstly, the individual consciousness is completely disintegrated. There is no awareness of 'I', no knowledge of time, space, objectivity or individuality. Even the breath stops in some cases. If one continues practising and experiencing this laya state, the whole body undergoes a condition like rigor mortis. This could continue for half an hour, one hour or a whole night, during which the body is devoid of prana.

In the state of laya the mind reverts from the state of manifestation to the state of dissolution. During this period the mind returns to the causal state, to its original state which is called *moola prakriti*. In this state there is no creation, activity, movement or vibration. It is a state of status quo where everything stands still. There is no evolution or devolution, no time and no space. At this point, the mind enters anandamaya kosha, according to Vedanta, or the unconscious body, according to modern psychology. There the consciousness is refreshed and qualified with the unconscious self. The eight siddhis, expounded in the yoga of Patanjali, are also cultivated there, so that when the consciousness returns to the normal state, it is vested with spiritual power.

Controlling the prana
It can be said that laya is the state of disembodied samadhi which is achieved without any interference with the mind. In laya yoga, as in hatha yoga, there is no direct attempt to influence the mind. The mutual relationship between prana and the mind is recognized and the mind is brought under control by first controlling the prana. For those with very restless minds, this system is far easier to progress through than other systems such as raja yoga, which lay more stress on controlling the mind.

The practices of pranayama, mudra and bandha are indispensable in laya yoga. To perfect these three practices one must become an adept in hatha yoga. If seated in siddhasana, padmasana or any other position, the body has to be able to remain totally immobile, because in the practice of pranayama the prana moves throughout the body at a terrific speed. One must assist the movement of prana at that time by maintaining total immobility.

The interior of the body must also be pure. For example, fermented mucus will interfere with pranic activities, which is why the stomach, intestines, nose, mouth and whole body have to be properly cleaned. The physical body is a combination and permutation of the five elements: ether, air, fire, water and earth, and if the elements are not purified by hatha yoga, it will interfere with the activities of prana. After purification, the practices of pranayama are utilized as a basis for controlling the prana and dissolving the mind. These practices are regarded as the most powerful aid to laya samadhi.

Patanjali describes a number of yoga practices, including mantra japa of Aum, trataka, etc, in the first chapter of the Yoga Sutras. Are these sadhanas capable of leading an aspirant directly to samadhi?
Samadhi cannot be attained through these practices, but one can definitely attain the psychic or spiritual power necessary for the finer stages of samadhi. By practising the various sadhanas mentioned by Patanjali, the aspirant acquires mastery over the finest atom as well as infinity. He becomes a master of the finest as well as the largest forces. These practices are necessary for making progress towards the subtle perception of the finer states of samadhi. Just as the scientist arrives at the finer conception of matter and energy, likewise the yogi becomes capable of practising concentration even on subtle thought and also on infinity.

We find people who are unable to grasp the subtle meaning of things because they have no mastery over their mind. The concentration practices Patanjali mentions can make the consciousness very refined, and the mind can be introverted at will. This is observed equally in the case of solving problems of mathematics or science or meditation. With training, the mind can be made to concentrate properly. In yoga the first psychic power is achieving this mastery, then the mind can be fixed on any object, gross or subtle.

There is an interesting example. When Swami Vivekananda was in the USA, he used to borrow several books from a library every day and return them the next day. The librarian, wondering if so many books could be read in a single day, wanted to test the swami, but to his astonishment he noticed that the swami remembered every word and line he had read. This is how a yogi has control over the finest and largest.

A person can go into samadhi only when he is able to perceive even the ideas and thoughts. This is because in the finer states of samadhi one has to pick up the dynamic consciousness and hold on to it. There are states of samadhi wherein the aspirant has nothing but the awareness of the effort of control that he has been making. That effort has to be brought into his consciousness as an idea and then it has to be thrown out. It is very difficult to understand this.

Patanjali also says that faith (shraddha), strong will (veerya), memory (smriti) and intelligence (prajna) will lead to samadhi. How is this possible?

There are two types of yogis, *videha* and *prakritilaya*, those who are disembodied and those who are merged in prakriti, who are able to attain samadhi from birth and do not have to practise preliminary stages like dharana, dhyana or vitarka, vichara, etc., but such yogis are rare. The vast multitude of aspirants have to go through regular practice of different yogic techniques to enable the development of qualities essential for making the perception more subtle. According to the intensity of application and urge, it is possible that through the faith, courage, memory and a higher form of intelligence, the student can attain samadhi sooner or later.

Shraddha means 'that which holds the truth', rather than faith. It arises from true experience, and is different from mere belief, which is not an outcome of realizing the truth. Shraddha never fails and it is the first essential principle required by a student of yoga. Shraddha can be had only after having a glimpse of the highest truth, just as Swami Vivekananda and Swami Yogananda had a glimpse of the truth when they came in contact with their gurus. It is, however, not the whole truth, but only a glimpse; it is just the beginning of the path of yoga. The guru induces in the disciple an experience of truth or samadhi through his own power and thus shraddha arises.

The next essential quality is *veerya*, energy, physical as well as mental. In the context of samadhi, veerya means courage through which the many impediments on the path of yoga can be overcome. It involves strong will and determination, one must continue on the path at any cost. The mind is to be properly controlled and full of courage.

The third factor is memory. *Smriti* here actually means *dhyana*, meditation, in which the aspirant remembers the symbol. Through smriti the realization of consciousness can be brought into the conscious field.

Prajna is intelligence. *Samadhi prajna* is higher knowledge attained through samadhi. It may be described as a favourable angle of vision. It presupposes spiritual realization. It is essential for attaining asamprajnata samadhi. According to yoga, intelligence is of two types: worldly intelligence, which is required to be successful in daily life, and a higher type of consciousness which develops as a result of samprajnata samadhi. This kind of intelligence is not present in most of us, but it can be developed through regular practice. Once it is developed, the aspirant can make tremendous progress in a very short time.

It may be said that Swami Vivekananda had this faculty in him and due to it could make very swift spiritual progress, in spite of various conflicting ideas in his mind regarding religion, God, human destiny, etc. Samadhi prajna is the spiritual attitude or spiritual vision that one develops by constant satsang and by constant self-purification.

However, we find many people who have practised nothing reaching the state of samadhi very easily. This is because at the time of birth they received all the traces of their past karma in the form of samadhi prajna. Thus there are examples of persons going beyond the barriers of lower consciousness at a very young age; for example, the great saint Jnaneshwar and, similarly, Ramana Maharshi of Arunachala, who attained samadhi when in his teens.

29

Realization to Overcome Suffering

The subject of God-realization can never be communicated successfully until it has been personally experienced. This supreme state can solve some of the burning problems being encountered at both individual and social levels. The restlessness, confusion and tensions operating at physical, mental and emotional levels are only symptoms, only effects. To uproot sorrow and suffering we have to go to the root cause, which is located in the deeper layers of consciousness. There is a definite method of arriving at the cause and becoming acquainted with its contents. We know that the root cause of our problems, at any level, is *avidya*, ignorance. The great spiritual personalities who mastered the technique of penetrating into the deepest layers of the mind also confirm that ignorance is the main cause of our maladies.

Discover the permanent source of light

The rishis, munis and great seers experimented throughout their lives in an unceasing effort to discover and to popularize the method by which the endless suffering of humankind may be destroyed. But somehow or other from time to time their dictates have been disobeyed and often misunderstood. Even the latest scientific discoveries, technological advancements and well-organized social, political and economic institutions have failed to find a solution for mental and spiritual suffering.

With the progress of civilization, suffering is multiplying. The further we go into the realm of matter, the more disquiet we face. Tranquillizers are used by large sections of society, suicide and juvenile delinquency are rising rapidly. We cannot understand or face the facts. When we see wrinkles on our face, we feel perturbed. When the truth is spoken, we cannot stand it. We do not possess sufficient mental power or strength. We may have expanded our intellectual knowledge and extended it to cover the invisible realms, yet we are totally ignorant of ourselves. However, the time has come to make an effort in that direction, and when we learn the method of going within, then the total annihilation of suffering may even become within easy reach.

You may have been studying Vedanta and the various categories such as reality, homogeneous consciousness, maya, avidya, illusion, and so-called appearances, but you must know the method to gain first-hand knowledge of them. How can homogeneous consciousness be realized? Is it enough to merely have intellectual comprehension of the truth as recorded in the Upanishads? Broadly speaking, there are two forms of acquiring knowledge. One is indirect in which the senses, mind and intellect act as mediums. The other is direct and immediate, it is transcendental in character. Here, knowledge of the object is acquired intuitively, directly through one's innermost being; the mind is dispensed with.

For a long time scholars have been following the path of Vedanta which consists of listening and contemplating, but their path has been confined to the intellectual level only. Their convictions regarding identity with the supreme never penetrated beyond the intellect and so they were victimized by personal suffering.

In spite of the bold assertions we make about the divinity of the soul, when we face the world with all its difficulties, which are an integral part of life, we cannot stand them. The light is there, but it is flickering. Intellectual knowledge gives only momentary peace and calmness. We have to discover the permanent source of light so we can understand the difficulties we face in society, in the family, in economic and political life, and are able to stand with dignity, courage, knowledge and complete understanding.

Employ yogic techniques

Yoga is a practical method where there is not much to be learned but a lot to be followed. Yoga is not to be practised for hours and hours, as even a little practice of yoga brings relief. People think the practice of asanas and pranayama alone constitutes yoga, and while they are very beneficial for the body, it is not the whole of yoga. Some people practise yoga to develop their psychic faculties, which is also a part of the science of yoga, but we are trying to understand the problem of human suffering.

It has to be understood that unless one realizes one's own self, not the lower self but the supreme self, the atman, Brahman, unless one is able to communicate with that supreme self in the depth of meditation by withdrawing oneself temporarily from all forms of the outer dimension and external experiences, it is not possible to go beyond suffering. It is here that yoga lifts you from the conscious, subconscious and unconscious and lands you into the realm of super-consciousness. You may call it samadhi or God-realization or nirvana or whatever you like, but there is an individual, personal state of awareness which is highly sensitive.

Intensify awareness

Animals move on the instinctive plane, unaware of what they are doing. Human beings have the gift of awareness, yet generally live on an instinctive plane. We must leave the instinctive plane and learn to live on the plane of awareness. This awareness, which manifests the moment we are born, is called *jnanam*. It is not merely knowledge but awareness. We are aware of what we are doing, what we are thinking and what we did and will do. We are aware that we are alive, 'I am and I am aware that I am'. This awareness which has just evolved in the human being should be intensified and its duration increased. Whatever we do should be done with complete awareness. Yoga is a method of developing this type of awareness, so much so that it is completely separated from body awareness.

At present I am aware that I am giving a discourse on yoga. I am aware that this awareness is mixed with body awareness, with mind awareness and with sense awareness. When I know that 'I am', I am also aware that I have a body, so this awareness is not purified. It is not non-sensual awareness, but there is no doubt it is awareness. This awareness should be separated step by step, stage by stage, so much so that it remains intact and keeps on expanding. But, at the same time, all the other elements, physical, sensual, mental and psychic, must be removed from its body.

Self-purification
From this perspective yoga is a process of purification. It is an act of separation in which we separate the non-self elements from the atman. This awareness is atman, it is pure, undifferentiated, always homogeneous, always eternal, always unchanging, in everyone.

Focus on yourself. Think, "I am aware that I am listening to a discourse." This fraction of awareness, which is not complete in itself, which is not pure but tainted and mixed up with mental awareness, is to be separated from other forms of awareness and from other confusions. How? Through the practice of yoga, through *viveka*, discrimination, through *yama* and *niyama*, self-controls and personal disciplines, through *pratyahara*, the process of withdrawal, or by *dharana*, concentration, or through *dhyana*, meditation.

Do nothing, except keep on eliminating all those foreign elements which have through habit become part and parcel of your pure awareness and which completely cloud the real structure of this awareness. This can be done through bhakti yoga, raja yoga, karma yoga, jnana yoga, etc., through yogic methods and techniques like mantra japa, concentration on a symbol, devotion, prayers, serving humanity with absolute unselfishness, serving the guru or following the path of knowledge. You may choose any path according to your temperament. All yogic techniques are used to free the atman from lower turmoil.

Raja yoga is the method of meditation through which you go deeper and deeper, and become free from physical awareness, transcend all sense experiences and finally merge with your own highest self. But this is not as easy as people think. Unless the personality is purified and freed of its burdens and tensions, it is not possible to go into deep meditation. Raja yoga is not easy, but it is certainly a method to take one to the ultimate of human evolution.

Preparation for raja yoga

Karma yoga purifies the heart, which leads to mental peace. *Bhakti yoga*, the yoga of devotion, brings about a spontaneous state of concentration, which is otherwise very difficult for the lay practitioner to acquire. When that concentration has been brought about and dissipations have been overcome, then we move more easily into raja yoga. When we sit for meditation, we find it difficult because the spinal cord does not remain erect. The lotus posture is very difficult to maintain so we want to practise meditation sitting in a chair, which obstructs the flow of magnetic currents otherwise created by yogic postures. The energy flow also becomes less intense in the spinal area, which in turn shifts the centres of gravity.

The inevitable obstructions are to be removed through the practices of hatha yoga, asanas and pranayama. Now, when you sit down for meditation practice, inertia or lethargy, *tamoguna*, overpowers you. The moment you arrive at the point of concentration, unification of thoughts, either you land in the realm of visions or you sleep. That state like sleep is often mistaken for samadhi.

If you are asked to hold a form, image or symbol in the mind, you may begin to disagree due to your religious beliefs. But this should not interfere with the yoga practice because during meditation, the light within will be your proper guide and carry your consciousness further and further. It is an indicator of whether you have slipped into *tamas*, inertia, or if you are proceeding in the right direction in raja yoga, in this yoga of meditation, in this yoga of finding the source of the atma, your deepest and highest and eternal being.

Avoid siddhis
For those who want to practise yoga for the purpose of God-realization, it is necessary to shake off the temptations of psychic powers, *siddhis*, because in the end they will only lead one back into suffering, which is what happens to most yoga aspirants. The majority of people take up yoga with the sole view of achieving psychic powers to become mediums, and exercise telepathy and so on. These powers are referred to in detail in the *Yoga Sutras* of Patanjali. Patanjali considers psychic powers as hindrances on the path to higher realization because they make the mind restless, and have to be shaken off.

Yoga is the path of absolute hypnotism, but do not misunderstand me here. The practices of hypnotism and yoga follow the same path until they branch off at the point of dharana; then yoga branches off into the path of expansion of consciousness. Whereas an aspirant of hypnotism undergoes a process whereby his consciousness diminishes until it is completely overtaken by a state of hypnotism, the aspirant of yoga widens his frontiers of consciousness. His consciousness assumes the form of a symbol, a deity, ishta devata, the form of a mantra, the form of a sound, or any concrete form. But, of course it is only his consciousness. It keeps on expanding and this act of expansion is spontaneous.

Yoga in its highest form
Theoretically, we cannot expand our consciousness because it is eternal and infinite. Expansion of consciousness is the unveiling of avidya which was covering the consciousness. When the clouds disperse, the sun begins to shine. It does not mean the sun has been affected, but that the clouds have been removed from in front of ever-shining sun. In

exactly the same way, our consciousness, atman, universal self or Brahman is forever infinite. When the temporary clouds of avidya disappear, the infiniteness of atman manifests again.

Self-realization is only an act of eliminating the layers of ignorance. So one proceeds through the path of dharana. It is a practice of retaining a form of consciousness within and not allowing that form of consciousness to disappear from the mind, so much so that in the act of holding the consciousness, all other dissimilar forms drop away and the original form always remains. It shines in all its infinite glory and infinite beauty, and samadhi dawns. This is possible through employing yogic techniques.

Once that state has been reached through the systematic methods and practices of integral yoga, then the layers of avidya are completely eliminated. You can live as a family man, a technician, an industrialist, or as anything you choose. You may not possess the power to perform miracles, you may not be a healer, but you will be the happiest person on earth. At the same time, your personality, presence, thought currents and blessings will enable others to overcome suffering and achieve everlasting happiness. It is a state of nectar, a state of immortality, and therefore God-realization is yoga in its highest form.

God-realization is the prime purpose of life. We are born to realize God and until that becomes our aim, suffering will not end and society will not progress, whether we introduce the greatest prosperity or the most developed political order.

30

Karma Yoga and Samadhi

The *Yoga Vasishtha* emphasizes that this life and body should not be taken as it seems. The body is a manifestation of life, life is not due to the body. There is another part of life which is separate from this body. All these realms of life can be manifest simultaneously. Most people experience only one realm. We feel the body only, we cannot know the origin of our thoughts; we are just like a machine. What is thought? Is it some electrical power, or sensation, or a psychological process? Where and how does it originate? Does it depend upon the body or does it exist without the body?

When thought is replaced by inner wisdom, there is the experience of 'I am'. We can conclude from this that man is looking at himself from a very limited angle, as a physical body with a mind, or even a soul, and there is confusion. Yet we know that when the veil of confusion is removed, immortal life can be experienced. When the realms of consciousness are extinguished, turiya illumines and samadhi dawns.

Beyond the unconscious

You may be able to sit for meditation and become completely unconscious and think you have attained samadhi, but what is this unconsciousness? Here something needs to be eliminated. It is true that you have become unconscious to the outside world, but what about the inner awareness? Here something still remains to be achieved. This state of unconsciousness is an obstruction, due to which nothing is visible deep within and we are only able to experience this body with its pains, attachment, pleasure, birth and death. This obstruction is also termed *avidya*, ignorance. Only when it is removed can man's outlook expand. Outlook does not mean to see with the eyes; it is not an external view but a divine experience. How can that screen, that veil, that obstruction be removed?

Yogis have found that according to the aspirant's point of evolution, the path of karma yoga becomes important, because karma is the cause of ignorance and illusions. When an aspirant on the spiritual path practises meditation and kundalini yoga, his progress becomes bogged down at a certain point because the karmas are not exhausted. We must realize that every action, thought and place is an experience which produces karma. A satsang or a lecture on the *Bhagavad Gita* is an experience. Even an ordinary experience can become very consequential in later life.

There are many types of karma. Charity is a karma and plundering someone's property is another. Even if one does not do these things, still one is making karma. In the *Bhagavad Gita*, it is said that there is not one moment where one is free of karma. Therefore, in spiritual life karma yoga is not merely a means to pass the time or to serve society, but a means of liberation from karma. Only in samadhi can karma be completely done away with.

According to Manu, only karma yoga roots out the karmas. It is the accumulated karma which shapes our destiny, which causes our pleasure and pain, and this very destiny can lead us to either rise or fall. Do we know how to become free of the self-created boundaries that encircle our lives? The saints and sages advised a change in the direction of the karmas, a change in the number of actions done as karma. Changing the direction of karma will lead to liberation and bliss.

Karma and spiritual life

Respect for karma and the relationship of karma with spiritual life should be understood if the development of spiritual life to the ultimate state of samadhi is to be possible. Spiritual life does not mean sitting in padmasana all day and meditating. *Karma yoga* is a part of spiritual life. It means any karma done without the involvement of ego, with total awareness and total interest, but without any selfish motive, for the sake of others. Karma executed without attachment to the results is karma yoga and becomes a part of spiritual life. Accept karma yoga as a sadhana and combine bhakti yoga and jnana yoga with it. Thus your spiritual life will rise very high and you will be able to transcend the limitations of this present life to a greater extent.

Success in human life depends on the attainment of self-knowledge. Self-knowledge, knowledge of the absolute, is a different level of experience. It is not non-existence or a state of void, but absolute fulfilment. This is the whole purpose of the human incarnation, life after life. There is a desire to achieve that experience, yet that state of *mukti*, liberation, is very difficult to attain. It is time consuming and labour consuming, and without the grace of guru and God, it cannot be realized. It is not true to think that mukti can only be attained by awakening kundalini or by attaining samadhi. Although samadhi does destroy karma, it cannnot be obtained without the elimination or obliteration of karma, which is an effect of karma yoga.

Karma yoga

Karma yoga is the foundation of spiritual practices. It is very difficult to practise. Karma yoga is not charitable work or honorary work. The art of karma yoga can be acquired by living and working in an ashram, and then applying the same philosophy and art in one's daily life at home. Everyone can practise karma yoga in their own family. Are you able to separate the karma from its results? Are you able to separate the result and your ego? Are you able to understand what attachment is? If it is possible, then you have practised karma yoga. When you are attached to the fruits and the results of life, it is karma, but when you have not identified with or attached yourself to the fruits of karma, it is karma yoga.

If aspirants living in the ashram only meditate and do not practise karma yoga, then as soon as they begin to achieve higher experiences all the samskaras will come out, because they have not been cleared away from time to time during the process of daily life. When we practise karma yoga in the ashram every day, we may feel anger, hatred or jealousy, but every now and again these are cleared away. We go on analyzing our behaviour and purifying the mind in this way, so by the time the state of awakening is arrived at, most of the negative tendencies have already been cleared away, and then the awakening will not cause any adverse effects. All the great swamis who did not involve themselves in karma yoga faced this problem, but ordinary swamis who involved themselves in karma yoga did not.

The awakening of kundalini gives siddhis, but it does not eliminate karma. One who has attained that state of siddhi has to suffer karma, and will have to face karma either in this life or in another life, because certain samskaras have to be undergone. There is no way out. As long as one has a human body there are certain karmas and samskaras which cannot be wiped out. Birth is one karma, death is another karma. These are the karmas of the body and incarnation that have to be undergone.

The fire of samadhi

However, there are other forms of karma which can be managed very well. Many ways of wiping out the samskaras have been suggested. One of the most important methods for becoming free from samskaras is to practise higher sadhana, under guidance, as these practices prise out the seeds of karma. During the process of practising higher sadhana leading to samadhi, these samskaras come up in the conscious mind and then they can be analyzed, rationalized and completely destroyed. Many karmas that come up during sadhana automatically die. Many of the samskaras in us are very ordinary ones, and also create problems, but once they come up on the mental plane they are vacated.

There are other types of samskaras called illusory samskaras which are created due to the quality of the mind and emotions. Love and hatred, separation, death and destruction all cause very strong samskaras. If the quality and perception of the mind could have been changed, then the agonies would have been less, but as this did not happen, a samskara developed. During the practices leading to samadhi the aspirant realizes this. One realizes detachment, one realizes the falsity of relationships and one realizes disidentification. During the stages of practising samadhi, many of one's past experiences are realized as foolishness. Many of these strong samskaras die immediately. In this way many, many samskaras can be eliminated during higher sadhana.

To have that experience, the whole process of karma has to be worked out through karma yoga. What is the use of suppressing the desires as long as the volcano of karma is inside you? No amount of suppression will manage it. A karma yogi will have to decide the purpose and objective of work, karma. Do we work for money, for name and fame, for attachment and to fulfil passions, or in order to work out our karma of the past? Or are we working to work out our primordial, archetypal and primitive karma?

Karma affects the mind and emotions and creates further karma because in reality we do not own the result of the karma. We are only the doer, *karta*, not the enjoyer, *bhokta*, but when we are doing karma, we are both a doer and an enjoyer. However, a karma yogi ceases to be an enjoyer and just remains a doer. Finally, in jnana yoga, one ceases to be a doer also. Then one realizes that one is not the doer, not the enjoyer, but a *drashta*, a seer, a spectator. Side by side, other yogas such as hatha yoga, mantra yoga, bhakti yoga, etc. should be practised. Only then can liberation or mukti or samadhi be attained.

Mental balance through karma yoga

When we practise karma yoga, when we are expressing our body and mind, and not creating tension and fighting with our conflicts, we grow side by side with the passions, desires and instincts, but at the same time internal purification is taking place, the result of which is mental balance. Mental balance is not the psychological process in which externally we are trying to maintain balance of mind, because we think it is necessary to have good health, good relationships, a good home and a good society, although inside everything is totally imbalanced and in turmoil. Real mental balance is the result of the mental purification that takes place through a constant, relentless and prolonged process of elimination of karma.

The mind cannot be cleaned without undergoing a process of purging. Nature has created many ways of purging. We think many of them are unethical and immoral, but passions, desires, anger, frustration, disappointment, greed, jealousy and fear are all outlets created by nature for human beings to practise mental shankhaprakshalana. They are nature's way of cleaning the mind.

In bhakti yoga there is no such provision for cleaning the mind. In bhakti yoga, God, His glory, His creation is fine, His devotees are fine, the sanctum sanctorum is fine, the flowers and the priest are fine. Everything is so nice there. In raja yoga everything is wonderful and clean: truth, non-violence, celibacy, contentment, non-greed, non-aggrandizement, physical and mental purity. We understand how good these systems are, but we are not facing life or ourselves there.

However, in karma yoga everything has to be faced. When one is concerned with the affairs of life, when the body and emotions are in demand, and when one is relating to every Tom, Dick and Harry, at that time, when the mind is gossiping, a clear classification of the sattwic, rajasic and tamasic nature of individuals can be made. Observe everybody's behaviour impartially without judgement, and just see on which level your mind is floating. Sometimes you are full of remorse and guilt. Sometimes you are arrogant and sometimes you are as idiotic as a pig. Sometimes you are as angry as a demon and sometimes you are a gentleman. Sometimes you are a saint. The process of the threefold universal nature of man can only be realized in karma yoga. If you do not know yourself in external life, how can you purify yourself and undertake higher sadhana?

Gradually, through karma yoga the mind obtains absolute tranquillity within and without. One is at peace with oneself and with everybody else. At this time, when one sits for meditation with the eyes closed or open, the mind begins to drop away without any effort and one does not what is happening.

Just as sleep comes to a person who is tired after the day's work, in the same way, one who has practised karma yoga without the sense of ego, with total detachment and dedication, who has yoked the body, mind, emotions, passions and violence, the demonical and animal nature, completely to work, experiences spontaneous samadhi. This is *sahaja samadhi*, which can be had in this very life if one understands the role of karma yoga.

31

Bhakti Yoga and Samadhi

Those who follow the path of bhakti yoga exclusively have an experience called trance. Trance is a kind of samadhi in which merging of the individual mind takes place through growing emotion and devotion. In raja yoga one is controlling the patterns of the mind, controlling every *vritti* or thought formation, and by stopping the manifestations of the mind one comes to a state of *shoonya* or void. In raja yoga the process is suppression, whereas in bhakti yoga there is no suppression. One awakens the emotions, ecstatic feelings or *bhava*. Just as passion is emotion directed towards empirical things, devotion is the same emotion directed towards divinity. This devotion and emotion has to be expressed and when it is awakened, one enters into a state of trance, called *bhava samadhi*, by which one awakens the emotion through devotion.

From time to time, many great souls have descended to demonstrate how to practise bhakti. The bhakta Mirabai immersed her total mind in God. She could sing the name of God and enter into samadhi or trance. When she sang God's name in kirtan and bhajan, she would forget herself completely. When the mind is impure and tainted by passions, when the mind is full of petty and insignificant worries, when even the smallest event becomes great to you, when you are not able to concentrate your mind and when your faith faces a crisis every time, then at that time, if you sing the name of

God repeatedly, ten to thirty times or more, you enter into a state called bhava samadhi.

Bhava samadhi is a little different from raja yoga samadhi. In raja yoga samadhi there is external and internal mobility. In bhava samadhi, the inner self is quiet, but externally the emotions are charged with high-powered energy. It is as if one is suffering from separation from the beloved. The relationship between the individual soul and the universal soul is the same as between husband and wife. That is also the concept voiced by Christ in the Bible.

I am the wife, God is the husband, and I want to be one with Him. I suffer from separation and we are trying to unite with each other. But as long as there is individuality, one cannot merge in God. In order to shake off the individuality, the cloaks caused by ignorance will have to be removed. If you feel that you are a man or a woman, or an intellectual, engineer or doctor, or a Muslim, Hindu or Christian, when you stand before God, these are complexes.

Unless both husband and wife forget what they are, they cannot become one. That is exactly what happens in bhakti yoga. The *bhakta*, the devotee, represents individual consciousness, God represents spiritual consciousness, and the ultimate purpose of the bhakta is to merge in God. Just as all the rivers are flowing only to unite and merge in the ocean, in the same way, all devotees must try to move towards God and merge in Him. That is samadhi. Mirabai had such devotion.

Power of music and dance
In India, there lived a great bhakta named Chaitanya, who became God-intoxicated. He would wander through the streets singing and at times hundreds and thousands of people followed him with drums and other instruments. He became so God-intoxicated that he forgot who he was. At one stage he thought he was Radha, searching for Sri Krishna. This kind of metamorphosis can take place through music. Kirtan is singing and becoming one with the melody so much so

that you forget your own self and the music lives while you die.

Kirtan is the most important practice of bhakti yoga. We call music sankirtan yoga, or *nada yoga*, the yoga of sound. If you can give yourself totally to music, not just enjoy it through the senses, then the senses can be transcended. Sometimes music just gives comfort to the senses, and then it becomes a source of sensual pleasure. The mind must transcend its relationship with the senses. With the ears plugged you should be able to receive the vibrations of music through your skin, and your soul must dance with it. Music is not only the way to *shanti* or relaxation, it is a way to samadhi. Through chanting God's name for more than an hour, with rapt devotion, in the same rhythm, slowly and steadily, and then climaxing very slowly, many people go into a trance, into bhava samadhi.

Music and kirtan are so powerful that they can free the purusha from prakriti, free the individual soul from the bondage of maya. Music has so much inherent power that it can free you of your ego. It does the most important groundwork of taking your self away from you. Even in the western world, where people generally do not have spiritual feelings, where boys and girls sing just for pleasure and entertainment, they also lose self-awareness. They become so emotional and crazy about the music that they forget their self-identity.

Swami Sivananda used to say, "God's name is the quickest, safest, cheapest, surest and best way to reach God." He said 'safest'. Kundalini yoga is not the safest. Tantra is not the safest. No other way is sure except kirtan. Chanting God's name with devotion is the highway to reach God. Through kirtan the highest pinnacle of spiritual experience can be reached. The ego is totally eliminated. One can have the vision of the divine, the vision of one's highest self, the vision of God, the vision of Christ, the vision of Mary, the vision of Krishna, the vision of Rama. It is possible. This is the power of bhakti yoga.

When the atma reveals itself

Bhakti is the simplest way to manifest the *nirakara* or formless soul. This soul, the great power dormant in us, manifests through sattwic, rajasic and tamasic forms. Sattwic materialization gives peace, bliss and moksha. Rajasic and tamasic materializations react upon a sadhaka and cause misery, pain and sometimes even death.

When we perfect meditation on Rama's picture, we can see him before us as real as anything. The formless becomes *sakara*, with form. The consciousness is separated from matter or prakriti. The mind does not exist at this moment. When we concentrate on him, we actually concentrate upon our atma which reveals itself before us in our cherished form. It is our atma which comes to us from beyond the seven gates. It is the swan of the temple which we see in the medium of the form we meditate upon.

When you are in samadhi, the seven gates are opened, the veils are rent asunder. That is the reason why meditation is so important. When the mind merges and the meditation is keen and progressive, the soul will begin to express itself. The light is seen clearly. The same soul that makes your body and mind work comes before you as in a form.

Give the heart to the self

The heart which God has given you should be given to the ideal. When it is given to desires, passions and sense pleasures, it causes restlessness and dissipation. But when the same heart is given to a great ideal, union with the self in samadhi or self-realization, it experiences peace, attains power, perceives light and gains wisdom. By heart, I do not mean the biological or psychological stuff, which has a tendency to love and hate, and is always in need of someone upon which it can rest. When the heart is given to such associations, then longing and clinging, frustration and insanity, result, but when the heart is utilized for sadhana, it becomes a link between divine and human experiences.

The heart is to be absorbed in the thought of one's self; it is there that it should abide. Love, which is an expression of the heart, should be made to flow towards one who can consume it without becoming agitated, like an ocean which consumes all the rivers and yet remains undisturbed. If any mental activity such as love or hatred disturbs the heart or excites more longings, then the heart is shallow and narrow and miserly, for it cannot consume either love or hatred. One who has consumed them remains undisturbed and unruffled.

Since divine vision illumines one's inner life, and since the self abides in the inner altar, it is necessary to render the inner state smooth, clear, balanced and happy. So the heart is to be united, love is to be consumed, and the personality must become free from psychological taints and strains with the help of regular and proper understanding, without any prejudice or reservations.

The senses are turbulent. It is no use curbing them because they revive like the ten heads of Ravana, and mislead the mind. God-given understanding alone can drive away the senses and control them with the help of the mind. The emotions make the senses unruly. Sensitivity causes the mind to make inaccurate judgements. Brooding destroys hard-earned self-confidence. Hatred pollutes the inner temple. Passions of all kinds persuade the jiva to undertake indiscriminate actions.

Buddhi, or higher intelligence, will tell you that inner relationships with sensual objects disturb the tempo of meditation and cause delays in the attainment of higher realization. The sadhaka should give the heart entirely to one ideal. Only then will the strains of daily life not interfere in meditation. All other longings except the desire to attain divine realization are born of lack of wisdom and lead to mental distortion. Only the desire to see Him face to face in His divine essence is helpful to a sadhaka. Blessed is the person who has turned his gaze, withdrawn the senses, dedicated his heart and started the quest for samadhi.

The cosmic dance within

In the spiritual realm *maha rasa* is the process of yoga where everything dissolves into one purusha, into one supreme self, one great spirit. The gopis lose themselves and become one with the form of Sri Krishna. When he played his flute, the gopis heard and they thought he was calling them. They went running after him in the middle of the night. Sri Krishna asked why they had come and he tried to discourage them. He told them over and over again to go home, but they were determined. They said, "No, you are our sole refuge. You are our centre and you are the goal of life."

Ultimately, they said, "Lord, you told us to renounce everything and take shelter in you. Why then are you telling us to go home?" Sri Krishna had no answer. Gradually, he submits to the demands of the gopis and ultimately the rasalila takes place. Prakriti will move into conjunction with purusha and then there will be creation. There will be that spiritual experience which yoga calls nirvikalpa samadhi or *Bhagavata darshan*, the vision of God, or whatever you want to call it.

God is the centre of life. Bhakti and love are the main duty of every human being. Only man can think of God, investigate God and dedicate his whole life to God. An animal or bird cannot do it. If that is the truth and the law of nature, then divine bhakti is the prime duty of everyone. Bhakti is the first duty, family is the next duty. This is what the gopis told Sri Krishna. He tried to discourage them by saying, "Go home and look after your children and your husbands." But they said, "No, those are secondary duties!" Vedic dharma also says the same thing. Even Christianity and Islam say the same thing. God is first, everything else comes second, if at all it is necessary.

So to enter into the depths of your consciousness, you definitely have to transcend the duality of nature with which you have constantly intertwined your life. The real cosmic dance is when you are within yourself.

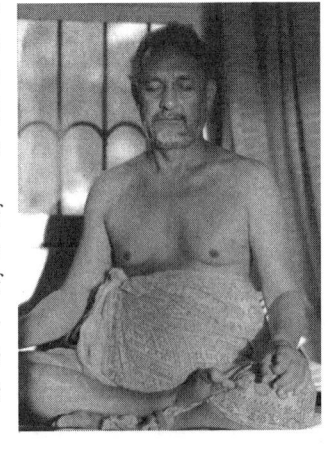

32

Samadhi – Culmination of Yogic Effort

There are many wrong notions about samadhi. According to some, samadhi is a state in which one's body becomes like stone, the pulse rate slows down and the metabolic process stops. No doubt, suspended animation is a great science mastered and perfected by some yogis but it is not samadhi. Trance, ecstasy, or suspension of consciousness is not samadhi. In the state of suspended animation, or *jada samadhi*, there is no awareness or knowledge, and the stock of subconscious or subliminal impressions remains unexhausted and dormant.

If samadhi merely meant a stage of steady posture and total unconsciousness, very few spiritual seekers would be successful in attaining it. A person who has been able to make the conscious and subconscious forces dormant deserves to be commended, but that has nothing to do with yoga and the ordinary person. If the state does not exhaust muscular, emotional and other tensions, if it does not bestow peace, power and enlightenment, if it does not remove the complexes, conflicts, schizophrenia and other such psychological disorders, it is certainly not samadhi.

What then is samadhi? Can everyone achieve samadhi? Is samadhi total awareness or complete forgetfulness? In samadhi are we conscious or unconscious? Is samadhi total suspension, unconsciousness, inertia, or is it absolute consciousness or total awareness? The mind is a bundle of mental patterns of awareness. When every pattern of awareness has been rejected and annihilated, what remains is the ultimate form of consciousness and it is here that peace is experienced within.

Original source of tension
Modern man feels tension in day-to-day life. The busy mechanical life of cities, the congestion due to industrial development, family problems, all lead to increased tension. Tension is that state where two forces pull in opposite directions, when we want to do something, but some force within dissuades us from doing so. This is tension or conflict between the ego and superego, as psychoanalysts would describe it.

There are divine as well as evil elements in us. The war between the dark and the divine forces in us is the real tension. A psychologist will make you relax by certain methods, but there is still an inexhaustible stock of dormant subliminal and unsubliminal tendencies within, called *anadi vasanas*, which the psychologist cannot help you to exhaust. It is here that yoga comes to the rescue.

If you wish to remove your tensions, the first step is to relax yourself. Find out the ultimate and original cause of tension. That tension is the constant struggle between the ego and superconscious, the dark and the divine forces in us, between the devil and God. The practices of yoga remove the mental, muscular and emotional tensions and a stage dawns where there is an end to this eternal fight within. This is the supreme stage of sublime equanimity. Suspended animation has nothing to do with this. Yoga helps to make life powerful, to awaken the dormant genius within, to gain insight and to activate the 'third eye', the centre of intuition. This is the stage of superconsciousness.

Balance of mind
If we close our eyes, we will feel blankness and darkness within, but in the yogic state of samadhi we are aware both internally and externally. However, this is not the highest

samadhi. The greatest samadhi is balance of mind, not just balance of consciousness, not intellectual balance, but total balance. Sometimes when you feel free of tension, the tension has actually passed on from the conscious level to the subconscious or the unconscious.

The greatest tension one feels when one advances in the stage of meditation is in the innermost body. The individual soul is in a wilderness. The ten senses have taken away the peace of the individual soul. The individual soul comes into being out of intelligence, restlessness and inertia, *sattwa*, *rajas* and *tamas*. Due to inertia the individual wanders in worldliness and runs after a shadow, greed, etc., and gives up the four factors necessary for peace: satsang, introspection, spiritual practice and inner silence.

This is the point where real tension starts. First you found pleasure in the world, and developed cravings and desires. The fight is now with sloth, lethargy and indolence. You also have to fight with the unseen forces of the mind, the conflicts in your consciousness. Devotion, spiritual and vital strength, constant vigilance and mindfulness are essential to progress. Spiritual sadhana must be continuous, constant and regular. But sometimes, even vigilance and mindfulness fail. Eclipsed by lethargy, vigilance is relaxed because the senses are very powerful.

The individual has to take to spiritual practice in earnest without any postponement. If you postpone spiritual sadhana, it will never come in your life. The spiritual personality will fade into oblivion. Therefore, always remain awake. Passion, anger and greed are the great thieves hidden in us which loot our divine treasures.

How can these inner tensions be removed? So long as the mind is not introverted and the senses controlled, tensions cannot be removed. However, there is no use curbing the senses and suppressing the mind and sensual desires. The senses and mind are indestructible. Without craving, there can be no mental activity. Craving or desire is the root cause of the war between the divine and the devil.

If you want spiritual peace, sublime equanimity, or the ultimate eternal peace, you will have to burn or annihilate attachment and perfect the art of detachment. There should be no liking for pleasant things and no dislike of unpleasant things. Physical, mental or intellectual detachment will not help much. Spiritual detachment is the real thing.

Culmination of yoga
When the stock of emotions and desires are exhausted, there comes a state of perfect balance and peace. Samadhi is the state of absolute sense, intelligence and vigilance. In samadhi you will recognize and know everything just as you know people in the waking state. You will maintain this normal sense of discrimination but your mental, intellectual, political, social and sexual jaundice, your physical, mental and intellectual crises will be overcome.

You do not become inactive after samadhi. Rather, you become very powerful and active. Hard work for days at a time does not tire you. Sleeping pills and tranquillizers are not needed. No incident of tragedy or joy has any influence. There is equipoise in joy and sorrow, death and birth, loss and gain, insult and praise, notoriety and fame. One is full of indescribable serenity. You must have experienced the serenity of deep sleep during which you are in the lap of a blissful experience and nothing disturbs you. The only difference between deep sleep and samadhi is that in sleep one is unconscious while in samadhi one is conscious of everything, yet serene, equibalanced and cheerful. Imagine this highest state of bliss, peace and joy!

Every individual needs this attainment to face the storms of day-to-day life with a balanced mind. You must have such strength that you do not get tired even after long working hours. It is possible to live without eating, sleeping, etc., but only after the attainment of samadhi, not before. However, samadhi should not be considered as the final thing, not merely as a practice. We must strive to attain perennial samadhi and personify it. Ours should be what Kabir called *sahaja samadhi,* effortless samadhi. In that state we attain and retain all the qualities of *sthitaprajna*, steady wisdom, described by Lord Krishna in the *Bhagavad Gita*.

Accept yoga in your daily life. Yoga is a way of life, the culture of tomorrow. It is not necessary to go to a temple or meditate on your deity, but wherever and whatever you perceive do so with sublime equanimity. Yoga will fulfil your worldly ambitions and quench your spiritual thirst, whether you wish for good health, a happy marital life, prosperity or spiritual enlightenment. The starting point of yoga is satsang, the company of holy people and good books. Its culmination is samadhi.

33

The Spiritual Quest

The purpose of yoga is to evolve the human being. Everyone, whether young or old, modern or old-fashioned, wants to discover a meaning and value in life. If the purpose of life were just to follow the four basic instincts of eating, sleeping, fear and sexual behaviour, there would be no difference between human beings and animals. There are people who believe that the purpose of life is to live in God, or to realize the highest spirit, or to merge this finite mind with the cosmic self, or to stop all the desires and mental functions and enter into samadhi or nirvana. There are those who believe that the purpose of life is to help their less privileged fellow beings. Then there are those who think that the only purpose of life is to live as God wishes them to. Everyone has to find a goal to suit themselves.

There is only one governing philosophy of life – to experience illumination, to become enlightened, to attain nirvana or samadhi, to realize 'I am All'. This should be the guiding philosophy. Yoga has opened people's minds to the possibility of spiritual evolution. They start practising yoga, learn to concentrate, go to the guru's ashram, do some anushthana or pooja, slowly learn about kundalini shakti and the possibility of awakening kundalini and attaining samadhi. Yoga gives this kind of meaning and philosophy to people today, and it has truly come as a boon.

There are many levels of consciousness and we have to discover them one by one, because that is the purpose of human life. Man's advent is to discover the man behind the man, the mind behind the mind, the consciousness behind the consciousness, until he comes to the point of universal evolution, samadhi. At that point of evolution he comes out of the circle of birth and rebirth and then becomes what we call a junior god. When that experience comes, everything becomes *shoonya*, null, void. It is a moment when the notion of time and the idea of space are terminated. You forget who you are, you don't even know where you are or what you are doing or experiencing. There is a supramental experience, which is the discovery of the universe in you.

The universe is microcosmic and macrocosmic. The macrocosmic universe is outside, millions and millions and millions of light years, but the microcosmic universe is enshrined in one point, in one *bindu*, in an atom or something smaller than an atom. This little particle or bindu is beyond time and space. The supramental experience is much subtler than that bindu, and comes in many forms. It can come in the form of sounds, sometimes music, sometimes another sound. It can come again in the form of geometrical figures, symbols of the inner universe. The universe is not trees, mountains, the sun, moon or stars; it is geometrical in form, mathematical, not an artist's painting. What we see now is an appearance, a manifestation; not reality, not the seed.

Just as a gold bangle is a manifestation of gold, in the same way, this universe we see is a manifestation, not the total universe, so it is incorrect to define the universe in terms of the sun, moon, stars, planets, mountains and oceans. Physicists and scientists say exactly the same thing. If you are to experience the universe, it will not be in this form but in its real, potential and deeper form.

Spiritual evolution

The spiritual quest is therefore not a religious quest or a moral quest, not a quest for goodness or purity. A spiritual quest means having the particular experience of something which is beyond the mind and beyond this ordinary everyday consciousness. As the ancient seers said, the human birth is given to us to have this experience, not for anything else.

Man is not a product of a solitary action, but an outcome of a long chain of evolution in the realm of nature. He has been fashioned by nature over millions of years, and nature's purpose for performing this evolutionary process is to ultimately transform you into a transcendental being. This experience is close to you, not very far away. It is not in paradise, not in another country, not in the Himalayas, not in the mountains or caves. It is within you, closer than your own breath and much closer than your own mind. But the problem is that you can feel your breath, you can feel your mind, you are able to experience pain and pleasure, but you cannot experience the transcendental universal experience. Why? Where is the obstacle? What stands between you and the experience? That problem can be solved by the practices of yoga and tantra.

Even if you are interested in the spiritual quest, you do not really know exactly what you are looking for or what you are talking about. You may say, "God, grant me that divine experience. I want to have that transcendental experience." But how will you go about it? How will you face the experiences that will come to you, when you are not even able to face an upsetting dream? If you begin to hear birds chirping inside your head, you will immediately go to a doctor. If it feels as though an ant is crawling up your spine, you will think something is wrong with your nervous system. Therefore, the spiritual quest must begin, must continue and must end with the guru.

When you follow the spiritual path, there will be experiences which are not spiritual, but simply patterns and impressions that have been buried deep within and which must come out. Those experiences do not last long and are succeeded by other experiences. Many types of experiences will come and go provided you continue your sadhana, but if you are frightened and discontinue your sadhana before these experiences are worked through, then nothing further is possible.

The experiences you undergo during your spiritual quest are some of the most valuable experiences in human life. True spiritual experiences will completely transform the quality of your life, wherever and whoever you are. That experience is inner peace and inner bliss. The ultimate spiritual experience has come to many saints, such as Ramakrishna Paramahamsa, Ramana Maharishi, Aurobindo and St Francis of Assisi. Thousands and thousands of people in history have been illumined by that experience. Today we are at the crossroads, we have reached a climax in our point of evolution and now we must return to our spiritual quest, to experience the universal or transcendental consciousness. There is really no other choice, neither for the East nor for the West. All people of all nations will have to return to the spiritual quest designed by nature for humankind. That is the direction in which man is now meant to move.

Is samadhi the end point of our evolution?
Darwin's theory of evolution pertains to the evolution of nature, but in the universe, evolution has taken place first from the unmanifest to the manifest, from invisible to visible. The second phase is evolution from the visible to man. That is the law of natural evolution as propounded by Darwin and also by Indian philosophy. Man has completed his physio-biological evolution; natural evolution is now complete in us.

Spiritual evolution is now beginning, the third evolution, from the awakening of kundalini to samadhi. That is the completion of evolution. After awakening the chakras and sushumna, the awakening of kundalini takes place. The awakening of kundalini is the greatest event in man's life, the climax of spiritual evolution. It is the destiny of everyone. If you do not awaken your kundalini, nature will do it for you. A superhuman or supramental race will be the outcome of this awakening. For this purpose the science of yoga and tantra has come about. There is a great awakening throughout the world. Everywhere people want to realize and experience the man behind the man, the existence behind this existence, and they know this can be done through the practices of yoga and tantra.

Is it possible to regress in evolution?

No. You only move forward, you cannot go back. If you want to look back and see the previous stages of consciousness, it is usually difficult unless, of course, you are at the highest stage of samadhi. At a particular point of samadhi all the previous stages of consciousness are revealed in a flash and all the past incarnations are remembered.

Ego seems to be the major barrier on the path to samadhi? How can it be overcome?

The ego stands in the way of truth. We live in the body, we are aware of the body, but we are not able to transcend it unless we are deeply asleep. We have to discover a conscious practice by which we can gradually transcend the experience of duality, of name and form, until we are able to jump over the ego principle. Jumping over the ego principle is samadhi. It is not easy, but it is something we have to accomplish eventually. This is the purpose of human existence, otherwise life has no logical justification.

If we are born as human beings only for what we have been doing until now, then there is no fun or logic in it. We have just been living a superior kind of animal life; we are civilized animals doing the same things in a different way. If animals eat grass, we cook it and eat it. If animals procreate in the field or forest, we procreate in a modern home. Animal life belongs to the dimension of instinct. In the process of evolution there are three distinct divisions: instinct, intellect and intuition. Instinct is the quality we have inherited from the unevolved, tamasic animal kingdom, where there is no spiritual response. The moment one has a spiritual response, a spiritual hunger, one is out of the area of instinct.

The ego dies when meditation is born. The ego dies when bhakti is in her full bloom. The ego dies when awareness becomes overwhelming. Out of the death of the ego is born darshan. Out of the death of the ego is born *atma anubhuti*, spiritual perception, and *aparoksha jnana*, direct knowledge. The most important thing in yoga is *dhyana*, meditation. It is the answer; it is the way. When you are able to transcend the idea of the body through meditation, to forget the notion of name and form, to rise above past memories and to have even a blurred vision of something non-physical, then you are on the path of samadhi. Those who are able to see the light, to experience the space or the sound within, are on the path.

When the ego is destroyed, tensions will leave, cravings for pleasurable experiences will dwindle into nothing, idleness will dissipate. Then the light will be switched on. Then the light will be switched off. Then the light will shine all over. Then the light will be extinguished. Then the light will emerge. Then the light will merge. Sages call it moksha and nirvana. When awareness of God dawns, awareness of the rest dies. When self-awareness stretches itself to every side of experience, sense awareness ceases to function. Samadhi is the consummation of all vrittis in one supreme awareness.

34

The Necessity of Sadhana

One cannot have samadhi, kundalini awakening, the vision of God or God's blessing by doing sadhana. All these totally depend upon the will of God. So why is it necessary to do sadhana? Sadhana is done to pacify the wavering mind. Due to the wayward plays of the mind people suffer a lot of misery, due to uneasiness, anger, frustration, guilt, and so on. The role of sadhana is to control the mischievous mind.

This mind is an outcome of the three gunas, *tamas*, lethargy, *rajas*, dynamism, and *sattwa*, purity. Due to their interplay there is conflict within the mind, which is the main cause of all the so-called miseries and bad habits. Sadhana not only controls the mind, but also erases tamas and rajas and establishes a sattwic state of mind, by means of which one can lead a happy, peaceful life.

There is a barrier between God and the human being. This wall is caused by *maya*, illusion. Maya is the production of our mind. All the functions of the mind are performed due to maya. Maya is the cause all the delusions which cause pain, false ideas about life and so on. If the barrier of maya is broken down, then the human being will be united with God. This can only happen through sadhana, and hence sadhana is essential for spiritual aspirants.

Kabir gives a good example of maya. If water from a well is poured into ten earthen pots, due to maya people will think that the water in each pot is different. The pots may be different but the content, the water, is the same. Just break all the pots and see. In the same way if this barricade, this wall, this veil, is dissolved, there will be union between God and the sadhaka. The imaginary difference between the creator and the aspirant, the duality of 'I and you', will also disappear and all will be one, all will be God. This understanding is *atma jnana*, knowledge of the self, self-realization. Due to this knowledge the sadhaka, who until now has called himself the *jivatma*, individual soul, and looks on God as a different entity, has his ignorance of duality dispelled and sees that God and he are one and the same. Hence, to control the mind, to dispel the illusion of maya, sadhana is absolutely essential.

Be an instrument

In the *Bhagavad Gita,* Lord Krishna impresses upon Arjuna that he should to do his duty and play his role, acting only as an instrument. A spiritual aspirant has to perform sadhana in the same manner. Once while performing sadhana, I felt a sort of egoistic notion that 'I am doing sadhana for God- realization'. But after deep thinking I realized that it is the will of God and I am only an instrument. Why then run after sadhana or realization? So I gave up everything. Again after deep thinking I realized my mistake; it is totally wrong to give up sadhana, because thereafter my mind began to play its wicked tricks again, causing agony, misery and anger. Therefore, to control the mind and win over its wayward tendencies, one has to practise sadhana.

Due to sadhana the mind becomes calm and quiet. Once the mind is controlled the aspirant realizes that a divine power is causing him to do sadhana and finally knows that God and himself are one and the same. Therefore, sadhana should be performed without ego and with the feeling that one is doing sadhana only as an instrument in the hands of a divine power. Always have the feeling that you are performing asanas, pranayama and meditation as an instrument, that you are only playing the role of a sadhaka. We have to face many problems in daily life such as anger, displeasure and insults, which cause depression, frustration and helplessness, but these are illusionary, an outwardly imaginary play of the mind. Hence to pacify and control the mind sadhana is absolutely necessary.

Abhyasa

Abhyasa means to be perfectly fixed or firmly established in spiritual effort or sadhana. The effort here involves the practice of *chitta vritti nirodhah*, blocking the patterns of consciousness, a definition of yoga given in Patanjali's *Yoga Sutras* (1:2). It may include meditation or karma yoga or bhakti or self-introspection and other practices. It should be remembered that just practising something for a short period is not abhyasa.

Abhyasa means continued practice with full dedication; it cannot be left at all, whether it is kriya yoga, hatha yoga or meditation. It must become a part of one's personality. Every student must pay utmost attention to regular and continued practice, which, when perfected, leads to the complete blocking of the vrittis. When abhyasa becomes natural, firmly rooted and complete, it leads to samadhi.

Three conditions must be fulfilled for the practice of abhyasa. It should be practised with complete faith, it should continue uninterrupted and it should go on for quite a long time. When these three conditions are fulfilled, abhyasa becomes firmly established and a part of one's nature. It is often observed that many aspirants are very enthusiastic in the beginning, but their faith dwindles away later on. This should never happen with a student of yoga who wants to achieve samadhi in this very birth. A spiritual aspirant must continue sadhana until he is able to receive something very concrete and very substantial, but very few aspirants can do this.

Foundation of abhyasa

Patanjali says that spiritual practice "becomes firmly grounded by being continued for a long time with reverence and without interruption." (*Yoga Sutras* 1:14) This is very important because if the practices are interrupted now and then, the student cannot gain the full benefit. To attain spiritual maturity the practices must continue for a long time. Sometimes we observe a misconception in many people that the task of spiritual evolution can be completed within a few months, but this is wrong. It may take many births to achieve. The aspirant should not be impatient; there should be no hurry or haste.

Our ancient literature is full of stories wherein it is declared that it may take many births for an individual to attain the highest goal of yoga. What is important is not the length of time, but the fact that one has to continue the practices without any interruption and until the goal is achieved, whatever time it may take to reach there. One should not lose heart; one should continue the practices with faith.

Faith is the most important factor, for it is only through faith that we have the patience and energy to continue the practice against the odds of life. If the aspirant has complete faith in the fact that he will surely achieve the goal through sadhana, then it matters little to him when he reaches the goal.

The next important point is that one should like sadhana to the highest extent. Just as a mother becomes disturbed if her child does not return home on time, so the aspirant should become disturbed if he does not do his daily practices. You should love your practices as much as you love your body. The practices can produce the desired result only if they are done willingly with love and attraction; there should be no feeling of compulsion. If one has these qualities, earnestness, respect and devotion, good results are assured. Attachment to the practices can be developed through constant self-analysis and satsang.

In the *Yoga Sutras*, Patanjali declares that if we practise abhyasa with faith and conviction continuously for a long time, it will definitely bring about a blockage of the fivefold vrittis of the mind.

Degree of eagerness

It is observed that out of a number of aspirants practising the same type of sadhana, some reach the goal of samadhi more quickly and others linger on. The speed of attainment depends upon one's earnestness and sincerity. Earnestness is a mental attitude. It should be as intense as that which was exemplified by Dhruva, the great devotee of Lord Vishnu, who reached God because of intense sincerity. Samadhi is quite close for those who are earnest, but earnestness does not mean hard or difficult sadhana. Even the easiest sadhana can bring one nearest to realization provided the urge is intense. Nor is intensity of speed to be confused with impatience. That is very different from eagerness.

We can describe increasingly intense stages of earnestness as mild, medium or extremely strong. Many aspirants are found to be very enthusiastic in the beginning, but their urge is rather weak and so they do not have very promising results. Even if they practise sadhana for a long time when they begin, in the course of time their interest fades and they lose the courage and energy with which they started. They may carry on in that state without much hope. They are examples of mild intensity of earnestness.

The medium type of aspirants are no doubt earnest, but they are not ready to go through intense sadhana to reach samadhi quickly. Intensity of earnestness is rare, but if it is there, it makes the aspirant so intent upon achieving his goal at once that he does not rest until the goal is achieved.

These three classes of aspirants have three different sadhanas, according to the intensity of their eagerness. Usually teachers who give spiritual lessons judge the intensity of the aspirants and guide them accordingly. A good student should not demand a higher sadhana in the beginning. One should practise with earnestness whatever sadhana one receives from the guru, for, in fact, no such differentiation into higher or lower sadhana should matter in the beginning. It is the earnestness which is more important.

The path to samadhi is such a long one. How can I overcome my impatience?

The most intense crisis in spiritual life is impatience. Aspirants want to get there overnight. They do not really understand what they want and as a result they want practices that will give them samadhi in the shortest possible time. It needs to be understood that we are dealing with the evolution of consciousness in our practices, so attaining samadhi should definitely take more than one lifetime. If everybody were to realize in one lifetime, there would be a universal crisis. Your sadhana should be an integration of the elements of karma yoga, which should then be tempered with bhakti yoga, which should then be improved by raja yoga, which should be surveyed properly through jnana yoga. Since the body and mind are interacting with each other, it is necessary to understand that whatever sadhana you do should be properly graduated. Then there will be less impatience and intense crisis.

How do we qualify ourselves for the higher experiences of samadhi ?

Samadhi is within you always. You can attain samadhi and have higher experiences, but you must prepare and qualify yourself through the practices of yoga. Yoga is not the end, it is the means, the process, a method of self-purification. Yoga purifies the body and the three dimensions of the mind, conscious, subconscious and unconscious. Higher experiences beyond the subconscious and unconscious dimensions of personality can be attained. There is also a spiritual state called superconsciousness.

Take to the spiritual path once you have purified yourself internally. Go to a guru and ask for initiation. When everything is calm and quiet, when the samskaras and karmas have been exhausted and the afflictions are no more, then you should go on to the higher spiritual path, not before.

Although the aim of your life should be to attain spiritual realization, you should never seek that higher path unless mental health has been attained and the confusions and pandemonium in the personality have been completely calmed down. The practices of dhyana yoga or meditation are prescribed for this purpose.

Does yoga offer any shortcuts to samadhi, any special techniques that bypass the torture of discipline?
Yogic philosophy offers no shortcuts to the ultimate; it prescribes a long and tortuous way. The very brevity of our lives makes it imperative to understand the urgency of our mission. Spiritual liberation dawns only when inner equipoise is attained by disciplining the body and mind. There can be no collective realization of divinity. Each individual is left to himself; you are your own taskmaster and leader. Weak willpower, indecisiveness and vacillations of mind do not exist once yogic discipline is imbibed. A weak person is a strong person in embryo. Yoga philosophy delivers man from nescience to omniscience, from impotence to omnipotence, from the finite to the infinite. But there are no short cuts!

35

Awakening Inner Awareness

In the quest for spiritual awareness some people have by mistake taken to a path for the opening the third eye, the spiritual eye, which will give the experience of a trip into the superconscious. But sooner or later those seekers will realize that this way is incorrect. The opening of the third eye is only a state of the nervous system, a condition of the brain, not the ultimate condition of the supramental state.

Man wants enlightenment, to know the highest state of awareness. His soul has been passing through different grades of awareness from the mineral kingdom to the human kingdom: instinctive awareness, intellectual awareness, higher psychic awareness, then spiritual awareness. Spiritual awareness is also known as divine awareness, God awareness or enlightenment. It is said to be the highest awareness. The ultimate aim of yoga is to bring enlightenment to every individual.

Yoga does not believe that enlightenment comes from outside. Yoga believes that this supreme awareness is inherent in every human being. However, this awareness within has to be awakened separately by constant sadhana, by constant application. Only then is it possible to become a witness of one's own inner self. One keeps on removing layer after layer of consciousness, unfolding the different states and dimensions of consciousness. From consciousness one goes down to subconsciousness and then still deeper into the more dynamic state of unconsciousness, and then one takes a jump into superconsciousness.

Yoga is a method of communion, of joining two things together. The individual consciousness which you are today and the supreme consciousness which you want to attain have to be in communion. This lower consciousness has to be taken down deep into the superconsciousness, so as to have a glimpse of it. For this, different methods and techniques have been prescribed.

Yoga is a scientific methods of beholding the consciousness, tranquillizing the entire personality and then developing awareness with absolute consciousness. Yoga takes consciousness as its object or purpose, and then with the help of the mind tries to enquire into the deeper dimensions of personality. There are three stages: tranquillity, concentration or fixation, and meditation or awareness. When these three stages have been achieved, the final attainment is superconsciousness, samadhi.

Pratyahara

The first stage is tranquillity. If you want to be aware of the inner self, it is necessary to suppress or withdraw the senses from the outer personality. In the same manner, if you want to understand or become aware of the self in the deepest dimension, it is first of all necessary to settle the noise, dissipation and disturbances in the mental and sensual personality. When the senses become quiet and the thoughts become tranquil, you are able to witness your mind, personality and consciousness.

The first necessity is therefore tranquillity. In yoga it is called *pratyahara*, withdrawal of individual experiences from the medium of the senses. Listening to a discourse is an experience of the mind through the senses. However, when you want to go into the spiritual realm, the extrovert consciousness has to be completely stopped, external experiences have to cease. Tranquillity means withdrawal from sense experiences. When consciousness transcends outer experiences, forms are not seen, words are not heard, the skin does not feel sensations, fragrance is not experienced, and taste is not experienced even if a sweet is placed on the tongue.

The moment one starts to lose awareness of sense objects, samadhi begins. But this is not the final experience. The awareness must plunge deeper into this domain until ultimately it reaches the sphere of pure consciousness. Here the experiences are completely withdrawn just as in deep sleep. There is no motion, no object to be perceived by any medium or channel of the senses.

To accomplish the first stage there are hundreds of techniques, all of which are effective. Swami Yogananda used to teach kriya yoga, Mahesh Yogi taught transcendental meditation, and I teach ajapa japa for this purpose. In Christianity one prays and prostrates in absolute surrender. In Hinduism one sings God's names. These are all methods to pacify the disturbed personality. Then a stage of tranquillity and a stage of transcendence will arise. After that, yoga begins.

Dharana and beyond

In the second stage, the withdrawn sense consciousness is to be focused on an image, so much so that you are not aware of anything outside; for one minute, three minutes or longer there has to be unceasing awareness of that one form. The time will increase through practice. When the time increases, it means you are moving into a state called *dharana*, concentration, then *dhyana*, meditation, and finally samadhi. It can be called Godhood, it can be called nirvana in the language of the Buddhists, it can be called darshan in the language of Hindus, or it can be called samadhi in the language of yoga. This state can also be described as the divine state of oneness.

When pratyahara becomes complete, then for a moment you feel as if you have no mind; everything becomes completely silent. You are very happy at that time and give up your practices because you are under the wrong impression that you have gone to kaivalya or the higher state of samadhi. However, wherever there is complete blankness in the mind, when the mind does not seem to function, then at that point a symbol must be visualized. The symbol could be fire, the sun, the moon, the guru, a flower or a star; it could be one static substance. Even if you have been very poor at visualization, when the senses and mind have been completely cut off, you can easily visualize the symbol at the mid-eyebrow centre and continue seeing it. Then your sadhana, your personal efforts, are finished. Beyond that you cannot do anything. After the stage of dharana, concentration, one does not have to make any effort or think about what to do. Everything will depend upon the quality of your preparation leading up to dharana.

If you want to know what happens in dhyana and in samadhi, read the *Yoga Sutras* of Patanjali. The eightfold yoga, known as raja yoga, is important because it gives a codified system of practices. If a person is regular and sincere, it will take ten or twelve years, it is not possible in six months. It is a matter of time. After all, it takes ten or twelve years to become a doctor, thirty or forty years to own your own flat or house, and sometimes it takes eighty years to get a little common sense. So we should not be disappointed if we are told that it takes time to experience our real nature.

What are the rewards of yoga? There are three rewards: creative intelligence, freedom from the threefold afflictions caused by the body, mind and nature, and first-hand knowledge of the reality behind this appearance. Personal experience cannot be had from a book or a teacher, or even a guru. The reality behind the appearance may be God, it may be purusha, it may be nothing, it may be anything, but one must have personal knowledge of it.

How is sushumna awakening related to higher awareness?
Meditation cannot be achieved by effort alone. The methods we practise to bring about concentration do not help in achieving the final end, samadhi. Kabir calls it *shoonya* or

void, the state which lies beyond *jagrat*, the waking state, *swapna*, the dreaming state and *sushupti*, the sleeping state. It cannot be reached until sushumna is awakened.

The mind is subject to time. In yoga, time is considered as a moment, which is the smallest denomination of time. Time is an objective experience, just as objects are an experience. Time cannot be realized through the intellect, because time is an attribute of the intellect; the intellect cannot transcend time because it is governed by time, and so it cannot understand what one moment, two moments or three moments are. The mind binds all moments together, otherwise there is space between one moment and another. Yoga eliminates the mind, and extends the space between the moments. The space between two moments is shoonya, infinity. However, this is an experience, not an intellectual pursuit.

The bondage of the mind between two moments is snapped in the state of samadhi. That is why without awakening sushumna we cannot transcend time, and unless time is transcended, meditation cannot be achieved. When time is transcended, samadhi comes about. It is a strange cyclic riddle: without the egg there is no hen and without the hen there is no egg. Both are so deeply interdependent and inseparably connected happenings that we have to find the method for its release.

So, first of all awaken sushumna, and do not talk about concentration. While concentrating the mind, our awareness passes into the subconscious, into the realm of the unmanifest. We can also say that the role of concentration ends at the intellect; it cannot go beyond the intellect. It cannot reach the self, the unmanifest, which are finer states of the mind. One can have various experiences in sleep, in dream, in deep thought, in intoxicating illusion or in the deep state of concentration. Time, place, objects and the mind are so closely linked that it is impossible to separate them by intellectual analysis. The experience cannot be bound in figures or theorems. The observer, the observed and the act of observation are all completely fused. To separate these three is the subject matter of yoga.

According to the scriptures, sushumna nadi is sleeping, lying dormant in devastatingly destructive darkness. The Upanishads say there is neither day or night, light or darkness, but there is a hidden, dormant potential which contains the seed of creation. It has the potency of birth and death, but it is motionless and inactive. This sleeping power is called shakti in tantra. Samkhya calls it prakriti. Saints call it kundalini. Hatha yogis call it sushumna. Jnana yogis call it paramatma. Bhaktas have named it Lord Rama and Sri Krishna. It is all one and the same power which has to be awakened.

In yoga, the fusion of prana and apana in manipura and the confluence of ida and pingala nadis in ajna chakra means the awakening of sushumna. There are different means of doing this. Asanas are practised to awaken the chakras in the path of sushumna and to pierce through rudra, vishnu and brahma granthis. Pranayama extends the duration of the breath. Through pranayama, the prana shakti is taken into an invisible body beyond the physical, astral and causal bodies.

Symptoms of sushumna awakening

When sushumna flows, a number of symptoms appear. Mirabai, Kabir, Tulsidas and other saints have given us their experiences of this awakening. Those devotional songs tell us what happens when sushumna awakens. When Mirabai sings, "Here I hear the approach of Hari," it is the movement of sushumna she is describing. When she also sings, "I ascend the stories of my mansion and await the coming of my Lord," the stories of her mansion are the chakras. The ground floor is mooladhara, the top floor is ajna and the roof is sahasrara. In between lie the other four floors. Sushumna goes by this route.

If a person is tamasic, sushumna will surely destroy him, if he is rajasic, sushumna will lead him astray, but if he is sattwic, it will give him eternal knowledge and power. He will attain a treasure house of precious gems. Such great people have existed in our history. Not all were saints, many were poets, artists, painters, scientists, philosophers, warriors and statesmen. They were self-conquering mahatmas, who progressed not by their intellect or emotional strength, but purely by spiritual means. Their path was the spiritual path of awakening sushumna.

When awakening of kundalini takes place, sushumna becomes very active. When sushumna becomes active or is charged by kundalini energy, then the whole spinal passage becomes heated, active and full of experiences. Awakening of sushumna for a long period is an indication that either the person is about to die, or, in the case of a yogi, that the body, mind and object are going to be transcended and you will enjoy samadhi.

If ida nadi flows for a long time, beyond the usual healthy schedule of one or one and a half hours, then there is some abnormality in the mind. If pingala nadi flows for a long time beyond schedule, there is some abnormality in the pranic body. Sushumna nadi is very important. When both nostrils flow equally, sushumna is flowing and usually this equal flow can appear for a short period in twenty-four hours.

Whenever sushumna flows, the mind becomes absolutely tranquil because a balance takes place between prana and the mind at a deep level. At this time, if you sit for meditation, you can go inside with the least effort. And when sushumna nadi flows for a very long time, it means your mind is going to transcend the barriers of objects.

Can the practice of ajapa japa give direct experience of samadhi?

Ajapa japa is a complete sadhana through which one can have direct experience of samadhi. In order to attain samadhi, in other yogic practices one has to have complete control over the breath, because in samadhi the breath is suspended and kumbhaka takes place spontaneously. A difficulty is that many sadhakas become extroverted even after a short meditation if the lung capacity is not adequate. In the practice of ajapa japa, however, this problem is solved. Due to the continuity of breath and mantra, the breathing remains normal throughout, and even in samadhi there is no change.

In the scriptures it is said that one should practise *anahata japa*, which never ends, which extends into infinity. However, we do not know any such mantra and therefore we need a method of repeating the mantra so that it does not end. This is achieved through the practice of ajapa japa when the mantra is adjusted with the breathing process. Thus awareness of the mantra continues throughout the practice without a break.

In ajapa japa there is an efficient process of locating the awareness. If you are asked where your awareness is at this moment, you cannot locate it because it is extroverted and dissipated, but through a meditative practice it can be located at any particular centre of the body. In the practice of ajapa japa, the consciousness is located with the breath and mantra.

Ajapa japa is a complete practice in itself. Those who have read the *Yoga Sutras* of Patanjali know that first of all one has to concentrate on a concrete object. When that is complete with the eyes open, then one must meditate on the same object with the eyes closed. This is concentration on a subtle object. One must concentrate on the simple awareness of its presence. Through the practice of ajapa japa both stages of concentration can be achieved. Therefore, it is a complete practice in itself and through it one can enter the spiritual realms, even without the help of a guru.

Balancing ida and pingala

In ajapa japa, the breath is utilized to harmonize the body and mind and awaken the spirit. Two birds were tied to a peg with separate strings. They flew for a short distance, but had to return because they were tied to the peg. Thus they flew and returned many times. Finally they became tired and slept peacefully near the peg. Ida and pingala are the two birds.

The breath flow in the right nostril corresponds to *pingala* or *surya nadi*, representing the vital force, and the left nostril corresponds to *ida* or *chandra nadi*, representing the mental force. The alternate functioning of ida and pingala takes one away from inner consciousness. So long as ida and pingala function alternately, samadhi cannot be attained. Only when the two birds, ida and pingala, are tied and retire to the centre, the heart or the self, does sushumna awaken and the process of meditation takes place spontaneously.

According to swara yoga, when both nostrils flow equally, it indicates that sushumna is flowing. At this time one should give up all worldly pursuits and meditate. It is a common experience that when sushumna is flowing, meditation is wonderful because there is harmony in the entire system, but when sushumna is not flowing, concentration is not achieved even with a great effort. So it is important that ida and pingala should be balanced in the process of meditation, thus making it possible for sushumna to function.

How will the practice of witnessing the mind help me attain samadhi?

When you transcend the conscious plane and go to the subconscious plane, or what is called semi-samadhi, deep meditation, then the images that come cannot be controlled because the ego is not present. You do not know how to eliminate them. For example, if you are sitting somewhere and an unhappy idea comes, you can just eliminate it by willpower, but if you are dreaming at night that somebody is coming with a revolver to shoot you, you can do nothing because the ego is not there. Whatever is happening in the dream has to happen.

In the same way, in the stages of deep meditation there are experiences so compelling that you cannot get rid of them. So during the practice of dharana, when you are concentrating on the object, you must allow the purging to take place. A lot of ideas, images, memories, good and bad experiences, unhappiness, guilt, conflict, obsessions and complexes will come up and you must look at them. That is called witnessing the mind.

It is not just a few thoughts. The deeper you go, the greater the crowd. There could be moments during your mantra chanting or in ordinary meditation when there is confusion in the realm of thinking. So many thoughts come up at the same time that you cannot even distinguish them. That is purging, shankhaprakshalana of the psychic body. At that time, do not be discouraged or affected adversely. It has to happen.

Sometimes when a thought emerges on the conscious plane, it immediately releases a particular disease from the body. There are many cases where the most deadly diseases have just gone away miraculously overnight due to the witnessing and expansion of one thought. Witnessing the thoughts and images, everything that is taking place in the mind during mantra meditation or any type of meditation is a very powerful sadhana known as antar mouna. Meditation is the practice of mindfulness, and when it is perfected and mindfulness becomes constant and unbroken, it culminates in samadhi.

36

Samadhi – An Inner Journey Through Life

The superconscious state, or samadhi, or nirvana, or shoonya, or kaivalya is the highest stage of evolution. There must come a time when the mind, which is sattwic, rajasic and tamasic in nature, becomes able to transcend the realm of the three gunas. The search for the higher reality is an inward journey rather than an outward discovery. But exactly what is meant by inside? Is it in the body, brain or heart?

In the *Bhagavad Gita* Lord Krishna tells Arjuna that the supreme being lives in the heart of all living things, which is internal. This inner reality is the reality of personal consciousness. It is a most important path in spiritual life. When we travel this interior path, we follow the path of yoga. We have to go inside, through the personal mind to the higher mind, from the higher mind to the universal mind, from the universal mind to the cosmic mind, from the cosmic mind to total consciousness. It is not simple because the moment we go inside we face difficulties, barriers and diversions at every step, and all the paths look the same.

Sometimes two paths run parallel and very few people can distinguish between them. Both have the same direction, both are broad, but one is illumined and the other is dark. When the individual consciousness passes through the path of darkness, it comes back after some time to the point where it started. When the consciousness goes through the illumined path, it goes further and further and attains the great and total reality. To travel upon this illumined path requires a lot of preparation.

Steady wisdom

One fundamental quality has to be acquired: a mind fixed on wisdom and bound with determination. In the *Bhagavad Gita* this is known as steady wisdom, *sthitaprajna*, being able to keep the mind balanced in all conditions of life, being able to be forever serene, contented, calm and peaceful. In the second chapter, Arjuna asks Lord Krishna, "How does a person speak, sit, move and behave when he acquires a steady mind, when his consciousness does not fluctuate and is completely stabilized. When the mind is dissolved in samadhi, how can that be described?"

Lord Krishna replies that just as the tortoise draws in its limbs, in the same way the yogi draws in the sense experiences, places them in the centre of the mind and visualizes them, thereby destroying the dissipating experience. By practising awareness on the sense objects in this way, you do not kill the senses. The eyes will continue to see, the ears to hear and the tongue to taste, even though you are a yogi.

Buddha was asked, "Do you smell flowers?" He said, "Yes." "Can you see things?" "Yes." "Do you feel the sensations of touch cold, heat?" "Oh, yes." "Then you also have the same experience as I have, so where is the difference between you and me?" Buddha replied, "I experience not in the senses or in the object; my experience of everything is inherent within me, beyond the sun and beyond the moon." Buddha's sun and moon represent ida and pingala, mind and prana. He said, "When I sleep, I am the witness of the sleep, when I eat, I witness it, and when I experience, I am the witness of the experience." That is the idea of sense control when the mind is completely stabilized.

Stabilize the mind in spiritual awareness

A consistent, enduring, constant and unfluctuating mind is required to walk the spiritual path. Most people are so weak-minded that they are unable to bear their thoughts and emotions, and their reactions are over-exaggerated. The mind has to be strengthened because only then can one sit for meditation.

Many other factors have to be considered when one continues with spiritual sadhana and a meditative life. In its eighteen chapters the *Bhagavad Gita* talks about eighteen systems of yoga. Every aspirant who wants to succeed in the spiritual adventure must systematically follow at least one of these paths. Many of us do not really follow the path systematically. We just want to close our eyes and forget ourselves. But the *Bhagavad Gita* says that higher awareness, awareness of the spiritual self, can be maintained even while working and leading a normal life, just as one maintains awareness of one's child, wife or husband, while working elsewhere. This is ceaseless awareness.

When people practise mantra, love God, read the *Bhagavad Gita*, pray, and are eager for liberation, they know that this internal life is a must. But at the same time, this external life is something else. Why do people go to offices? Most will say to earn money. What is the difference between the person who works for money and the one who works for liberation? Both work in the same office, but the aim is not the same. The one who works for liberation throughout the day is constantly aware of the spiritual aim or motive, and motive is very important in spiritual life.

By developing this unconscious, spontaneous, natural awareness the individual consciousness evolves. It is not that one is operating a machine and thinking about samadhi. Mental awareness and spiritual awareness are different stages. Mental and intellectual consciousness are one dimension, but spiritual consciousness is a much deeper dimension. I may be talking to you about the *Bhagavad Gita*, but in the depths of my consciousness I am thinking of my guru. Similarly, one can be a commander-in-chief, a president, a mechanic, a doctor, a medical student or a shopkeeper, but the important thing is the content in the depths of one's consciousness. Just as a person fixes his mind on a vessel full of liquid he is carrying and carefully ascends a flight of stairs, so also the yogi fixes and absorbs his awareness in his atma, as he carefully ascends the rungs of the ladder of yoga. Thereby, he reaches the highest summit of nirvikalpa samadhi.

External life becomes a spiritual experience
If the aim of spiritual life is samadhi or nirvana, it does not matter if one is married or unmarried. This is the spiritual direction of the *Bhagavad Gita*. The principal teaching is discovery of the highest self, to act in the world but at the same time to live on the inner plane. It is possible, and there are many practical ways and teachers to guide aspirants. The path of yoga is open. Aspirants do not have to flounder in intellectual understanding.

When you develop a strong spiritual desire to attain liberation, you are maintaining a state of desire in the mind, but this desire for enlightenment nullifies all other desires. When it becomes stronger and all-permeating, other desires are rent asunder. If you have only one desire, the desire for enlightenment, then meditation and samadhi become very easy. After samadhi has been attained, even this desire is nullified. You are then able to live as a renunciate while actively carrying out your duties on the worldly plane.

If you have developed a spiritual level of consciousness through practice, any experience you have will be spiritual. External life will also become a path of spiritual experience. Therefore, those who have succeeded in yoga are called maha yogis. Then not only meditation is a spiritual experience; wherever they move, whatever they eat, say or do is a spiritual experience. All the saints who have gone into the spiritual realm say, "Whether I see a flower, a star, a moon, children, sinners, saints, a prostitute, a sattwic person or a criminal, I see the same thing." When one goes into that realm, every experience is spiritual. Everything, even pain and enjoyment, injustice, insult and abuse, is a spiritual experience.

Liberation in the Bhagavad Gita

Liberation is not closing the eyes, withdrawing the mind and entering into the great void. This experience is not related to real life. Renunciation is not liberation. Abstaining from duties and responsibilities is living an incomplete life. The *Bhagavad Gita* adds a new dimension to liberation by saying that it is living life without being affected by it at any time or at any cost. It is detachment in the midst of the holocaust. This is one meaning of samadhi.

When we face this peculiar and illogical life, the great void is completely eliminated. The *Bhagavad Gita* says that salvation is related to one's love, hatred, frustrations and accomplishments. People think, "I am Brahman, full of bliss," but this is not genuine realization because it does not transform their personality, emotions or ego. When they emerge from meditation, they exhibit the same tendencies as any ordinary human being.

The *Bhagavad Gita* states that complete freedom should be brought into daily life and not restricted to the meditation room. It must come into the kitchen, the workplace, when driving a car or about to face an emotional crisis. To experience complete freedom in every walk of life, meditation for one hour is not enough. What is needed is a completely reoriented philosophy, a retrained and healthy mind, and a cultured way of thinking with new dimensions of awareness.

Yoga of synthesis

The yoga of the *Bhagavad Gita* is *poorna* yoga, complete yoga. If you stress bhakti yoga and say, "Hatha yoga is only for sick people, raja yoga is only for swamis. No karma yoga, no jnana yoga; only singing the name of the Lord, playing the drum and dancing," that approach is *apoorna* or incomplete yoga. The personality is composed of four essential elements: dynamism, devotion, mysticism and rationalism. Accordingly, bhakti yoga should be practised for emotional expression or devotion, karma yoga for dynamism, raja yoga for mysticism and jnana yoga for rationalism.

To imbibe the philosophy of the *Bhagavad Gita* in daily life, just remember these few points. First of all work hard. Expect things, but if they do not come, do not be affected. Be courageous and go on with new ventures. Next, the mind must be balanced through a spontaneous culmination of the process of karma yoga. Whatever yoga you practise, never forget the atman within, which is the source of all yoga. For a yoga practitioner both dynamism, work, accomplishments and ambitions, and yogic life must be practised side by side.

Finally, do not condemn any phase of life because they are all phases of consciousness, not devoid of consciousness. If you condemn the life of a householder, or a sannyasin, or even a drunkard, you are creating a sickness in your mind. Whether a person is sick, great or helpless, Lord Krishna says that they are all his different points of evolution. If you practise hatha yoga, karma yoga, bhakti yoga, etc. with this broad and liberal attitude to life, you will not only be successful in every way but also gain enlightenment.

Contentment comes by a sense of enlightenment attained through yoga, not by achievement. Whatever you do, it is most important to have an experience. You should be able to awaken your prana shakti to such an extent that it will elevate the quality of your mind, which will influence the quality of your life and the quality of your achievement.

Even if you discover and understand your conflicts or problems, they still remain. For this reason you have to begin sadhana, the practical side of yoga. In the *Bhagavad Gita*, sadhana begins with karma yoga, the yoga of action. The daily activities have to be transformed in such a way that they are conducive to spiritual progress. Expressing oneself through action unburdens the soul. Side by side with karma yoga, raja yoga, then bhakti yoga, then jnana yoga should be practised in order to be victorious and eliminate the conflicts lurking in the personality. When the mind is completely free from the influence of conflicts, one is then a liberated person, a *jivanmukta*.

Those who sincerely practise yoga remain undisturbed like an ocean which receives the turbulent waters from inrushing rivers. While enjoying sense gratifications, a yogi is careful not to allow them to overpower him. It does not help to despise life. There is no virtue in retiring to a forest and sitting enchanted in the solitary grandeur of samadhi. Heroism lies in remaining steadfast in the tumult of life even when the scales are heavily loaded against you and in attaining equilibrium in the midst of all odds.

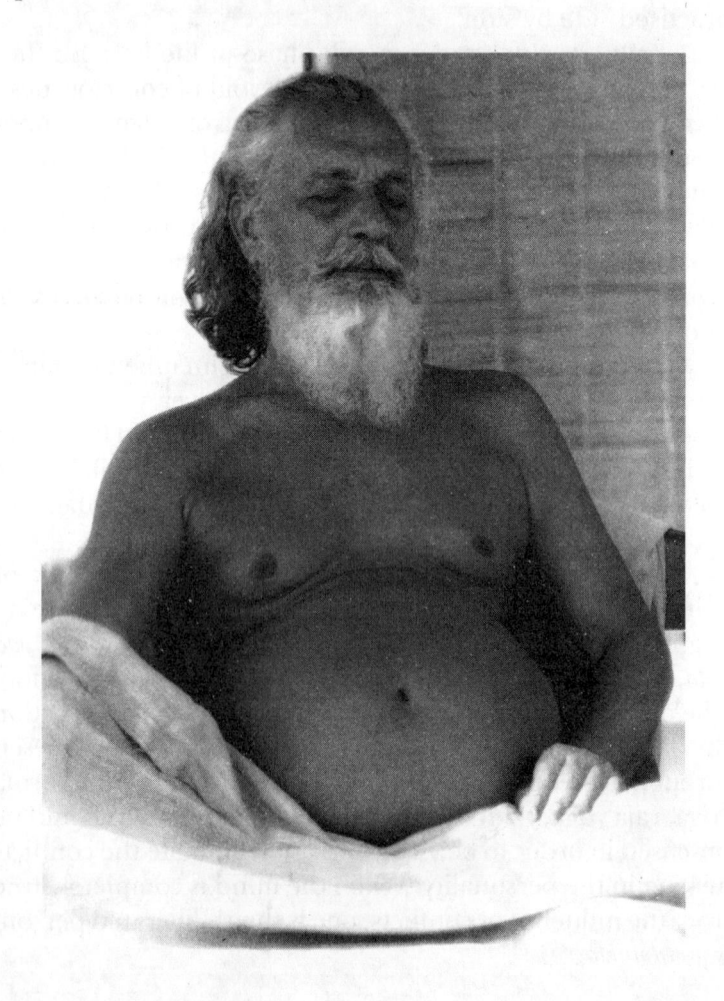

37

Enlightenment is a Process

With the help of the mind, one goes deeper and deeper into meditation until the point of enlightenment is reached. But what exactly is meant by the term enlightenment? We are aware of the outside world, we hear sounds, understand things and our senses are capable of cognition, but if we sleep we will not understand anything. At the most, if we try to concentrate and unify the tendencies of the mind, we become aware of dreams, visions and so on. But what about the innermost personality? What about the awareness of our innermost being? Enlightenment is being able to comprehend the most subtle aspect of one's personality. In the language of the Upanishads, enlightenment is being able to realize, understand and visualize the immortal personality, that which does not undergo death and decay.

During meditation, flashes of light come, sometimes body consciousness is lost, and beautiful scenes and experiences are revealed. We understand these expereinces to be the ultimate point of enlightenment, but it is not enlightenment. Those experiences are just proof that we are moving on and on. What then should happen during the ultimate process of enlightenment? How should one feel? One who has not attained enlightenment cannot talk about it, but even one who has attained enlightenment cannot talk about it. It is purely a matter of self-experience. Unless one has a tongue one cannot experience taste; it is impossible to convey the exact nature of sweetness through the ears.

Still, there are aspirants who would like to know. Enlightenment is said to be something like a drop of water which, having going into the ocean, cannot come back from the ocean. The small personality cannot come back again, but one comes back with a cosmic will, becomes an unlimited person with unlimited resources and unlimited knowledge.

Shun siddhis

At one stage of sadhana there is a tendency for the consciousness to become suspended. When sitting for meditation, there is awareness for some time, but from time to time it is overcome by a momentary void. Telepathic communication, the knowledge of things to come, may also be experienced. Such psychic powers or *siddhis* are considered to be distractions and it is difficult to avoid them.

Many spiritual aspirants become lost in these snares. They may become psychics, some begin to practise spiritual healing, others become telepathic mediums. These are held to be great achievements, but strictly speaking, according to yoga, these are downfalls in spiritual life. Aspirants have to be particularly careful of these attractions during meditation because if they become involved with them, they will be sidetracked from the main stream of consciousness. In order to avoid this, it is necessary to find a proper outlet for the correct expression of the current of spiritual power. The right direction must be given because one may have either siddhis or enlightenment, not both.

Aspirants wanting to attain higher spiritual states must shun psychic powers from the beginning. Therefore, when a person practising meditation finds himself succeeding on the spiritual path, he must also practise karma yoga. If physical, mental and intellectual karma yoga duties are performed sincerely, then the spiritual power generated through meditation will be utilized in a positive and uplifting way. The *Bhagavad Gita* says that spiritual aspirants must devote all their time to the performance of duty, to the performance of karma, and never shun the active life.

Exhaust the karmas

When I met Swami Sivananda in 1943 he just gave me one clear instruction. He said, "Exhaust your karmas. You will have to reduce the weight and grossness of karma. In your awareness there are layers and layers of grossness, impressions, dirt, distractions, *vasanas*, hidden desires and many other things. All those karmas should be exhausted. Exhausting the karma is an important sadhana in the process of enlightenment. Every karma brings an impression. In order to exhaust them, you will have to do karma yoga and not karma."

If the karmas are exhausted, then it is possible that the meditation experience will give positive rewards. But karma cannot be exhausted by karmas. Karma yoga is an impersonal action done without attachment. Karma is action done with absolute attachment. Karma brings anxiety, neurosis and exhaustion; karma yoga brings satisfaction. Karma yoga means dedication and karma means selfishness. By karma everything is for my self and by karma yoga everything is for the higher self. Performing karma adds to the karmas and the destiny becomes more and more gross. By practising karma yoga the personality becomes purer and purer, day by day, until the same thing is experienced continuously.

It is possible that the aspirant will then experience the point of enlightenment spoken about by Buddha, Christ, Mohammed and many others in many different ways. Sometimes it appears that you are nearing this point of enlightenment. The consciousness is intact and you have not lost touch with yourself, but at the same time you are not aware of the outer universe. Throughout the experience you feel that you are fully awake. After the experience of enlightenment, if you are asked, you reply that you don't know anything whatsoever. It is a point of consciousness where the world is lost for the time being. But in fact, the inner consciousness remains intact. Nothing of the inner light is lost. That is the state of enlightenment.

Realization of awareness

In the beginning enlightenment is a process, not an end in itself, because the area of enlightenment is too vast. It starts from an awareness of the self and then becomes a process of ascending, not a process of descending. It keeps on ascending and you keep on feeling the awareness expanding within you. Your awareness becomes more and more intense and more and more subtle. Just as you can feel the awareness around you, the awareness is also felt within. Some people might call it expansion of awareness, but it is better to say realization of awareness.

Knowledge and experience or realization become two different things. I may know that the electric current is flowing through the wire but if I happen to touch it, then I will experience it. In the same manner, I know that during the process of enlightenment the awareness becomes more and more prominent, but what exactly happens during the state of enlightenment is that the awareness is experienced at such a height or at such a depth that it is felt. In the process of enlightenment, the ignorance, distractions, impurities, difficulties and doubts are completely rent asunder, and then revelations start.

Revelation means a process of knowledge that comes. The spiritual being or the spiritual person or the inherent spiritual reality within you comes into prominence. It was not the speech, not the mind and not the lower body that was functioning. In reality, it was your higher spiritual personality that was operating. It is necessary to understand this most important point. Beyond the body there is the mind, and beyond the mental personality there is the higher spiritual personality.

The higher spiritual being is always operating, it is always there. It is never absent in us, even if we are unaware of it. We breathe twenty-four hours a day, our heart is continuously beating but we are unconscious of it. There are many events in our body, in our mind and in our life about which we are always unconscious. We are so extrovert that we do not know what is taking place inside us. In the same way there is one phase of awareness within us that we must become conscious of, but this can only come about by experience, not through the intellect.

The experience of Ramana Maharshi is an example. One day he felt he was dying. He lay down on the floor and saw himself split into two. He saw himself, he experienced it, even as you are seeing me and I am seeing you, and we know we are two different things. It is possible for us to become aware of the spiritual personality in that manner, but it is very rare. In most of us, there may be awareness of the existence of the body and even of the mind, but awareness of the higher self is absolutely absent. Just think, from morning until night, for how long were you aware of your physical existence, not to mention the subtle spiritual existence?

We are so unaware that it is not possible for us to be aware of our physical existence throughout the day. If it were, the tempo of our day-to-day life would be disturbed. It is possible to practise seeing your thoughts, but you can't be aware of the spirit, the atman, whenever you want to think about it. The immortal purusha, the part of you which does not die, is the one thing you have to know. This body dies, the mind, also dies, but the immortal personality does not die.

That immortal personality has no form and its experiences cannot be communicated, but at the same time it can be experienced. The saints have given it three names: *sat*, *chit* and *ananda*, existence, consciousness and bliss. These are the three attributes on the basis of which the experience of the purusha, this underlying consciousness, must take place. The Upanishads have said that the purusha is a golden colour and luminous, but whatever it is may be very difficult to say. All spiritual aspirants must become constantly aware of the spiritual person beyond the body and beyond the mind.

Discrimination, understanding the difference between real and unreal, must become known during the process of enlightenment. Once one attains enlightenment through the process of yoga – proper enlightenment, not just feelings of grandeur – then there is no darkness in any realm of life. There is no ignorance, the light within becomes very clear. The light is very quiet, there is tranquillity, no tension, and everything is full of bliss. In fact, when you have attained the light of enlightenment it can be seen; you do not need to prove that you have it.

Can enlightenment come at any time?
Enlightenment may come at any time. At first it may come like a flash from time to time until finally it stabilizes itself. It is not predestined, it is not your will. It is not an outcome of your sadhana, not an outcome of purity, not an outcome of tapasya or vairagya, which are for self-discipline. Enlightenment can come to anybody at any time. It can come to any person in the street while a saint may be waiting a hundred years.

I had always thought that enlightenment was only possible through absolute one-pointedness. However, I have come to the conclusion that enlightenment is the will of something else. If there is a will, it will come to you. Inner enlightenment can come and does come at any point. It has nothing to do with the vagabond thought process. Even while you are thinking rubbish, building castles in the air or worrying about your family, enlightenment can come. Enlightenment has nothing to do with cessation of the thought process. Even if you stop the thoughts, you cannot get enlightenment which is not there.

What is eternal enlightenment?
Within human consciousness there is a point that is light. When you have lost a valuable ornament in a room, you use a torchlight to search every corner, and when you eventually find it, you focus the torch so the ornament becomes illuminated and can be seen clearly. In the same way, in samadhi the focus of higher awareness is placed on the

inner self, which cannot be seen by the mind or experienced by any empirical sense. In order to apprehend the self, one has to jump over the mind.

There comes a stage when the mind stops for a moment. At that point of time your creation is destroyed because it is a concept of your mind. When the mind is destroyed, your creation is final. At that moment, shoonya appears. It is a state of consciousness where there is nothing, the whole process comes to a standstill. That is a wonderful moment in man's life. Suddenly there is a great experience from within called divine vision, in which one becomes aware of the divine. Buddha called it nirvana and yogis called it nirvikalpa samadhi. That is eternal enlightenment.

38

The Guru

The secret of inner awakening is the guru. No matter how much you practise yoga, if there is no guru, there can be no enlightenment. The quickest method to evolve the inner consciousness is through devotion and service to the guru. He may not be a literate or educated person, his external personality may not be in accordance with yours, but the light of his soul will enlighten all devoted to him. His words are the *atma shakti*, spiritual energy, which is transmitted to you. They are the seeds which you water when you apply and practise what he has said. When the seeds bloom forth, his words become the living reality.

Samadhi and the guru
Guru means one who has experienced the light and who has the capacity to illumine others by the light of that illumination. The guru can be anyone, but he should definitely have realized the spiritual light or knowledge. He should have become one with cosmic existence during the period of samadhi. A guru is one who dies at least once in the body and comes back. Whether for one or two nights, two or three days, twenty or thirty days, for a few days one should 'not exist'. The awareness must be withdrawn. That is the state of samadhi, the state of timelessness, when time, space and object are transcended, and then again you will have to come back into this body. Then you are not the

same person as you were last week or last year. In the state of samadhi you are totally transformed. The previous 'person' is totally dead. Such a person is known as a guru. Once you experience samadhi you will understand what guru means, because once you have attained samadhi you are a guru.

Guru does not mean a teacher or professor or trainer. People have misunderstood what a guru is, thinking he is an eminent or famous personality, a scholar, a beautiful person or a person with a flowing beard and robes. But a guru can be anyone, a Hindu, a Muslim, a Christian, a beggar, a joker, a man or a woman. The guru may prepare you adequately for samadhi; he may guide you through the awakening of all phases of consciousness, into finer and higher realms. Then again, he may not even speak to you at all. However, if the link of bhakti, an experience of inner union, is established between you and your guru, his energy can flow incessantly to you and keep your spiritual inspiration always kindled.

Not everyone can be a guru. Gurus are not made in universities but within the university of God. When one sees tragedies, comedies, laughter, crimes and people living and dying, the beauties of nature, swirling oceans and other external things, then one begins to realize that there is something more than this worldly realm. Gurus are cast in this university.

Guru's grace
A living guru is the manifestation of your own atma, and atma only appears when you have reached a certain stage of inner awareness. What the external guru says and wants for you is the voice of your own atma. Therefore, without his will there is nothing you can do. The guru can give you instant awakening if he wants to. So, the one way to samadhi is grace or *anugraha* from the guru.

The *Gheranda Samhita* (7:1–2) states that, "Samadhi, the supreme yoga, is attained by great merit earned previously. It is achieved by the grace of the guru and by devotion to him. That yogi soon acquires this exquisite experience who is convinced by what he has learnt and heard from his guru, who has developed self-confidence and whose mind is becoming more and more enlightened."

Grace or anugraha is also known as *shaktipat*. The intensity of shaktipat depends on the intensity of a disciple's desire to attain realization, and his previous samskaras. Spiritually evolved souls can attain enlightenment through intense or *tivra* shaktipat without performing much sadhana. Those who are less evolved receive intermediate or *madhyama* shaktipat to help them realize their guru and to be initiated into yoga. Through regular practice of sadhana and patience they can attain liberation. The third type of shaktipat is moderate or *manda*, which instils a yearning for spiritual knowledge, and if the desire and perseverance in the quest is pursued, there can be enlightenment.

A living tradition in India

Enlightenment is the birthright of everyone, not the monopoly of any creed. There have been many enlightened people and gurus in the West, but they lack cultural, social or governmental support. In India, we have realized the necessity and value of an enlightened guide amidst us. Even today if the prime minister goes to meet a guru, he or she will behave like a disciple. A true guru is considered to be above all. We have never seen God, but by seeing such a realized person we can at least experience the fragrance of divinity.

One does not become a guru in one day; it takes many years or lifetimes of discipline. The body, mind, emotions and psyche have to be disciplined by exposure to every kind of experience. To produce a guru requires the right environment. In India the orthodox religious communities do not interfere with sannyasins because they know yogic experience enriches the scope of religion. The spiritual endeavours of sincere sadhakas or sannyasins are respected and they are taken care of by society. This is a living tradition in India even today.

In India, many yogis did not follow the necessary disciplines and yet they attained high states of realization, but they had many problems. Such yogis are unknown, unheard, unseen, sometimes very unimpressive and very eccentric in their behaviour. They do not know how to behave socially. They may just look at you like a crazy person and shoo you away. There were many gurus like that who were enlightened people.

My guru, Swami Sivananda, was enlightened. Anandamayi Ma, who died in the 1980s, was a guru. Ramana Maharshi, who died in 1946, was a guru who lived in South India in Tiruvannamalai. Ramakrishna Paramahamsa was a guru. Swami Nityananda was the guru of Swami Muktananda. These people attained cosmic consciousness in their lifetimes. Sometimes they remained merged in samadhi consciousness for long periods, but every now and then they would come out in order to work with us.

Brahma vidya guru

In India there is the tradition of brahma vidya gurus, enlightened people who teach the science of the absolute nature of the soul. *Brahman* means absolute or expanding consciousnesses, and *vidya* means inner experience. Therefore, *brahma vidya* is the experience of expanding consciousness, and such gurus are known as brahma vidya gurus.

It is very important to understand that an enlightened guru is a product and quality of society. Although ancient India was very wealthy, for over a thousand years India has suffered from utter poverty, but in spite of the economic struggles the guru tradition has not changed. This tradition has been maintained in India, and we are very careful about it, because we know that if the gurus die, then true religion will become closed.

It is most important to realize the necessity of the guru in the context of our society because without a guru spiritual guidance will become very difficult to obtain. In order to receive spiritual guidance, an experienced, enlightened person is absolutely essential, and that is only possible if there is a cultural and social awareness of the necessity of a guru or an enlightened being amidst us.

The guru-disciple relationship is the best and highest relationship for the fulfilment of one's spiritual destiny. For those who are just practising yoga it is definitely very good to have a guru, but those who want to go further towards the highest accomplishments in spiritual life should ardently pray, "Let me have a guru; let me come to his door!"

Anywhere, in any place on the earth, you may be fortunate enough to find a spiritually illuminated person. But do not say, "Guruji, give me moksha, give me samadhi," or "Give me blessings." Just stay with him without even thinking that he will is going to give you a meditation technique or kundalini or enlightenment. The guru may only tell you to practise karma yoga, to exhaust the last remnant of karma, then the light will shine by itself. He knows that you do not have to bring the light because it is shining all the time. He has seen and is always seeing that light which we are unable to see. We are blind, and a blind person needs to be given eyes with which to see the light.

In the same way, when you go to the guru, you do not have to think or imagine or wish for the light. The light is within you. The cover of *avidya*, ignorance, constituted by the mind and samskaras must be rent asunder by karma yoga, and then light will come by itself. If you do not do it, then even though you may be a renunciate, without the responsibilities of a householder, still you will be regressing on the spiritual path day by day.

How can the inner power in the form of guru be awakened?
The higher power is formless. It is an all-pervading essence. Ordinary mortal eyes and mortal beings cannot comprehend that higher power. The transcendental forms of reality or the transcendental aspect of reality is formless, and therefore the mortal mind cannot comprehend it. However, there is a way to realize that power. You have to create an image, a form, and that form can be anything, a flower, a symbol,

your guru; there is not just one shape in which to formulate that abstract reality. Realizing that higher power in the form of your guru is the realization of savikalpa samadhi.

In raja yoga it has been explained that the highest stages of realization are twofold. One is called savikalpa samadhi and higher than that or the highest is called nirvikalpa samadhi. Nirvikalpa samadhi means that highest state of consciousness where there is no archetype, no form, no name and no limiting dimensions, where you become total and do not remain an individual. The ego is finished.

There are no means to realize the state of nirvikalpa samadhi because the very process of realization postulates duality. But when there is non-dual existence who is going to perceive whom? How can one know the knower? That is what is written in *Brihadaranyaka Upanishad*. That is the state of nirvikalpa samadhi. It has been a matter of great adventure and research for many thousands of yogis who have tried to get into that mood of experience and at the same time maintain this lower consciousness of duality so that they could say what it was. They could not do it.

Lower than nirvikalpa samadhi is savikalpa samadhi, where there is total realization of atma or *paramatma*, the highest being or the supreme essence. At the same time from some corner of the experience there is slight awareness of the existence of that, and what it is. It is because of that partial knowledge that the great yogis of the past have been able to talk about God or about consciousness. This is what is called the notion of duality, although the aspirant or the yogi or the great saint himself is beyond duality. Therefore, the process is a very simple one and you do not have to think too much about it.

Inner experience

When you look at a flower, a rose, a lotus or whatever it is, with your eyes open, it is sensorial experience. When you close your eyes and try to formulate a flower or any other object within you, and you are able to see it in the form of a vision, as a little experience, then what is it? The experience of the inner rose which you are imagining within is your mind; it is mental stuff. Therefore, that experience of a flower, of a symbol, of Krishna or Christ or guru, or anybody, is made up of your own consciousness and is said to be totally subjective. You are realizing yourself in that form. The experiences you have within during the deeper stages of meditation are manifestations of yourself, not of anybody or anything from outside.

Realization is an expression of one's higher self, *darshan*, divine vision. Passion, anger, greed, desires, anxiety, all these mental patterns experienced in day-to-day life are manifestations of the lower self. Compassion, mercy, love, sacrifice, dedication, selflessness are manifestations of the higher self. Inner visions and experiences are manifestations of one's evolving higher self. As you go deeper and deeper you become aware of the finest form of yourself.

The higher self can be realized up to savikalpa samadhi in any form you like, for example, in the form of your guru, if there is no conflict between you and your guru. If you have any conflict, then there is going to be trouble in that area of consciousness. Therefore, the Upanishads and other scriptures have very clearly stated that there should be no conflict between the guru and disciple under any circumstances because ultimately it will destroy your own patterns. You will be the loser, not the guru. Therefore, the relationship between you and your guru has to be established in such a way that the image within yourself does not fluctuate, does not extinguish, does not die, does not break, does not get disturbed and does not cause any spiritual problem, whether it is guru or Sri Krishna or Lord Rama or any other symbol. That is the form of the supreme self.

39

Awaken God From Within

In the *Ishavasya Upanishad*, we read that "the face of truth is covered with a golden cover". This all-blissful soul is as if covered by three veils. We have to tear away these veils. There are three veils and seven doors. Beyond them is the field of atma or purusha where there is infinite light and bliss. As long as we do not know these three veils, those seven gates and that inner purusha, and as long as we do not realize that there is a great power in us, we cannot get rid of our sorrows and miseries.

This body is not only as much as you see. Beyond the phases of perception and experience, beyond the seven gates, yogis have seen an infinite power within the folds of the body. Therein lies hidden the power of homogeneous consciousness. Climb those seven staircases and unlock the gates one by one. Beyond the seventh is a temple resplendent with lights, equivalent to infinite suns. He is there. There is a pure bird sitting on a thousand-petalled lotus, silent and sweet. This temple is in you, and this bird is within that temple.

Split purusha from prakriti
Our great Upanishads tell us that "the one who stays in me, who is my essence but whom I do not know, and who governs me from inside, is the soul, the inner ruler and immortal." The soul is *in* this body and not *the* body. You will discover it

at the eighth gate. But how to realize this purusha? The purusha can be attained by controlling the mind.

By practising concentration and meditation, one-pointed introversion can be attained, and gradually the mind can be brought under control. *Dhyana*, meditation, perfects the process of splitting purusha from prakriti. When you are in samadhi, the seven gates are opened and the veils are rent asunder. Once the mind merges and the meditation is keen and progressive, the soul will begin to express itself, and the light is seen clearly. That same soul which makes your body and mind work comes before you now as *sakara*, with form. At that particular moment you forget everything.

Although you know how to experience divine bliss, in order to retain that joy permanently, you must have the inner strength to bear it. The mind has to be prepared. So long as the senses wander among objects, that bliss will not be obtained. So long as the gopis are engrossed in their family affairs, they will not hear Krishna's flute. Simply saying that you are the blissful soul will not do. You might sit in silence and think over it and believe that you are not this body, but by merely saying that you are bliss absolute, you cannot become that. You must know how to realize and experience it.

Dhyana is the key

Concentration is the key to open the gates of that greatest power. When you can successfully concentrate on one idea or form, you enter into meditation. Whether you are a devotee of God or an atheist, you can realize the glory through meditation. A person with faith in God can meditate on any chosen form of God and realize Him through that form. An atheist can also be given a way to reach the destination. He can meditate on either a flower, a star, the tip of the nose, between the eyebrows, on the heart and so on. He can concentrate on *nada*, inner sound, according to the advice of an experienced master of nada yoga.

As long as you do not realize your real *swaroopa* or form, you will continue to suffer from the positive and negative charges of nature. You will not experience that supreme bliss which is your personal property. This is your first and foremost duty. Whether you are a father or mother, a husband or wife, you can walk upon this divine path to samadhi. This path is not only accessible to a brahmin or a sannyasin, every sincere soul can start on this pilgrimage to peace and power. Virtuous and saintly souls are ever ready to guide you at every step.

The path of God is the only path, the glory of God is the only glory. All else is transitory and fleeting. Here is the way to maintain that divine happiness. Life is wasted without God-realization. Intellectual achievements are futile without meditation, prosperity is a curse without peace. In short, you are dead without eternal life.

Meditation is the prerequisite for samadhi. Concentration precedes meditation as an essential step. Concentration presupposes name and form for its basis. Thus concentration culminates in meditation, and meditation terminates in samadhi and self-realization. Yoga sadhana has to be looked at in this respect.

Unlocking the secret chambers

Just going to temples and churches and discharging your religious obligations as taught by your tradition will not help to unlock the secret chambers. At best it will maintain a sense of fulfilment in your psychological condition. However much you may sit for pooja, lack of concentration will render all your efforts futile. It is always best to aim first and then shoot; there is practically no use shooting in the air. Intense practice of concentration is essential. Only then will real bliss be experienced.

Concentration is a permanent aid to success in every sphere of life. It paves the way for intuitional flashes of discovery in different fields of knowledge. It bestows keen insight and a ready reckoner of intellectual capacity. It somehow acts as a potential medium to unearth occult treasures.

The right and proper way to attain permanent joy and happiness is to regain your lost vision by the practice of yoga sadhana. Awaken God from within. Wake up, O Shiva, from within, from Kailash and dance on the bosom of your Mansarovar. I know you as my Shiva, my inner light, my Rama. Do you descend upon your children!

Samadhi and divine life

There is a boundary wall which hangs before samadhi and after meditation. Only the aspirant can remove that wall, no one else can eliminate it. But not everyone will be able to go through it, as it is such a solid wall. How can that wall be removed? Swami Sivananda used to tell everyone that life had to be lived in all its nobility and fullness, so that the onslaughts, tremors and shocks from family members, friends and enemies, well-wishers and ill-wishers, would have no effect. Every day, therefore, you must try to adjust to insult, injury, pain and pleasure alike.

You have to test yourself and see how you fare. Analyze yourself: what am I feeling? Find out how you become affected or shocked, how you respond to the negative things in life. Try to perfect divine life because constant application to this higher side of life should go hand in hand with other yogic practices and meditation.

Some kind of philosophy will help in life. It may be based on religion, or it may be that of a yogi, that of a devotee or *bhakta*, but that philosophy has to emerge from the depths of your heart, so that one day when you sit down for meditation, your consciousness shoots up like a rocket and goes to the highest point of samadhi.

There appear to be two different standards in life. In human life our contacts are good and bad. In divine life everything is judged from a higher standard. The human standard is if anyone is inflicting injury on you, give it back the same way. The divine standard is if anyone inflicts injury on you, then you must bear it.

Swami Sivananda used to believe that for a yogi, for one who wants to attain the higher spiritual path, divine life must be practised side by side with meditation. For him the ethical way of living was not merely an adjustment with society, but an act of self-purification. The sadhana is as follows: I will not rob you, not because I might go to jail, but because being honest is an act of purity. Similarly, I observe non-violence, kindness and compassion for everyone, not because it is ethics or part of morality, but because acting in this way will exhaust my karma and purify my heart. So in this way we can exhaust the dross, the density and thickness of our karma, the residue of our past actions. Only when the impressions are cleaned will life be illumined from inside.

You may attain a very high state of meditation, yet become unconscious because you are unable to develop supreme awareness within. Why? Meditation is the easiest thing, but the trouble is that your life, thinking, concepts, reactions and responses are not in accordance with the laws that meditation demands. This is the necessary relationship between divine life and the final point of yoga. Therefore, side by side with yogic techniques, practise divine life little by little. If it is not possible to practise it today, I assure you that after having attained the highest state of meditation, you will have to come back down.

Samadhi at any point
It is said, "Wherever the mind goes, on whichever object the mind is fixed, it just goes into samadhi." What a fine concept! When you look at something dirty, you go into samadhi. When you look at sensual objects, you go into samadhi. When you look at Lord Rama or Sri Krishna or the guru, you go into samadhi. When you look at a beautiful man or woman, you go into samadhi. Wherever you fix the mind, you can just go into samadhi. You have that much control of the mind, that much *samyama*, that you can experience samadhi at any point.

How does this happen? When your consciousness is fixed in the higher self and the ego is melting, when awareness of objects, space and time is completely dissolved, and the mind sees just one point before it, this is the state of samadhi.

If you are concentrating on a light, there is nothing but the light; if you are concentrating on a shivalingam, there is nothing but a shivalingam; when you are concentrating on a flower, there is nothing but a flower; when you are concentrating on a bad idea, there is nothing but that evil idea. Everything else must be forgotten. That should be the efficiency and capacity of the mind, to grasp the totality of the object and merge itself in that object. It is then that the mind transforms.

Therefore, it is important for everyone to practise sadhana systematically. If time permits, if opportunities come, you should not lose even one moment of sadhana. Our ancestors have said that it is difficult to obtain a human birth. We are not sure that we will be as born human beings again. What is the guarantee that we are going to be born with the same chances and the same opportunity? If you lose this chance for sadhana, you may it lose forever.

Jivanmukti and the final samadhi

A little drop of water went into the ocean with one purpose, not to lose itself, but to discover its depth. However, once that little drop went inside it completely lost its identity and became one with the infinite ocean. Similarly, after our own little 'I' consciousness merges with the infinite oneness, the individual consciousness no longer remains. Awareness of the self dissolves.

After that merger, the individual just moves about according to the dictates of nature. His movements are beyond ego, beyond 'I'. He lives without ego; his body and senses perform their own natural actions of seeing and hearing. It is said in the Upanishads that even after the merger of this 'I', ego consciousness, the individual lives in the state of *jivanmukti*, liberated while living. The liberated individual still has certain karmas to perform in the world, but they are higher karmas, acts of compassion for all living beings.

A jivanmukta lives for some time in order to fulfil divine acts of compassion. Then the final state of liberation comes and not only the spiritual consciousness, but also the physical consciousness is dissolved. When that state begins, the aspirant lives for only twenty-one days. He then departs this life, and there is no rebirth.

In my life I have seen such a man in the final state of liberation – Swami Sivananda. With him there was no physical consciousness, he was always in samadhi. When he achieved the state of final liberation, he told everyone to do his respective work and that he wanted to enter into samadhi. He became absolutely unconscious for twenty-one days; there were no physical actions at all. However, on the twenty-first day he opened his eyes and said, "Is this the twenty-first day?" He asked just that much. We did not know what was happening to him. We thought that maybe he had fallen ill or that he had fainted, or that he had had some kind of coronary or some other disease. You see, we are mere human beings, we cannot understand these highest states of existence!

At this time he asked a lady doctor to bring a piece of paper and a fountain pen and he wrote an important sentence: "My message is that God is real, everything else is unreal," and under that Sivananda. That was the end of his message. It appeared that Swamiji was unconscious during those twenty-one days, but how did he know that it was the twenty-first day? There is some other consciousness which keeps on functioning.

Liberation is a continuous process
When the final liberation takes place, the physical body survives for a maximum period of twenty-one days. The body can only survive for this long because it is not protected and it is not nourished, there is no circulation, respiration or prana. This body only survives on one's will to live. So because the liberated person has become completely oblivious to the body, disintegration or death takes place. If one has no interest in one's body, one cannot remain with it.

Although *jivanmuktas* or liberated saints may no longer have any need for a body, some still incarnate because they have not yet permanently removed themselves from the cycle of rebirth. Jivanmuktas incarnate, paramahamsas incarnate, and so do rishis and saints. Only *videhamuktas* do not incarnate, those who have become completely free from the tentacles of life and the superficial structures of body consciousness. Some of the saints from the Christian, Hindu, Jain and Muslim traditions have been videhamuktas, and some of the Greek saints, who were called cynics, have also been videhamuktas.

It is important to understand that liberation is a continual process. You are already liberated but at a subtle level, not completely. If you were not liberated, then you would be behaving like a cow, a buffalo or a donkey. As the process of liberation continues, more and more light becomes vivid before you and things become better and clearer. Liberation is not like magic in which something is removed and something else appears in its place. It is always going on.

Liberation is a continuous process, and it has already occurred when the spirit was liberated from the mineral kingdom to the herbal kingdom. Then again it was liberated from the herbal kingdom to the animal kingdom, and then from the animal kingdom to the human kingdom. Again it was liberated from the lower human kingdom to the higher intelligent human kingdom. And then it was liberated from the higher intelligent human kingdom to the spiritually intelligent kingdom, as many people are. Liberation is another name for the outcome of evolution.

The supreme abode

The supreme abode is for everyone, it is not reserved only for the righteous few. If the doors of heaven were only open for holy people, then I think it would be God's greatest disappointment. He would have to wait and wait. There would be very few entries because man's evolution is incomplete, and he is suffering from infirm willpower. He is not perfect. If the doors of hell were open for every sinner, there would surely be an overpopulation problem there. This is not a joke, it is a very serious matter. I have never believed in sin and I do not think that man is a sinner. We meet obstacles, we falter and we fall, that is all. Every time we fall, we make a fresh attempt to evolve. It is very important to know that the spiritual light is for everyone. Samadhi and spiritual evolution can be had by all. We are born for this purpose.

It is only in samadhi that all the highest purities of peace, light, bliss and ecstasy appear. No amount of enjoyment in life can equal this rare experience. Whether you call it emancipation, salvation, darshan, enlightenment, nirvikalpa samadhi, *adwaita anubhuti*, the non-dual experience, moksha, nirvana, shoonya, kaivalya, kundalini awakening, God-realization, union with God or absolute experience, it's all the same. There are many, many other names for the experience of samadhi. It has no name and it has every name. It is beautiful, it is splendid. It is the last door which opens into the temple of unimaginable bliss. It is the final goal and ultimate purpose of human existence.

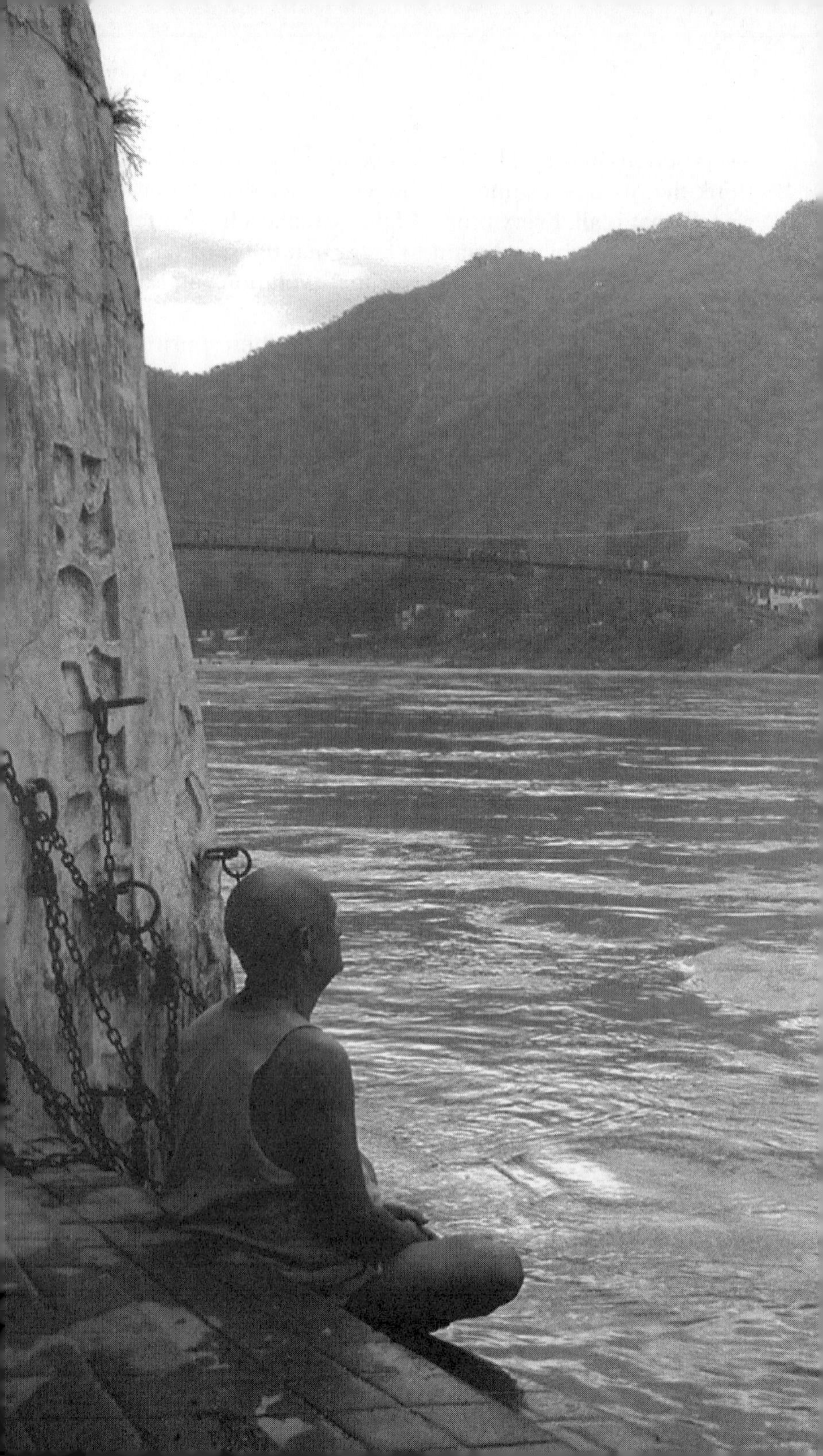

The Form of Ishta

Samadhi is a blissful state of mind
Where there is no other experience except atma.
This too is consumed in full-fledged nirvikalpa
When not even a bit of the individual functions.
Savikalpa retains the experiences of atma
In the form of Ishta;
Nirvikalpa is at once homogeneous
Devoid of any subject or object.
Bhakta can talk to Ishta in the state of savikalpa,
There he feels close to his Lord,
He is so aware of his Lord
That he loses all self-consciousness.
He hears the divine speech of his Lord,
He finds all questions answered and wishes fulfilled,
He is taken back into the arena of his previous lives
Which he views with awe and wonder.
Then God becomes a concrete reality to him,
Guru becomes a divine power.
He truly feels his Ishta before him
Just as you see your living father before you.
The only difference is that you see your father
While you are aware of yourself
But in samadhi you see the Ishta
While you are unaware of yourself.
Having attained samadhi, bhakta becomes calm,
Peaceful, cheerful, powerful and intuitive;
A veritable medium of his grace and lila,
Atma manifests through him.
Body, action and thought are divinized,
Everything moves according to his wish.
This is difficult to follow through intellect
But you will experience it when you attain samadhi.

—Rajnandgaon, 1960

Glossary

Abhyasa – constant uninterrupted practice for a prolonged period
Adhyatma vidya – knowledge of the self; spiritual wisdom
Adhyatmic anubhava – direct perception of the atma or soul
Adi Shankaracharya – enlightened sage who revitalized the Shaivite tradition, expounded and spread the Adwaita Vedanta philosophy throughout India, and founded the Dashnami order of sannyasa
Adwaita – non-dual experience; concept of oneness; monistic vision of reality; union with the supreme existence or Brahman
Adwaita anubhuti – experience of non-dual consciousness
Adwaita bhava – feeling of unity
Adwaita jnana – realization of oneness, non-duality, unity
Adwaita Vedanta – non-dualistic philosophy of Adi Shankaracharya based on the experience of Brahman as the absolute reality
Aham Brahmasmi – 'I am Brahman'; one of the four mahavakyas or greatest spiritual sayings of the Upanishads
Ahamkara – egoism, 'I am-ness'
Ahimsa – non-violence; one of the yamas described in Patanjali's *Yoga Sutras*
Ajapa japa – continuous, spontaneous repetition of mantra
Ajna chakra – pranic centre or chakra situated at the top of the spinal cord; seat of intuition; psychic centre where guru's commands are received
Ajnana – ignorance; unawareness
Akarta – non-doer
Akhanda – unbroken, continuous
Akhanda swaroopa – the eternal self
Alambana – support
Anadi – eternal; beginningless
Anahata nada – transcendental cosmic sound experienced only in the higher states of meditation; sound which cannot be grasped or heard externally
Ananda – pure, undying bliss
Ananda samadhi – blissful absorption; a phase of samprajnata awareness characterized by a state of bliss

Anandamaya kosha – sheath or body of bliss
Annamaya kosha – sheath or body of matter
Antar – inner, internal
Antaranga – inner limb; in raja yoga: sense withdrawal (pratyahara) leads to concentration (dharana), meditation (dhyana) and samadhi
Antarmukha vritti – state in which the mind is turned inward and withdrawn from external objects
Anubhava – knowledge derived from personal experience
Anugraha – divine grace
Anushthana – fixed course of sadhana; a resolve to perform sadhana with absolute discipline for a required period of time
Aparoksha anubhuti – direct, actual experience; state of intuitive experience
Aparoksha jnana – knowledge gained directly, without the medium of the senses
Apta kama – one who has renounced all worldly desires and attachments
Artha – real knowledge of the object of meditation; ultimate purpose
Asamprajnata samadhi – samadhi which occurs between the different stages of samprajnata samadhi; transitional stage of samadhi where the traces of the mind or samskaras become active according to their intensity
Asana – a physical posture in which one is at ease and in harmony with oneself; third limb of ashtanga yoga in Patanjali's *Yoga Sutras*
Ashanti – disturbed state of mind
Ashram – a place of spiritual retreat and inner growth through internal and external labour
Ashtanga yoga – the eight limbs of yoga described by Patanjali in the *Yoga Sutras*: yama, niyama, asana, pranayama, pratyahara, dharana, dhyana, samadhi
Asmita – sense of doership; 'I-ness'
Asmita samadhi – a state of samprajnata samadhi attained by dissolution of the ego; merging of body, mind and soul; samadhi with the seed of individual self-awareness; superconscious state immediately below seedless samadhi (nirbija samadhi) with only the feeling of 'I am' or 'I exist', 'Aham Asmi'
Atma(n) – the self beyond mind and body; supreme consciousness, spirit, soul

Atmabhava – seeing the atma or soul equally in all beings
Atma anubhuti – perception of the inner self or atma
Atma chetana – inner consciousness; state of suprasensual intuition
Atma drashta – seer of the self
Atma jnana – direct knowledge of the self; self-realization
Atma maya – the illusory force of the self responsible for the creation of matter
Atma shakti – spiritual force of energy
Atma vidya – the experience of the soul
Aum, Om – universal mantra considered to be the origin of all other mantras; cosmic vibration of the universe; represents four states of mind: conscious, subconscious, unconscious and supraconscious or cosmic mind
Avadhoota – one free from all worldly attachments or mental illusions
Avarana – veil of ignorance
Avasthanam – established
Avatara – descent, advent or incarnation of God
Avidya – ignorance; lack of conscious awareness
Avyakta – not manifest
Bahirmukha vritti – the outgoing tendency of the mind
Bhagavad Gita – Lord Krishna's discourse to Arjuna at the start of the Mahabharata war, containing the essence of yoga
Bhajan – devotional song
Bhakta – devotee
Bhakti – complete devotion to a higher reality of life; channelling of emotion to a higher purpose
Bhakti yoga – yoga of devotion; a systematic path with nine stages to purify the emotions
Bhava – feeling; love; inner attitude or subtle emotion
Bhava samadhi – absorption in meditation due to an emotional cause, such as kirtan; superconscious state of existence attained by intense emotion
Bhoktritva – enjoyership
Bhranti – illusory impression
Bhrumadhya – the mid-eyebrow centre; trigger point for ajna chakra
Bhu loka – terrestrial plane of existence
Bhuvar loka – intermediate realm between heaven and earth
Bija – seed, source, origin
Bindu – point; source of creation

Brahma, Brahman – God as creator; eternal, omnipresent principle of existence or ultimate reality
Brahma anubhava – self-realization; absolute experience
Brahma bhavana – feeling that all is Brahman
Brahma jnana – realization or immediate knowledge of Brahman
Brahma loka – the celestial sphere of Brahma; also called satya loka
Brahma vidya – knowledge of Brahman; science of the self
Brahmacharya – conduct suitable for proceeding to the highest state of existence, especially continence or control of sensual impulses; one of the yamas described in Patanjali's *Yoga Sutras*
Brahmakara vritti – the flow of the mind towards Brahman
Brahmanishtha – one who is established in direct knowledge of Brahman
Buddha – the enlightened one
Buddhi – discriminating aspect of mind; higher intelligence concerned with real wisdom; intuitive aspect of consciousness by which the essential self awakens to truth; creative intelligence
Chaitanya – absolute consciousness
Chaitanya samadhi – the state of superconsciousness marked by absolute self-awareness and illumination, as distinct from jada samadhi in which there is no such awareness
Chakra – wheel or vortex; centre of energy or psychic centre
Chidakasha – the inner space visualized in meditation behind the closed eyes or in the region of ajna chakra; the state of pure, unbounded consciousness
Chiranjivi – one who has obtained eternal life
Chit – thought; perception; intelligence; Brahman, the pure consciousness that lies beyond all phenomena
Chitta – individual consciousness, including the subconscious and unconscious layers of mind; storehouse of memory or samskaras; one of the four aspects of antahkarana or inner instrument; seat of consciousness, and as such includes the conscious, subconscious, unconscious and superconscious
Chitta vritti – disposition or state of the mind; mental fluctuation, movement or modification
Darshan – glimpse, seeing, observing; spiritual vision
Deva – luminous being; a god or divine being
Dharana – concentration or complete attention; sixth stage of ashtanga yoga described by Patanjali's *Yoga Sutras* as holding or binding of the mind to one point

Dharma – the natural role played in life; ethical law; duty; the laws or fundamental support of life; virtue, righteousness, good work; regarded as one of the four aims of human existence (purushartha)

Dharmamegha samadhi – state of superconsciousness or samadhi called 'cloud of virtue', as it showers nectar drops of immortality through the knowledge of Brahman when the deep impressions (vasanas) are entirely destroyed; the ultimate point of the aim of yoga; the final point of transformation in all realms of existence; finest type of samadhi

Dhyana – spontaneous state after deep concentration or meditation; the seventh of the eight steps described in raja yoga; the intermediate internal process where the power of attention becomes so steadily fixed upon the object of meditation that other thoughts do not enter the mind; natural expression of the sattwic state

Dhyana yoga – 'Yoga of meditation', the sixth chapter of the *Bhagavad Gita*, which explains the techniques of meditation resulting in mastery of the senses, self-control and the vision of the self in all beings

Dhyata – meditator

Dhyeya – object of meditation or worship; purpose behind action

Divya bhava – divine feeling

Divya chakshu – divine eye, associated with the third eye or the eye of Shiva

Divya drishti – divine sight; the divine eye, also called the third eye, located between the eyebrows or in ajna chakra; intuition; clairvoyance

Divya loka – plane of divine or transcendental experience

Drashta – witness, uninvolved observer, onlooker, seer; the consciousness which knows what is going on; atman or purusha

Drashta bhava – witnessing attitude

Dridha – strong, fixed

Drishyam – the seen

Drishyanuvid – a state of savikalpa samadhi connected with an object

Dukha – uneasiness; difficult; unpleasant; grief, pain, suffering

Dwesha – repulsion, aversion; hatred, enmity, dislike, repugnance, antagonism; one of the five afflictions (kleshas) described by Patanjali's *Yoga Sutras*

Ekagrata – one-pointedness of mind

Ekanta – solitary

Gopi – milkmaid; the gopis of Vrindavan were the transcendental devotees of Lord Krishna

Govinda – a name of Krishna

Granthi – psychic knot; the three granthis on sushumna nadi hinder the upward passage of kundalini: brahma granthi at mooladhara chakra, vishnu granthi at manipura chakra and rudra granthi at ajna chakra

Grihastha ashrama – second stage of life according to the ancient vedic tradition, i.e. household or married life

Guna – quality; the three aspects of nature (prakriti) which are present in every form of creation, known as sattwa, rajas and tamas

Guru – one who dispels the darkness caused by ignorance; spiritually enlightened soul who is able to guide others towards enlightenment

Hatha yoga – yoga of attaining physical and mental purity and balancing the prana (energy) in ida and pingala nadis so that sushumna nadi opens, enabling samadhi experiences

Hiranyagarbha – the golden egg or womb of creation; the first formation from the formless, the beginning of all time and space which spreads from the centre of the immeasurable present

Ida nadi – a major pranic channel in the subtle body which conducts the passive aspect of prana, manifesting as mental energy, throughout the body and mind; located on the left side of the body; lunar force or chitta shakti

Indriya – sense organ of cognition and action, ten in number; see jnanendriya and karmendriya

Ishta devata – personal, chosen deity, one's favourite god, the aspect of God which is dear to you

Ishwara – higher reality; unmanifest existence; principle of higher consciousness defined by Patanjali in the *Yoga Sutras* as a special purusha (soul) beyond the effect of karma (actions) and klesha (afflictions); a state of consciousness beyond the physical and mental realms governing the entire physical universe; supreme being

Ishwara pranidhana – cultivation of faith in the supreme or indestructible reality; surrender to God or the higher reality; one of the niyamas described by Patanjali in the *Yoga Sutras*

Jada samadhi – state of samadhi induced by the hatha yogic process in which there is no awareness or illumination, as opposed to chaitanya samadhi

Jagrat – state of consciousness related to the senses and the phenomenal material universe
Jana loka – plane of seers and sages; one of the seven higher planes of consciousness
Japa – conscious repetition of a mantra
Jiva – individual or personal soul; principle of life; living being
Jivanmukta – one who is liberated while living; a person who, being purified by true knowledge of the supreme reality, is freed from future births and all ceremonial rites while yet embodied in Vedanta, a person who has experienced all seven stages of wisdom
Jivanmukti – final liberation in the present state of life; expanded state of awareness
Jivatma – individual or personal soul
Jnana – knowing, understanding; higher knowledge derived from meditation or from inner experience; wisdom
Jnana chakshu – the eye of wisdom; the mind's eye; immediate vision of reality
Jnana yoga – yoga of knowledge and wisdom attained through spontaneous self-analysis and investigation of abstract or speculative ideas; contemplation as the principal means of attaining the higher knowledge of reality
Jnana yogi – one who practises the principles of jnana yoga; one who lives wisdom
Jnanasurya – the light of knowledge
Jnanendriya – five sensory organs of perception: ears, skin, eyes, tongue and nose
Jyoti – light, brightness
Kaivalya – final liberation; state of consciousness beyond duality
Kaivalyapragbharam – inclined towards oneness
Kalpa vriksha – wish-fulfilling tree; a psychic centre activated when anahata chakra is awakened, resulting in the ability to materialize what is desired
Kama – emotional need for fulfilment; wish, object of desire; one of the four purushartha
Karana sharira – causal body
Karma – action and result; action in the manifest and unmanifest dimension; universal law of cause and effect that shapes the destiny of each individual with actions inevitably bearing their fruit

Karma yoga – yogic path of selfless service; yogic discipline based on the law of cause and effect; gaining immunity to karma by dedicating one's actions to God or guru; action performed with meditative awareness; actions performed unselfishly for the welfare of others, without attachment to the fruit of one's action and renouncing the doership and enjoyership of any action

Karmendriya – five physical organs of action: vocal cords, hands, feet, reproductive and excretory organs

Karta – doer

Kartritva – doership

Kevala kumbhaka – spontaneous breath retention, the kumbhaka that occurs during samadhi when the consciousness transcends duality

Kirtan – singing of God's name

Klesha – pain, anguish, affliction, distress, suffering; clinging to mundane life; five afflictions described in Patanjali's *Yoga Sutras*: ignorance (avidya), ego or sense of doership (asmita), attraction (raga), aversion (dwesha) and fear of death (abhinivesha)

Kosha – body, sheath or realm of experience or existence; covering of the self which limits manifestation of the ultimate reality

Krama mukti – progressive emancipation of devotees in which they proceed from this world to the world of Brahma, and from there attain kaivalya

Kripa – grace; blessing; mercy

Krishna – eighth incarnation of Lord Vishnu, who lived in Dwapara yuga; his teachings are recorded in the *Bhagavad Gita*; beloved of the gopis of Vrindavan

Kritartha – a person whose purpose is fulfilled

Kriya – creative action or motion

Kriya yoga – practices of kundalini yoga designed to speed the evolution of humanity

Kriyamana – the effect of the deeds of the present life which are to be experienced in the future

Kumbhaka – internal or external retention of breath, a conscious process practised with shatkarma, asana, pranayama, mudra and bandha that aims at either retaining breath within the body (antar kumbhaka) or keeping it outside the body (bahir kumbhaka), and a spontaneous process accompanying samadhi states

Kundalini – spiritual energy; evolutionary potential related to the capacity and consciousness of human beings; the form of divine

cosmic energy lying dormant in mooladhara chakra, often referred to as the serpent power
Kundalini yoga – path of yoga which awakens the dormant spiritual force
Laya – dissolution
Laya yoga – yoga of conscious dissolution of individuality; system of yoga where suspended animation takes place; the preferred technique for samadhi explained in the final chapter of *Hatha Yoga Pradipika*
Lila – play; diversion, pleasure; activity of prakriti and its three gunas
Loka – plane of existence; seven higher dimensions of consciousness above sahasrara: bhu, bhuvar, maha, swah, tapo, jana and satya lokas
Lokasangraham – upliftment of society
Maha – great
Maha loka – one of the seven higher dimensions of consciousness; plane of saints and siddhas
Maha rasa – great cosmic dance: process where everything dissolves into the supreme self
Maha samadhi – final liberation experienced on the departure of the spirit from the body; death
Mahat – greater mind; the total mind which includes manas, buddhi, chitta and ahamkara; universal intellect (also called buddhi); in Samkhya philosophy, mahat is the first product from prakriti's process of manifestation and reflects the consciousness of purusha into the material realm of prakriti's evolutes
Mahavakya – four great statements of the Upanishads: 'Prajnanam Brahma': Consciousness is Brahman; 'Aham Brahmasmi': I am Brahman; 'Tat Tvam Asi': You are That; 'Ayam Atma Brahma': the soul is Brahman
Manasarovar – the lake of the greater mind
Manomaya kosha – mental body or sheath
Manonasha – dissolution of the conditioned mind, destruction of the mind (enabling one to see beyond it)
Manorajya – building castles in the air; realm of fancy
Mantra – subtle sound or combination of sound vibrations revealed to sages in deep meditation, used for liberating energy and consciousness from the limitations of mundane awareness
Maya – creative power; illusory force responsible for erroneous perception; cause of the phenomenal world

Mirabai – female saint born in the early 16th century in Rajasthan, India; a great devotee of Lord Krishna
Moha – delusion, confusion, error; infatuation; attachment
Moksha – liberation, freedom, release; in yoga, final emancipation, liberation from the wheel of births and deaths, the aim of yogic practices; one of the four purusharthas
Moola prakriti – the transcendental basis of physical nature; original source of all evolution
Mukti – release, liberation; according to Vedanta, liberation is due to right knowledge, or intuition of truth (tattwa jnana); final absolution of the self from the chain of birth and death
Nada – subtle sound vibration heard in the meditative state
Nadi – psychic current; flow of energy
Nama japa – repetition of God's name
Neti-neti – 'Not this! Not this!'; a famous exclamation of the Upanishads related to the impossibility of reducing divinity to any explanation or definition
Nididhyasana – profound, deep meditation
Nidra – deep sleep; isolation from mind and senses; unconscious state; one of the five vrittis listed in Patanjali's *Yoga Sutras*
Nirakara – without form, formless; unmanifest
Niranta – endless, continuous
Nirbija – seedless, without any seeds
Nirbija samadhi – final state of samadhi in which there is absorption without seed; total dissolution
Nirguna – formless; without qualities or attributes; beyond the three gunas
Nirodha – complete cessation of the patterns of consciousness when the mind is under perfect control; beyond the three gunas
Nirvana – cessation of suffering; final liberation or emancipation in Buddhist thought
Nirvichara – thoughtlessness (in meditation); without argumentation
Nirvichara samadhi – transitional stage of samadhi; absorption without reflection; superconscious state where there is no intellectual enquiry
Nirvikalpa – without any modifications or thoughts
Nirvikalpa samadhi – state in which the mind ceases to function and only pure consciousness remains, revealing itself to itself and there is no object of the mind; superconscious state where

mental modifications cease to exist, resulting in transcendence of the manifest world

Nirvitarka – without argumentation or logic

Nirvitarka samadhi – transitional stage of samadhi involving purification of memory, which gives rise to true knowledge of the object of perception; superconscious state where there is no intellectual argumentation or logic

Nishtha – steadfastness, established

Niyama – observances or rules of personal discipline to render the mind tranquil in preparation for meditation: purity (shaucha), satisfaction or contentment (santosha), austerity or penance (tapas), self-study (swadhyaya), and renunciation of the fruits of action or dedication to the Lord or to the highest principle (ishwara pranidhana); second step of ashtanga yoga in Patanjali's *Yoga Sutras*

Para bhakti – supreme devotion, which is said to accompany or follow the highest knowledge and be a state of consciousness which is self-contained

Para vairagya – absence of attachment in any form; highest type or state of dispassion (vairagya)

Para vidya – higher knowledge, transcendental knowledge, direct knowledge of Brahman

Param – the supreme being

Paramahamsa – supreme swan; one who is able to distinguish between reality and unreality; one who controls or subdues the passions; a sage, an ascetic; title of a person in the fourth stage of consciousness

Paramananda – supreme bliss

Paramatma – supreme soul

Parinama – transformation; according to Patanjali's *Yoga Sutras* transformation of the mind has three stages: in the form of tranquillity (samadhi parinama), in the form of Aum (ekagrata parinama), and suppression of the inner object (nirodha parinama)

Paripoorna – completely full

Pashu bhava – the animal nature

Patanjali – author of the *Yoga Sutras*; an ancient rishi who codified the meditative stages and states of samadhi into the system of raja yoga and is famous as the propounder of ashtanga yoga

Pingala nadi – a major pranic channel located on the right side of the body, which conducts the dynamic pranic force manifesting as prana shakti; also called surya nadi

Prajna – knowledge with awareness; awareness of the one without a second; understanding, wisdom, discrimination

Prakriti – individual nature; manifest and unmanifest nature; cosmic energy; the active principle of manifest energy; nature or primordial matter (source of the universe); according to Samkhya philosophy, insentient prakriti consists of three aspects or qualities called gunas: sattwa, rajas and tamas. They remain unmanifest (avyakta) when in equilibrium, but when this equilibrium is disturbed by the proximity of the witnessing purusha consciousness, manifestation, creation and evolution set in

Prakriti moksha – universal liberation; the end of a vast cycle

Prakritilaya – one who is submerged into prakriti

Prana – life force; vital energy permeating and sustaining life and creation, both in the micro and macrocosmos

Pranamaya kosha – energy sheath or pranic body

Pranava – another word for Aum (Om)

Pranayama – a series of techniques using the breath to control the flow of prana within the body; expansion of the range of vital energy

Prarabdha karma – actions already performed, the results of which cannot be avoided; that portion of one's actions which is bound to fructify in the present life and cannot be averted

Pratyabhijna – illumined knowledge; recognition

Pratyahara – restraining the sensory and motor organs; withdrawal and emancipation of the mind from the domination of the senses and sensual objects; training the senses to follow the mind within; prerequisite for dharana and higher stages of meditation; fifth stage of raja yoga

Pratyaksha – direct evidence or sense evidence, presented by Patanjali in the *Yoga Sutras* as one of the three sources for the vritti of right knowledge (pramana); present before the eyes

Pratyaya – seeds or impressions in the field of consciousness which do not disappear even in the first stages of samadhi; content of mind (in yoga philosophy)

Prem – love, affection

Purusha – 'who dwells in the city', the body being the dormant receptacle of consciousness, the soul; the totality of consciousness; the supreme being, God; in Samkhya philosophy purusha designates pure consciousness, undefiled and unlimited by contact with prakriti or matter

Purushartha – human attainment; the four goals to be fulfilled in life: wealth (artha), emotional fulfilment (kama), duty (dharma), and liberation (moksha)

Raga – attachment, attraction; one of the five afflictions (kleshas) described by Patanjali's *Yoga Sutras* as being attracted to (or attached to) what gives pleasure

Raja yoga – yoga of awakening the psychic awareness and faculties through meditation; the scientific method of union with the supreme universal being through control of the mental processes, which includes the eight limbs of ashtanga yoga; enquiry into the inner awareness of samadhi; the most authoritative text is Patanjali's *Yoga Sutras*

Rajas – one of the three gunas of nature (prakriti) and all matter; dynamism

Rasalila – cosmic dance where prakriti conjuncts with purusha and causes creation

Rasasvada – tasting the essence of the bliss of savikalpa samadhi

Ritambhara – full of experience; cosmic harmony

Ritambhara prajna – power or truth obtained in the super-reflective state of samadhi; cosmic experience

Roopa – form

Sabija – with seed

Sabija samadhi – absorption with seed (sabija); the state of samadhi in which the seeds of desire remain in the mind, and thus the seed of actions (karma) is not destroyed

Sadachara – good conduct

Sadhaka – spiritual aspirant established in sadhana

Sadhana – spiritual practice or discipline performed regularly for the attainment of inner experience and self-realization

Sadyomukti – immediate liberation

Saguna – with form or attributes; within the realm of the three gunas

Sahaja samadhi – spontaneous meditative experience where the mind is totally withdrawn from the external world

Sahasrara chakra – the thousand-petalled lotus; abode of super-consciousness; highest chakra or psychic centre which symbolizes the threshold between the psychic and spiritual realms, located at the crown of the head

Sakara – with form; manifest

Sakshi – eternal witness; that which passively observes the actions of the body, emotions, mind and senses without being at all affected

Sakshi bhava – attitude of remaining the witness; seer
Samadhi – culmination of meditation; state of unity with the object of meditation and the universal consciousness; final step of raja yoga; a state in which the mind is either completely concentrated on its object of contemplation (savikalpa samadhi), or ceases to function and only pure consciousness or pure awareness remains, revealing itself to itself (nirvikalpa samadhi)
Samadhi prajna – higher knowledge attained through samadhi
Samapatti – complete absorption; samadhi; a state of mind where there is complete acceptance and equilibrium; it includes a wide range of superconscious states in which absorption becomes deeper and deeper
Samkhya – one of the six systems of Indian philosophy, based on the division of all existence into the two eternal principles of purusha and prakriti, and the twenty-five elements of creation; the philosophical basis of the yoga system
Samprajnata – knowledge with awareness
Samprajnata samadhi – samadhi with intuitive awareness (prajna); transcendental state where the phases are vitarka, vichara, ananda and asmita. It alternates with asamprajnata samadhi and culminates in nirbija samadhi
Samsara – illusory world; cycle of birth, death and rebirth
Samskara – mental impression stored in the subtle body as an archetype; past patterns and mental impressions which remain unnoticed in the mind yet set up impulses and trains of thought; unconscious memories
Samyama – perfection of concentration; harmonious control of concentration (dharana), meditation (dhyana) and samadhi fused into one process, by which the yogi can know the inner cause of anything concentrated upon
Sanchita karma – the sum total of all actions done by the living being (jiva) during countless previous births, out of which a portion is allotted for every new birth
Sankalpa – positive resolve; desire, wish, thought, idea, reflection
Sankalpa-vikalpa – thought and counter-thought, awareness and counter-awareness
Sarvavid – one who knows everything in detail; a liberated sage
Satchidananda – the supreme reality as self-existent existence-consciousness-bliss

Satchidananda swaroopa – embodiment of existence-consciousness-bliss

Satsang – gathering in which the ideals and principles of truth are discussed; spiritual association; association with the wise and the good

Satsankalpa – true resolve; pure desire; perfect will

Sattwa – one of the three qualities (gunas) of nature (prakriti) and all matter; state of luminosity, harmony, equilibrium, steadiness and purity

Satya – absolute truth; one of the yamas described by Patanjali's *Yoga Sutras*, leading to a state where actions are based on and culminate in the truth

Satya loka – highest of the seven higher dimensions of consciousness; plane of truth and reality; also called Brahma loka

Savichara – with reflection

Savichara samadhi – a phase of samprajnata samadhi according to Patanjali's *Yoga Sutras*, where reflection alternates between time, space and object, but there is no thinking in words

Savikalpa – with imagination

Savikalpa samadhi – a kind of samadhi in which the mind still retains its material impressions (distinctions such as between subject and object, or of the knower and the known)

Savitarka – with logic and reasoning

Savitarka samadhi – a phase of samprajnata samadhi according to Patanjali's *Yoga Sutras*, where there is alternating association of the consciousness between word, knowledge and sensory perception

Shabda – word; thought process in the form of words

Shabdanuvid – a state of savikalpa samadhi connected with a sound

Shadsampat – sixfold virtues: equanimity (shama), self-control (dama), sensory withdrawal (uparati), endurance (titiksha), faith (shraddha) and constant concentration on reality (samadhana); one of the four necessary qualifications for a serious spiritual aspirant according to Adi Shankaracharya

Shakti – primal energy; manifest consciousness; power, energy; female aspect of creation; in samkhya, the power inherent in a cause; counterpart of Shiva

Shaktipat – higher energy or experience transmitted by the guru to a worthy disciple

Shanti – peace, tranquillity, inner serenity

Shastra – sacred book

Shiva – 'auspicious one'; name of the god of the Hindu trinity who is entrusted with the work of destruction; destroyer of the ego and duality; the first or original yoga; cosmic consciousness; counterpart of Shakti

Shivalingam – black oval-shaped stone; symbol of Lord Shiva; symbol of consciousness

Shoonya – void state of transcendental consciousness; state of darkness prior to enlightenment referred to as 'the dark night of the soul'; mental vacuum; state of nothingness

Shraddha – faith, trust; belief in divine revelation; an outcome of realizing the truth

Shuddha – pure in nature

Siddha – semi-divine being of great purity and holiness; accomplished soul particularly characterized by eight supernatural faculties called siddhis

Siddhi – paranormal or supernatural accomplishment; control of mind and prana; eight supernatural powers obtained by yogis as a result of sustained practice, which are considered to be obstacles on the path to realization because they maintain interest in samsara

Smriti – memory; one of the five vrittis described by Patanjali's *Yoga Sutras*

Soham – 'That am I', 'so' representing cosmic consciousness and 'ham' representing individual consciousness; mantra used in ajapa japa, said to be the unconscious repetitive prayer produced by the breath, inhalation sounding 'so' and exhalation 'ham'

Sthitaprajna – steady wisdom; one whose wisdom is firmly established and does not waver (due to fluctuations of the gunas), who is unmoved by the dualities of pleasure and pain, gain and loss, joy and sorrow, victory and defeat, and is unshakably established in superconsciousness

Sukha – happiness, pleasure, delight, joy; prosperity

Sukshma drishta – subtle inner vision

Sukshma sharira – subtle body or part of the subconscious which manifests in the dream state; the subtle body composed of pranamaya, manomaya and vijnanamaya koshas

Sushumna – central energy flow (nadi) in the spine which conducts the kundalini or spiritual force from mooladhara chakra to sahasrara chakra; the main energy flow related to transcendental awareness, 'situated' in the spinal cord of the human body, it opens when balance is achieved between ida and pingala nadis

Sushupti – third dimension of consciousness according to *Mandukya Upanishad*; deep sleep or unconscious realm of mind

Swabhava – one's inherent nature which is bliss and equipoise; therefore one seeks to re-attain that state

Swadhyaya – self-study, self-reflection; study of the scriptures

Swapna – second dimension of consciousness according to *Mandukya Upanishad*; subconscious realm of mind, state of dreaming

Swah loka – one of the seven higher dimensions of consciousness

Swaroopa – knowledge of one's own essential nature; knowledge of pure consciousness, which is the highest aim in life

Swaroopa avasthanam – being established in one's own form

Tadakarapatti – one unchanging form; unfluctuating pure consciousness

Tamas – one of the three qualities (gunas) of nature (prakriti); inertia, stability, ignorance, darkness

Tanmatra – subtle nature; quality or essence of the elements (tattwas) and the associated five senses (jnanendriyas), sound, touch, form, taste and smell

Tantra – ancient universal science, philosophy and culture which deals with the transition of human nature from the present level of evolution and understanding to a transcendental level of knowledge, experience and awareness

Tapa loka – one of the seven higher dimensions of consciousness

Tapasya – practice of austerity

Tattwa – an element, a primary substance; essence

Tattwa jnana – knowledge of the true principle or truth

Turiya – fourth dimension of consciousness; superconsciousness; simultaneous awareness of the conscious, subconscious and unconscious mind which links and transcends them; the final superconscious state of existence, a state of complete absorption of the mind in Brahman in which the individual self or soul becomes one with the universal spirit

Turiyatita – 'beyond the fetters of nature'; transcendental consciousness

Upanishads – vedantic texts conveyed by ancient sages and seers containing their experiences and teachings on the ultimate reality

Upasana – personalized form of worship

Vairagya – non-attachment, dispassion, detachment from the world and its cause; it is spoken of as lower (apara), when it denotes detachment from the objects of pleasure, and higher (para), when referring to a cleansing detachment from the gunas or nature (prakriti) due to the attraction to purusha

Vasana – subtle desires that are the driving force behind every thought and action in life; subtle impressions acting like seeds in the mind capable of germinating or developing into action; the cause of birth and experience in general; the impression of action that remains unconsciously in the mind

Vedanta – one of the six systems of Indian philosophy that teaches the ultimate aim and scope of the Vedas; teaches that there is one eternal principle (Brahman)

Vedas – the most ancient and authentic scriptures of India, revealed to sages and seers and expressing knowledge of the whole universe

Veerya – courage, heroism, valour

Vichara – reflection; enquiry into the nature of the self, Brahman or truth; ever-present reflection on the why and wherefore of things

Videha – unembodied

Videhamukti – freedom from body, a state of realization or liberation (mukti). It is not usually experienced by anyone with sufficient karma to warrant their still inhabiting a body, but in exceptional cases videhamukti is a state possible even with a body

Vidya – inner knowledge, higher knowledge, right knowledge, spiritual knowledge

Vijnana – intuitive ability of mind

Vijnanamaya kosha – astral or psychic (higher mental) sheath or body

Vikalpa – oscillation of the mind; very subtle fluctuations in the mind; fancy, unfounded belief, imagination; one of the five vrittis described by Patanjali's *Yoga Sutras*

Vikara – modification or change, generally with reference to the modifications of the mind

Vikshepa – dissipation; the tossing of the mind which obstructs concentration

Vikshipta – oscillating state of mind between one-pointedness and dissipation

Viparyaya – wrong knowledge; one of the five vrittis described by Patanjali's *Yoga Sutras*

Virama pratyaya – stopping the content of the mind
Vitarka – reasoning, argument, inference; fancy
Viveka – discrimination; right knowledge or understanding; sense of discrimination between the self and the not-self, between the eternal and the transitory, between consciousness and unconsciousness, between prakriti and purusha
Vivekakhyati – discriminative awareness
Vritti – a modification arising in consciousness; Patanjali's *Yoga Sutras* describes five mental modifications: right knowledge (pramana), wrong knowledge (viparyaya), dream or fancy (vikalpa), sleep (nidra) and memory (smriti)
Vyakta – manifest
Vyutthana – revival of previous consciousness
Yama – self-restraints or rules of conduct which render the emotions tranquil: non-violence (ahimsa), truth (satya), non-stealing (asteya), continence (brahmacharya), and non-covetousness (aparigraha); the first of eight limbs or means of attaining samadhi in the ashtanga yoga of Patanjali
Yoga – union; a systematic science of body and mind leading to union of the individual consciousness with the universal or cosmic consciousness; one of the six classical Indian philosophies
Yoga Sutras – ancient authoritative text on raja yoga by Patanjali